The HOLISTIC COOK

By the same author
ITALIAN DISHES
NATURAL SWEETS
PASTA DISHES
PIZZAS AND PANCAKES
QUICHES AND FLANS
THE RAW FOOD WAY TO HEALTH
SIMPLE AND SPEEDY WHOLEFOOD COOKING
A VEGETARIAN IN THE FAMILY
VEGETARIAN SNACKS AND STARTERS
THE VERY BEST OF VEGETARIAN COOKING
THE WHOLEFOOD LUNCH BOX

BRADY —
YOU'RE THE MOST AMAZING
COOK I KNOW — A TRUE
HOLISTIC COOK. ENJOY.
HAPPY EASTER!
LOVE — 03.25.91

The HOLISTIC COOK

Janet Hunt

Series editor: John Button

THORSONS PUBLISHING GROUP
Wellingborough • New York

First published 1986

Nutritional advisor: Joyce Treuhertz

British Library Cataloguing in Publication Data

Hunt, Janet
    The holistic cook.
    1. Food   2. Health
    I. Title
    613.2   TX353

ISBN 0-7225-1243-0

Printed in Great Britain by Butler & Tanner Ltd, Frome and London

With thanks to the very many people whose knowledge, advice and support not only made this book possible, but taught me much along the way. And with my apologies to the trees who gave their lives that the book might be printed.

Contents

How to use this book

Eating is one of the few activities we nearly all undertake several times a day—rarely do we go longer than three or four hours without food or drink in some form passing our lips. Because it is something we do so often, we are in danger of giving it too little thought and attention. Eating can become as automatic a process as sleeping, getting up in the morning, or washing. We forget where our food comes from and how it is produced—in fact we sometimes forget why we eat at all, except that it gives our mouth something to do when we're bored, and it's difficult to imagine any other way of spending our meal breaks.

Meals often become a chore. We are reluctant to waste precious time shopping for ingredients and preparing them for the pot. Instead we turn increasingly to convenience foods, to packets, boxes and tins, to complete frozen meals that only need to be heated up and gulped down. Even eating itself becomes a nuisance.

Conversely, food can become an obsession. It can even take the place of religion, filling our every waking hour as well as our dreams. We find it difficult to watch a film or a play without a box of chocolates on our lap. We cannot enjoy the company of friends unless there is a groaning table between us. We cannot travel through a foreign country without Egon Ronay to guide us. We grow fat and lethargic and—amazingly—can even suffer from malnutrition as a result.

In these and many more unnatural and unhealthy situations—some doctors and nutritionists estimate that seven-eighths of all disease may be related to diet—a whole new approach to food and eating is needed. With the death rate from heart and other stress-related disease on the increase, the National Health Service struggling under a deluge of ill-defined disease, and drug manufacturers recording enormous profits as more and more people turn to them for help, such a change is needed *now*.

This is why *The Holistic Cook* has been written.

It aims to help you to stop, think, and re-evaluate food and the place it has in your life, to promote a greater awareness of exactly what you are eating, and to encourage you to ask questions. To ask questions of your body, so that it can tell you what it needs to make it feel good and function like the finely tuned machine that it is. To ask questions of manufacturers, so that in time they will supply the foods you want rather than those which give them the healthiest profits. To ask questions of governments, so that they will be forced to take responsibility, not just for the whole of the human race, but for the planet itself, for a brilliant yet fragile eco-system that is in danger of being destroyed because we are no longer able or willing to see the havoc we are causing in order to cater for our insatiable appetites. Large aims for a small book, maybe. But with your help they can become a reality.

The Holistic Cook is divided into three sections. Each approaches the subject from a different angle. The first part explains why we in the Western world eat the way we do, what this is doing to us, and why we need to change. It explains not just how food can affect us bodily, mentally and spiritually, but how current methods of food production are harmful to human beings, animals, and the living earth without which life would be impossible.

The middle section of the book is practical. Having advised on the setting up of your kitchen, it gives a comprehensive glossary of over a hundred wholefood ingredients that will help you find new pleasure in cooking and eating, through the discovery of tastes and textures with which you may be unfamiliar, and through the rediscovery of foods with which you may be bored. You'll discover that many ingredients can often be produced in your own home or garden, and the book gives full instructions and illustrations. A selection of recipes will show you how to turn these ingredients into meals, and help you think of countless more ideas of your own. Cookery is, after all, a creative art. Learn the basics, then use this knowledge to go on to new things, make up your own recipes, surprise your friends and family. If you find that wholefood cookery takes longer than opening a packet, don't be discouraged. It may be more effort, but it's much more satisfying. Besides, once you're used to it, you'll discover all sorts of tricks for cutting corners—if you still want to.

The last portion of the book goes more deeply into subjects which are vital to a real understanding of the biology of food and nutrition. It is intended for those who want to understand how the human body works, what nutrients it needs to keep it in peak condition, and where those vital nutrients can be found. It also explains about the increasing use of additives and pesticides: what they are, why it is believed we need them if we are not to go hungry, and whether they are as dangerous as a growing number of ecologists and nutritionists believe.

Together the three sections will lead you towards an integrated way of life that will increase your awareness and understanding of all aspects of food, so that ultimately you will want to accept responsibility not just for yourself, but also for a world which we now know to be vulnerable and in desperate need of help, a world of which you are both a guardian and an integral part. Treat it kindly: it is the only one we have.

Conversion tables

OVEN TEMPERATURES

	°Fahrenheit	°Centigrade	Gas Mark
Very cool	225	110	¼
	250	130	½
Cool	275	140	1
	300	150	2
Warm	325	170	3
Moderate	350	180	4
Moderately hot	375	190	5
Fairly hot	400	200	6
Hot	425	220	7
Very hot	450	230	8
	475	240	9
Exceedingly hot	500	250	10

CONVERTING LIQUID MEASURES

British	Metric	American
¼ pint	140ml	⅔ cupful
⅓ pint	200ml	¾ cupful
½ pint	285ml	1⅓ cupsful
1 pint	570ml	2½ cupsful
1½ pints	850ml	4 cupsful
1¾ pints	1 litre	4⅔ cupsful

CONVERTING DRY MEASURES

British	Metric	American
½oz	15g	½ ounce
1oz	30g	1 ounce
2oz	55g	2 ounces
4oz	115g	4 ounces
8oz	225g	8 ounces
12oz	340g	12 ounces
16oz (1lb)	455g	1 pound

Note: 1 kilogram (kg) equals 2.2lbs

When using any of the recipes in this book, follow one kind of measurement only. They are not interchangeable.

SERVINGS

All recipes are for four average servings unless otherwise stated.

Food in Our Society

*Chief among the psychological and social forces
affecting food choice must be the idea that a mother
shows love for her family by feeding them well. Is it more
loving to provide chocolate biscuits or oranges?*

Christine Lewis
The Food Choice Jungle

Food in Our Society

Food, says *The Oxford English Dictionary*, is 'what one takes into the system to maintain life and growth'. In fact, nutrition is one of the last things most people think about when planning and preparing a meal. In recent years food has come to mean a multitude of different things to different people. To some it is a nuisance, a bother, a daily chore they could well do without. These, though, are in the minority. Many see it as something nice but naughty, a vice against which they must be on their guard for fear of becoming forever addicted to cakes, candies, thick creamy sauces, and other goodies guaranteed to expand the waistline and make them unappealing to the opposite sex, outcasts from society. For them life is a continual battle, a never-ending test of their will to say 'no' no matter what temptations are placed before them. Their stomachs may stay empty, but their heads are filled with the thought of food.

To others food can be a comfort, especially if it is sweet. Sweets are given as treats to children, hence in later years sweets have the ability to console in the way that a nice, crisp salad rarely can. A salad *could* also help someone who eats because they are nervy; digging your teeth into something crisp can certainly help to relieve tension. Because they are readily available, however, crisps or crackers are the more common substitutes. Those who nibble because they are bored are inclined to eat anything that is handy, presumably unaware that if they took the time to consider exactly what it was that they really fancied, then obtained and prepared it for themselves, they would no longer be bored, nor badly nourished, as they so often are. Those who never nibble, but instead sit

down to several large meals during the day, often based on red meat—and the bloodier the better—may be doing a lot for their macho image, but they won't be doing a great deal for their cholesterol levels.

As a status symbol, food compares well with cars and ex-wives. The wise hostess realizes that it is not her conversation, or the music, or the company that makes a successful dinner party; it is the food. The out-of-season asparagus, the duck or quail or venison cooked according to the Bible of cordon bleu cookery, the chocolate mousse that melts in the mouth—these are the things on which her popularity depends, which guarantee her a place on the committee and ensure her husband's promotion. Easier still, but just as impressive, is inviting someone to join you for a meal at a very chic and very expensive restaurant where the head waiter knows your name.

As well as leading to popularity and promotion, it is widely believed that food can lead to love. How many romances begin over candlelit suppers for two? Possibly most importantly it is a way of *showing* love, tangible proof that you are concerned for someone, their pleasure, their wellbeing. You feed them, therefore you must love them. The illogical conclusion is that the more you feed them, the more you love them. Fat children who grow into fat adults are too often the sad result of a mother who could find no better way to show her love for her offspring than through food.

Conversely, there is no snub as powerful as the refusal of food. To turn down the cheesecake for which a friend is famed, or your mother's casserole, or to turn your nose up at a gift of chocolates because you prefer a different brand, is tantamount to refusing their love. The child who won't eat, the political prisoner who goes on hunger strike, the elderly widow, lonely and afraid, who claims to have no appetite—all are using the refusal of food to attract attention, to make their grievances known

Food. A token of love. A panacea. A powerful weapon. What is it to *you*? Do you see yourself in any of the following examples?

Mary, housewife, mother of two young children

Brought up at a time when convenience foods were just being introduced to wives who were now working, had money of their own, and wanted free time to enjoy it, Mary never gives a thought to feeding her own family in any other way. Besides, she has more than enough to do, what with keeping the house reasonably clean and tidy, making sure her husband and children have freshly-laundered clothes to wear each morning, walking the dog, attending her aerobics class, and working three days a week in a local draper's shop. Why should she take on the chore of preparing meals from basic ingredients when she can buy foods that need little more than heating and serving?

Mary's children are, in any case, faddy about their food. At an age when they need to conform, to be seen to be normal, they won't try anything with which they are unfamiliar. Their friends live on sweets, crisps, cakes, colas, hamburgers and tinned peas—and so do they. If Mary ever has a twinge of concern about their diets, she consoles herself with the thought that they are not alone in their eating habits. And if they seem prone to hyperactivity—well, it's all part of growing up. No doubt they'll grow out of it.

She usually does her weekly shop on a Thursday evening when her local supermarket stays open late. Often she takes the children. With a choice of ten thousand items neatly displayed all around her, deciding what to buy could be a nightmare. In fact it isn't. Instinctively she reaches for the names with which she is familiar, those which are advertized regularly in the two women's magazines she reads, and on the television set which is on almost continually when the children are at home. She may even hum a jingle as she glides down the aisles. The children help her, piling things on to the trolley, choosing not so much by name as by packaging. The more amusing and colourful the product, the more desirable: blue and green ice cream cornets, cakes with yellow icing, animal-shaped biscuits, ring-shaped crisps, bright orange drinks, a never-ending selection of products specially created and marketed to appeal to youngsters.

'Sauce without the saucepan . . .', the appeal of convenience.

Of course Mary cannot help but be aware of some of the controversies that surround food and eating habits. When a friend's husband has a heart attack, Mary decides her man should be spreading soft margarine on his morning toast, though she doesn't realize that only soft margarines high in polyunsaturates are of any benefit. Occasionally she buys brown bread; unfortunately it is the kind made from dyed, refined flour. The breakfast fruit juice that she puts on the table owes its sweetness and flavour not to the fruit so attractively shown on the pack, but to chemicals. The bran cereal is oversweetened, the 'diet' marmalade contains a host of additives. But these token efforts make Mary feel good; she is trying at least. As a reward for such stringencies, she treats the family to a frozen gateau. After all, Mary reasons, life is too short to go without.

David, student

Living on a student grant isn't easy for David, especially as his parents cannot afford to subsidize him. Though he knows a little about nutrition, he finds it hard enough to eke out his cash without forking out for fancy foods. And though he used to enjoy conjuring up the occasional meal, it's just too much of a challenge to cook on one ring of a Belling in the corner of a tiny room, with a saucepan so warped that it tips over when set down, and nowhere to store the ingredients he needs.

Instead, David makes do. In his room he prepares bean sprout sandwiches and muesli and drinks decaffeinated coffee, though since he often shops at the late-night delicatessen on the way home, he cannot always get even these simple basics. Sometimes he treats himself to a Chinese take-away or fish and chips.

Most of the time he eats at the university canteen, where the mass-produced meals, based on convenience foods and overcooked, are nutritionally poor. But they're cheap and filling, and for now that is enough. Other students demand more, and there are rumours that a salad bar is to be opened, that vegetarian dishes are to be included on the menu, that Things Are Going To Improve. David will believe it when he sees it.

Meanwhile he is keeping his eyes open for a small second-hand fridge. Then, he reasons, he will at least be able to have a small supply of salad ingredients, yogurt, cheese, wheatgerm and tofu in his room—all the natural foods he enjoys but which, because they are natural and therefore not full of preservatives, just won't stay edible without refrigeration. And because he knows that studying and partying put a strain on one's body and nerves, he tries to remember to take a multivitamin pill daily. It may not be the answer, but it helps.

Sarah, assistant at a garden centre

Sarah, like so many girls of nineteen, is almost always on a diet. 'Thin is in' say the media, backed by boutiques which sell clothes for skeletons, by boys who make never-ending fun of fatties, and girl friends who are as obsessed as she is. Even more persuasive is the widespread theory that thinness equates with happiness. Slimming magazines head success stories with lines such as 'I was a failure, alone and penniless, until I lost 3 stone'. Sarah is impressionable. Not wanting to be a failure, alone and penniless, she knows she must stay thin.

For breakfast she usually has half a grapefruit and a cup of black coffee, for lunch a carton of yogurt, and in the evening a salad with cottage cheese. Or she'll buy one of the many meal substitutes for dieters: biscuits, chocolate bars, cereal bars, soup, milk shakes, all containing as many if not more calories than the more traditional versions, but fortified with a few synthetic vitamins so that they qualify for the words 'meal

'. . . bring back your taste for slimming', the emotional pull - 'we understand . . .'

replacement'. Despite their higher prices, Sarah is convinced they are worth it.

When she's feeling really on top of things, she may even skip meals altogether.

Like most compulsive dieters, however, she also has a tendency to compulsive overeating. Able to keep to her stringent diet only as long as all is going well, she comes off it regularly—whenever she has an argument or a disappointment, or the weather turns suddenly cold, or her period is about to start. At times like this she'll indulge in all the foods she has been craving whilst dieting: crisps, chocolate, salted peanuts, plates piled high with chips. And she'll eat twice as much as she ought because at the back of her mind she knows that tomorrow, or the day after at the latest, she must get back on to her diet.

The result of this starving-eating pattern is that her weight soars up and down. When she is slim she enjoys wearing crazy clothes, meeting friends, and puts energy and enthusiasm into her work. When on an eating binge she withdraws into herself, stops bothering about how she looks, refuses to see people. Sometimes she can't face working, and makes excuses about migraines or other health problems, then spends the day eating whatever she can find in the cupboard. Eventually she regains control, fasts for a few days, finds she can fit into her favourite skirt—and once more can face the world.

Her attitude to remaining thin very much affects her pleasure in eating and in life. If someone invites her out for a meal at a time when she is dieting, she may well plead a previous engagement simply to avoid having to overeat. Or she'll go along and pick at food she would really like to tuck into, irritated that others around her are doing so, and comparing her slimness with their dimples and curves for consolation. If someone at the garden centre has a birthday and hands round cake, she'll insist that she doesn't like cake, then feel miserable at being left out. She may even feel so miserable that later—alone—she'll scoff a whole packet of biscuits to cheer herself up.

When a friend told her how, after eating binges, she forces herself to vomit, Sarah was revolted. Later, however, she tried it. It wasn't so bad. And it meant that she could enjoy eating whatever she wanted without having to worry about getting fat. Though she still thinks it's unnatural and can't do her much good, she can't see that it will do much harm either, especially if she only does it occasionally.

Robert, account executive

Though Robert is without doubt an intelligent and wordly man, conscientious and much respected at work, a good husband and loving father, he nonetheless considers it beneath him to be concerned about what he eats. At home he leaves it to his wife to stock up the cupboards, fridge and freezer with items of her choice, and will always eat and enjoy the meals she serves up. During the week, however, he eats nothing for breakfast, and only a snack in the evening, lunch being the main meal of the day.

Business lunches are, in fact, an integral part of his work, wining and dining clients and getting to know them, fostering their trust in a way he never could over an office desk. It is a part of the job he particularly enjoys. In his address book is a list of the very best restaurants in the area, serving between them a wide selection of foods. After dry martinis he will tuck in along with his guest, enjoying favourites like vol-au-vents, paté, creamy soups, duck à l'orange, or a three-quarter-pound steak, which he can put away with no trouble at all, preferably with a jacket potato and soured cream. Though he has a weakness for profiteroles, he often uses a little restraint and chooses Brie and crackers to finish the meal. Wine, of course, flows continually, brandy accompanies the coffee.

Back at the office, Robert is inclined to feel heavy and sluggish. His secretary keeps a supply of indigestion tablets in her top drawer. No one expects him to do much work in the afternoons, so it doesn't matter. Sometimes he can even sneak forty winks. He puts the need for an afternoon nap down to his age; after all, he is fifty now. His secretary hints that he is getting a paunch. She points out a newspaper report stating that research shows that men who are only 10% overweight show a 20% greater risk of dying young than do men of normal weight. Robert jokes about women and their obsession with weight.

He cannot deny that he has put on a little weight over recent years, but he puts this down to lack of exercise. Business has come first and left very little time for the cricket and swimming he used to enjoy. He actually tried jogging when it first became fashionable, but it made his legs ache and his heart pound quite painfully. More recently he paid a year's subscription to a gym, but he just cannot find time to get along there. One day soon he really will make an effort. Once he gets started on a training schedule he'll soon lose that extra stone.

Arthur, old-age pensioner

Since his wife died three years ago, Arthur has aged rapidly. It isn't just that he misses her, though that certainly has a lot to do with his deterioration. She was not just a strong, determined woman who treated him like a child, taking care of his every need from dawn to dusk; she was also a good friend. With her he could have discussed the things which irritate him so much: the noise made by the people upstairs, the social worker who is always nagging him and never really listens, the way he keeps forgetting where he puts things.

She would also have made sure he ate. After sitting back and letting her cook for him for forty years, he has no idea where to start. During the first year of living alone he made an effort, but most of the foods he was used to such as meat, fish and cheese came in large family packs that he couldn't afford, and would never have got through anyway. Sometimes he heated up tins of beans or soup, but now he relies on the occasional meals-on-wheels, packets of biscuits, and tea. Very occasionally his granddaughter brings him a wholefood flan, but he has trouble chewing the crunchy pastry, and

digesting the salad she insists he ought to eat with it. He's flattered by the thought, but once she's gone he puts the food out on the window ledge for the birds, and makes another cup of tea.

To be honest, Arthur doesn't have much of an appetite these days. He rarely leaves the house so gets no exercise or air. And as his sense of smell and his tastebuds have deteriorated, he doesn't get much pleasure from food anyway. Besides, he reasons, why do the elderly need nourishing? They're not growing, they don't do much, they hardly use any calories. The fact that he feels tired and listless most of the time, suffers terribly from the cold, is one of the quarter of all people over 65 who suffer from deafness, is invariably constipated, sleeps badly except during the day when if he sits down he drops off—these, he believes, are all part of growing old. You can't expect things to be any different.

If anyone were to tell him that because his body is working less efficiently than it used to, and absorbing fewer vitamins and minerals, he should be eating *more* nourishing foods, not less, and that if he did many of the symptoms he dismisses as part of growing old may well disappear, he'd shake his head. He wouldn't believe it. Besides, he would say, it's too late to change his eating habits now, and how could he buy them in any case, it's hard enough to live on his pension without buying expensive new-fangled foods? At which point he'd go off to make himself a fish paste sandwich. On white bread, of course.

The affluent West

Such eating habits are endemic only in the affluent West. In Third World countries, where any kind of food is often in desperately short supply, there is little evidence of such aberrations. People eat simply to stay alive. Yet even in areas where they find it difficult to obtain sufficient food, their diet being based on a few basic ingredients such as grains and vegetables, with a piece of meat or fish or a drop of milk included only as the rarest of luxuries, people often tend to be stronger and healthier than the average Westerner.

We in the West are a sickly lot, with the lowest social classes often being the worst affected. More people in their middle years are suffering from coronary heart disease, cancer and strokes than ever before, these illnesses now accounting for over 66% of all mortalities in England and Wales. One in four of us can expect to have cancer, with Britain leading the world for deaths from lung cancer. Scotland has the highest rate for death from heart disease. We are also prone to obesity, headaches, diarrhoea, constipation, tooth decay, depression, migraines, anaemia, appendicitis, arthritis, catarrh, diverticular disease, piles, ulcers, varicose veins, and a rapidly growing list of allergies. These, and many more maladies, are now being linked with diet.

Undoubtedly, diet is not the only contributing factor. Our frenetic beat-the-clock lifestyle, lack of exercise, the water we drink, the air we breathe, our addiction to coffee, tea, alcohol and cigarettes, all must play a part in our health. But barring accidents, the food we take into our bodies still plays a more important role than any other single factor. We need it to supply us with energy and warmth, to help us grow, to repair tissues, to keep our blood healthy and our inner organs functioning, and to build resistance to disease. Our eating habits, formed so early in our lives, are critical to our health and wellbeing; we need a nourishing diet if we are to be alert, positive and happy. Food is our lifeline. There is no saying more

true than 'we are what we eat'. But what exactly *are* we eating?

The question shouldn't need to be asked. It arises simply because the main criterion for the production of food in the Western world today is not to nourish, but to increase profits. The food industry is one of the biggest success stories of post-war years. We now spend a fifth of our incomes on food to be consumed in the home, in addition to a sizeable proportion on eating out in restaurants, pubs, hotels, buying take-away meals, or on those strategically-placed vending machines you can't miss on underground platforms, cinema foyers, street corners and petrol stations—wherever the sudden need to nibble might strike.

Neither does the food industry stop at food. Kitchen shops are springing up in towns and villages across the country, often within larger stores, their shelves groaning beneath saucepans, frying pans, steamers, pressure cookers, food processors, microwave ovens, slow cookers, fast cookers, cooking bricks, fondue sets, cutlery, crockery, glasses, special dishes for avocados, sweetcorn and grapefruit halves. There are fridges and freezers so you can stock up against the threat of famine, dishwashers to clean up after you've eaten. Eating is, no doubt about it, Big Business, and growing all the time.

Unfortunately, all this attention to ceremony tends to distract us from the original reason for eating. We eat to be nourished. Yet how much nourishment is there in the refined and highly-processed foods that form 70% of what we consume? Maybe even more important, how many potentially dangerous substances are we consuming, substances which could well be responsible for many of the illnesses that are prevalent in our society today?

Products of unknown hazard

No-one really knows. The food industry denies any danger, pointing out that without preservatives our food choice would be restricted, our diets dull. A growing number of nutritionists seem to think that this may not be a bad thing. Over ten years ago Dr A. E. M. McLean told an international symposium on 'The Health Challenge of Foods' that the food industry 'may now be selling the customer a product of unknown hazard'. If anything, the situation has worsened. New lines are continually being introduced to tempt shoppers to buy, many of them identical to products already on the market and often produced by the same company. The word 'new' is what the producer hopes will sell the product, and to make it more interesting, colourful, easier to prepare and with a longer shelf life, an increasing number of additives, preservatives, flavourings, colourings, pesticides, hormones and antibiotics are being used.

It isn't only chemicals as such that are being overused in this way. Sugar, for example, is a non-food we know to be bad for us. Yet it is added to a huge range of processed foods including tomato ketchup, corned beef, beef extract, tinned soups, corn-flakes, macaroni cheese, baked beans, and chicken supreme. On average we now consume some two pounds of sugar per person per week, a vast and dangerous overconsumption of an ingredient that medical evidence has indicated as a contributory cause of many of the diseases associated with affluence. Just to make sure we get off to a really good start on our sugar addiction, it was until recently added to many baby foods, and is made into the sweets with which we are encouraged to quieten, reward and tempt our children—and one of the most popular teaching kits used by schools is produced by the British Sugar Bureau!

Salt, now suspected to be a causative factor in high blood pressure for susceptible people if taken in amounts present in the average modern diet, is added indiscriminately, presumably in order to give some kind of taste to foods with none of their own. Apart from the harm that salt does, it can also dull our palates, so that we need to add even more to our food to make it seem edible.

The government-sponsored Health Education Council tells us that our health is our own responsibility, that we must look after ourselves, thus relieving the government of any guilt as our national health continues to decline. The theory is sound, but how can we avoid potentially dangerous foods when most of those available are polluted in one way or another? How can we make the right choices when we don't have the full information, and even if we did, may not be sufficiently knowledgeable about nutrition to know what is what? Who can we turn to for help? Who is to be believed?

Certainly not the advertizers who are bombarding us from all sides, using any ploy they can to make us buy, particularly emotional blackmail. By buying this product we prove our love for our children, by buying that one we are guaranteed to impress friends and influence people. Life will be more fun if we eat yet another, or more exciting, or more sensual. Look through someone's kitchen cupboards and you will know everything about their innermost feelings and insecurities! And just to assure us that there is nothing unnatural about the products, packages show pastoral scenes, or vignettes from the past, when foods really were freshly picked or fresh from the oven. Or they show flowers or sunshine or smiling faces, none of which has anything to do with the contents, but give you a nice warm glow. The words 'real', 'fresh', and best of all 'natural', are the clinchers.

To be fair, there has been a lot of media interest in various aspects of nutrition over the past few years. The food industry, never slow, has turned each of them to its advantage. An interest in protein led to the magic word being added to all sorts of food, foods that contained some protein certainly—they always had—but not necessarily in impressive amounts. Potato crisps were an example. 'Added vitamins' became the next big selling gimmick. Undoubtedly they existed, but what kind, in what quantity, and whether or not they would be assimilated into the body in combination with the foods they were added to was not mentioned.

'Fibre', the cult of the 80s, was the best thing that had happened to the food industry since sliced bread. Bran is inexpensive, can be added in small quantities to the widest range of ingredients without ruining the taste or texture, and is absolutely guaranteed to boost sales. Hi-fi foods now proliferate to such an extent that it's sometimes hard to find something that doesn't have bran added. The benefits to the purchaser are debatable for a whole list of reasons, not least the fact that the manufacturer need only add the smallest quantity to be able to sell his product as containing bran. The benefits to the manufacturer, however, are obvious.

The adverse effect of too much salt has recently come into people's awareness. No problem. By using just a little less a producer can quite truthfully put 'reduced salt' on the tin or packet.

Animal fats have become suspect as contributing to heart disease and various other serious health problems. Many manufacturers now make a point of stressing that their product contains vegetable or non-dairy fats. In some cases, especially in dessert toppings and cream substitutes, this is coconut oil, an inexpensive and easy-to-use fat which also happens to be a saturated fat, and can therefore cause the same problems as the saturated animal fats it is replacing. The labelling is not incorrect, but it is designed to mislead.

As for the national preoccupation with dieting, this has resulted in a separate industry of its own. Rather than using willpower to eat less, we are tempted with a variety of 'diet foods' that include marmalades and jams, 'cream toppings' and 'ice creams', tinned fruit, bread, mayonnaise, margarine, milk, lemonade, tuna fish, coleslaw, sugar substitutes—and even that dieter's favourite, cottage cheese, now further reduced in calories. An even more brilliant idea is that of putting the calorie count on frozen, tinned and packet foods that have a low calorie count. The food may have been on sale for some time in exactly the same form, but it

THE THINKING WOMAN'S DIET.

You're thinking about watching your weight. And you're thinking sensibly. No crash diets. No fads. Then here's your first thought for the day.

The *Kellogg's Special K* Breakfast. It adds up to 250 calories as part of a calorie-controlled diet. And there's enough protein in it to keep you ticking over nicely, until lunchtime.

So if you can pinch more than an inch start the day with *Kellogg's Special K*. You'll end up sliding into your jeans and pinching nothing but compliments. Think about it.

YOUR FIRST EXERCISE OF THE DAY.

Food for the intelligent

...and only 65 calories.

Fresh Spring Vegetable is a new addition to the Heinz SlimWay Soup range. Fresh, ripe vegetables in a traditional recipe to give a true Heinz taste. And to give you extra variety, there are now 8 other recipes in the range, all 70 calories, or less.

HEINZ SlimWay SPRING VEGETABLE SOUP

'. . . and only 65 calories', eat and be beautiful

now has a whole new appeal for millions of potential customers who may not have been aware of it before, and the manufacturer hasn't had to do a thing except change the label. Anyone who thinks that the desire to lose weight might rob the food industry of some of its profits isn't giving credit to the way the industry works. Weight Watchers International, the company that runs classes across the country, belongs to Heinz.

Even healthy foods—real genuine wholefoods—are subject to marketing hype and the fastest possible sell. It's good to see big department stores and supermarkets—Boots and Sainsbury's for instance—selling some wholefoods, though the category of 'health foods' often includes some very suspect delicatessen lines like tea, coffee, jams and chocolate spread.

Staff or crutch?

The arguments about the advantages and disadvantages of white bread have been going on for decades. It is only recently that the general consensus of opinion—not just wholefood cranks, but doctors and nutritionists too—is moving in favour of wholemeal bread. Despite this, white bread still accounts for 77% of all bread sales. A new trend is in-store bakeries where the baking is done on the premises, allowing the wafting fragrance to do as good a job as any advertisement when it comes to pulling in customers. Somehow 'baked on the premises' has become synonymous with 'wholesome', though most of the bread produced in this way is made from the same refined white flour and using a similar process to bread made in a factory. The different, less precise shape of the loaf may in the end be what gives it more sales appeal.

There is also confusion about the kinds of brown bread that can be passed off as wholemeal bread, though if they contain white flour that has been dyed brown they are no more nutritious than white bread. New labelling laws due to come into force in 1986 should help clear up some of this confusion.

Labelling is, of course, vitally important as far as all foods are concerned. It brings us to the ultimate question of who is responsible for the foods that are put on sale, and will therefore be consumed by millions of people. Should it be the government? Or the manufacturers themselves? Or is it up to us, the consumers, to take the matter into our own hands by refusing to buy any products about which we have the slightest doubt? Would there in that case be anything left to buy?

There is now a widespread and growing agreement amongst leading medical people that we should stop and look closely at the way we eat. In September 1983, after two years of government delay, almost certainly prompted by the economic implications for the British farming and food producing industries, the Health Education Council issued a report showing that we are consuming too much saturated fat, too much refined sugar and too much salt. It also stressed the need to increase the amount of dietary fibre we include in our diets. In Holland and Norway governments have not only accepted such reports, but have acted on them. The *British Medical Journal* called on our government in 1984 to recognize the need for urgent action. Although several reports and surveys have been published since then, there has been little official action.

The British government does have the problem of having to conform, to a certain extent, with EEC regulations. One result of this—and also of a strong farmers' lobby in several of the member countries—is that large subsidies are being paid for the overproduction of beef, milk, butter and sugar, items which then need to be stored. The cost of both the subsidies and the storage comes out of our taxes, and the only dubious advantage is that occasionally some of these surpluses are sold off to us at reduced prices. Beef, milk, butter and sugar are generally agreed to be harmful to health, and best consumed in limited quantities. We are therefore, through the government,

actually being encouraged to eat unhealthily!

The now compulsory contents list which appears on packets of processed foods does at least give an indication of how many additives are present, though individual items are not always given, so cannot be checked for safety. In any case, without a science degree you may well not understand what they are. There are now a number of books coming on to the market that help the non-expert to find a way through the maze, and it is to be hoped that the media will take up the cause and help to educate anyone concerned enough to want to find out about the food they are eating. It would also be extremely useful to have a guide to the nutritional content of each item—explicit labelling which would indicate whether a food was high or low in saturated fats, salt, sugar, fibre, and so on.

One argument against labelling of this kind is that people are not in a position to be able to use the information given—but it is a weak one. Those who do not want to know need do no more than ignore the label and continue eating the way they always have. Cigarettes carry a government health warning, and though there is no direct proof as to whether ths helps reduce smoking, purchasers are at least forewarned. If they choose to smoke it is an informed choice. Surely everyone who buys, prepares and eats food deserves to be given the same sort of choice.

The Holistic Approach

*Breathe lightly: life is delicate and subtle;
the universe is like a fine workshop of the maker of glass*

Mohammid Taqi Mir, 1723-1810

The Holistic Approach

Water, air, earth, rock, plants, fish, insects, humankind—all are part of an integrated whole. Though each part may appear to exist in isolation, to survive in different and quite unique ways, every part needs the others. They are the elements which, when added together, form the single organism that we know as the planet earth.

Ecologically speaking, our planet presents a brilliant balance which makes life not just possible, but exciting, challenging, illuminating, a beautiful and constantly changing experience. Yet the planet is threatened. As the human population of the planet increases and much of it becomes more affluent, the growing demands for space, fuel, food and resources are forcing ecosystems to change faster than they are able to. To an extent the planet is able to take care of itself, to adapt and survive. Pests can develop immunity to

pesticides, fish can recolonize once-polluted rivers, dead forests can revive. But the balance is precarious; tip it slightly and the effects can be rapid and far-reaching, push it too far and the results can be disastrous.

Living holistically means living consciously. It means being aware of the balance of nature and doing our best to maintain it, remembering that every action we take, no matter how small or insignificant it may seem, has a consequence. Everything we do affects the world around us, and we in turn feel the effects of what is happening in the world. We need to be aware of the links between all the parts of the planetary ecosystem, respect each part, tread carefully and live lightly. We need to be aware of the needs of others and turn our back on unnecessary consumerism, taking and using less, discov-

ering pleasure in restraint rather than excess, in the simple rather than the sophisticated.

In Greek mythology, Gaia was the name given to Mother Earth. It is a name coming back into use today, reminding us that the earth is a living entity. Like any good parent, Gaia provides for her children, giving us the materials and tools we need to build shelter, to create heat and light, food and drink. We should never take what the planet provides for granted, and although we should certainly enjoy it, we should also be constantly grateful, ready to share and to give freely and lovingly.

Food—an essential of life

For human beings, air and water are the first essentials for life. Without air we can only survive for minutes. Without water we can live for several days, sometimes longer, depending on our surroundings and the temperature of the air. After air and water, food is the next most important essential for life. Most certainly we can live for weeks, even months, without eating. Fasting can sometimes be beneficial to our health, but eventually we must eat again. Food gives us energy, repairs tissues, nourishes our bodies so that they work efficiently, keeps us warm.

Though less than one-tenth of the total land mass of the planet has the right conditions of climate and soil for agriculture, there are still something like 3.6 billion acres under cultivation. This area produces more food than ever before, enough to provide just about enough energy food to feed every single person in the world reasonably adequately. Yet five hundred million people—equivalent to the entire population of Europe—go hungry every day. One in five of the world's children is undernourished; every two seconds a child dies of hunger or a hunger-related disease.

The reasons for this apparent paradox are extremely complex. The inhabitants of affluent countries tend to oversimplify, and to blame hunger in the Third World on overpopulation, yet though this is a key factor, it is also a convenient excuse for ignoring the fact that we in the West consume a disproportionately large amount of the world's food resources. The USA, for example, contains only 6% of the world's population, yet consumes 25% of its food resources. Our sisters and brothers in the Third World are going hungry partly because of the size of their families, because of droughts and other natural disasters, because of ignorance. But they are also going hungry because we are exploiting them.

Cash crops are one of the ways in which we are doing this. These are luxury crops grown specially for the European and North American markets which bring in money for the lucky few, whilst taking up land—usually the best—which could be growing food for those who need it so desperately. Ethiopia exports coffee, melons, sugar cane. Sri Lanka supplies most of Britain's huge demand for tea while at the same time buying food amounting to half the value of the total import bill—food there is no space to grow because most of the land is taken up with tea plantations. In Senegal, European aid is helping to irrigate desert areas, not to grow millet, a staple food in that area, but to produce aubergines and mangoes for export. In Africa in general—a continent where starvation is rife—the production of sugar cane has doubled in the last twenty years, the production of tea quadrupled. In Brazil over much the same period, land used for growing oranges for export has increased whilst land used for growing maize, the local staple, has decreased proportionately. Mothers living in the shanty towns around Brazilian cities frequently abandon their small children because they are unable to feed them, and unwilling to stand by and watch them die.

Some countries fare better, though the price may be high. Despite a history that has included some very difficult periods, Kenya is at the moment relatively well-fed. One reason is that the military cooperation deal made with the USA, which ensures a market and a fair price for many of the luxury crops grown in Kenya, such as pineapples, while in return Kenya provides the US Air Force with a base within easy reach of the valuable Middle East oil supplies.

Bertold Brecht once said that 'famines do not occur, they are organized by the grain trade'. Though this may be an oversimplification, our use of cereals is another way in which we contribute to hunger in the Third World. Cereals have always been staple foods, and still are for most people. In the Far East, 90% of the cereal crop is still consumed directly by human beings, yet worldwide, over 40% of all cereals produced are fed not to humans, but to livestock for the production of meat, milk and eggs. Using grain to produce meat is very wasteful—it takes 3lb of grain to produce 1lb of chicken, 10lb of grain to produce 1lb of beef. In Mexico, where 80% of the children in rural areas are undernourished, livestock consume more grain than the entire population—livestock destined to become hamburgers for the US and Canadian markets. Even in Britain we feed two-thirds of our home-grown grain to our animals, and then import more from Third World countries for the same purpose. In 1983 we imported 4 million of the 14 million tons of grain imported by the EEC. Many of the animals fed on this grain are destined to be added to the 'beef mountain', one result of EEC farming policies based on subsidizing farmers to overproduce. Skimmed milk and butter are other valuable foods which are stockpiled instead of being sold at reduced prices—or used to help feed starving people in the Third World.

Feeding livestock does not stop with cereals. In Peru, where fishmeal for animal feed is now a major export, fish is too expensive for ordinary people to be able to afford. In parts of West Africa the sale of peanuts is banned locally so that the maximum amount can be exported, most of the crop coming to Europe to be fed to pigs and cows.

Disposing of surpluses

Even when surpluses do occur, Third World countries are unlikely to benefit. Milk lakes and food mountains in Europe follow deliberate overproduction, and the only way of dealing with such surpluses, as far as European decision-makers are concerned, is to store them at vast expense, since gluts, which force prices down, must be avoided at all costs. Sometimes climatic conditions lead to bumper crops, and if the crops concerned cannot easily be stored, they are often destroyed rather than processed into forms which could help alleviate world hunger. In South Africa, pineapples have been thrown into the sea; French growers have thrown away tomatoes and peaches. In 1977, the UK Potato Marketing Board bought 200,000 tons of potatoes from farmers at £44 a ton, then sold them back at £12 a ton for animal feed.

Some surpluses do reach the Third World, but can cause more harm than good. A massive advertizing campaign persuaded many African mothers to stop breast-feeding their babies and give them artificial milk formula instead. The lack of clean water with which to make up the powder and the inability of most of the mothers to read and follow the instructions is still leading to thousands of deaths.

It is both unfair and incorrect to say—as many critics do—that Third World countries are doing nothing to help themselves, though their efforts frequently compound the problems, since the solutions offered by profit-motivated Western manufacturers are totally inappropriate. They have been exhorted to update and improve their agricultural techniques with the use of specially produced high-yield seeds, together with fertilizers, pesticides, herbicides and fungicides, and many countries have been willing to try it out. Apart from the inherent dangers of importing techniques which ignore tried and tested local methods, the purchase of the necessary machinery, tools and chemicals involves huge sums of money. Soaring interest rates make borrowing a never-ending nightmare. Struggling under the weight of foreign debts, governments are forced to put up the prices of what foods are available locally, turning basics into luxuries. More cash crops are grown to make money to pay off the debts, and since these crops are subject to widely fluctuating prices, their profitable sale can never be assured. Thus the land available to grow food for local people is reduced still further. It is a vicious circle with the poor coming off worst all the time.

Aid from the more affluent countries can help, though it still tends to be linked with trade deals and politics, rather than the needs of the people concerned. This means it is not always given where it will do the most good. The British government, for example, gave aid amounting to £528 per head to the Falkland islanders following the conflict with Argentina, compared with 25p per head to India. Aid can spend so long getting through red tape and reaching the people who need it that it often arrives too late, most of it having been misappropriated along the way. It is estimated that only 10% of all food aid is used for vital emergency relief. In addition, food aid undercuts the price of locally-grown food, so that local farmers are forced out of business, making the community more dependent than ever on help from the outside world. In the short term, especially in the wake of natural catastrophes, food aid is essential, and it doubtless saves many lives. As a long-term project it does little to help solve the problem of world hunger.

Financial aid coupled with the teaching of skills and the giving of advice can be far more beneficial, though even this can misfire. A factory was built in Kenya recently to freeze fish, which could then be distributed throughout the country and provide a source of income for local people. After the huge factory had been completed it was realised that there were so few freezers in Kenya that the market did not justify the setting up of the project. The factory still stands, its machinery unused. It has instead become a store for fish dried in the time-honoured way by local people for local consumption.

And so, while most of the world's population goes hungry, the rest of us strive to have more and yet more. Rain forests are destroyed so cattle can be raised for meat—it is estimated that, at the present rate of felling, there will be no rain forests left at the end of the century. Vast plains are forced to grow crops until the life is drained from them and they turn to dust. Insects, plants and animals become extinct as their habitats disappear. Birds, poisoned with pesticides, fall silent and give way to the sound of machines. The world around us is crumbling, and it is our greed for ever more food that is very much responsible.

What do we do with all that food? We put on weight and have heart attacks. We go on diets that do not, of course, mean eating less, but instead encourage us to eat specially-produced low-calorie foods. Food permeates our life at every level. We read about it, go to classes to learn how to prepare it, spend much of our time shopping for it, and then we throw a quarter of it away. There's nothing wrong with most of the food we throw out. There's just too much of it.

The world on our doorstep

Television and newspapers bring the world into our homes, making it part of our lives, our responsibility. Events that may once have happened unseen and unquestioned are now daily news. With the growth of this supply of information comes the sense of frustration of being concerned about the state of the world, yet being able to do so little. But major changes are the end result of many minor shifts, and there is much that an individual can do to improve the health of our planet.

Live holistically, change your attitudes through a new understanding of ecological principles, change your lifestyle to live more lightly on the earth. You will find yourself in the company of many other people interested in living more simply, a movement of people wanting to give life back to the soil, the air, the seas and the rivers, as well as to all the living inhabitants of our planet. You will find yourself part of a movement bringing about changes with kindness and not by force, with love and not with laws.

It has been suggested that rather than living organisms—including human beings—adapting to conditions on earth, our being here actually *creates* those conditions. If this is the case, it means that our responsibility for the world around us is that much greater, our unity with our environment that much stronger. If by our very existence we help to create the right conditions for all life to exist, it is surely the more foolish and dangerous to tamper with the links that tie everything together. We may literally be destroying ourselves each time a forest is killed, a field poisoned, a so-called pest exterminated.

When it comes to food, there is no magic to living simply. There is nothing complicated about eating holistically, no club to be joined, no vows to be sworn. It simply means eating wholefoods which contain the minimum of additives. It means choosing locally-grown produce in preference to foods which have been transported vast distances and may have deprived other people of essential sustenance. It means growing and producing your own foods whenever possible, rediscovering their natural unadulterated taste, and feeling the satisfaction that comes when you take full responsibility for feeding yourself rather than picking your food from a supermarket shelf. It means having planetary awareness, informing yourself about how and where food is produced, and how this affects other human beings. It means having the courage to make a conscious decision not to buy any products that you feel uncomfortable about.

Like Gaia, the word 'holistic' also comes from the Greek; it means 'whole'. In the context of the holistic cook it describes a way of eating that embraces the world around you, and the world that *is* you. It embraces the past, everything that has led up to this moment in time which is responsible for the way things are now, both the good and the not-so-good. And to a very large extent it also embraces the future, because every choice you make is a chance to make the future the way you want it to be. Your decisions and actions today will result in the way you feel tomorrow, how you look, how you will cope with problems, your future happiness and success.

If you have children, you have a responsibility for their future too. Start them early on the habit of eating holistically. Teach them to enjoy wholefoods rather than numbing their tastebuds with chemicals. Encourage them to have an awareness of why they eat, of where food comes from. Let them help you to prepare meals—not as a chore, but as a joyful experience. Guide them gently along the holistic path, but don't force them. Overenthusiasm on your part can lead to a distinct lack of it on theirs. Let them discover what is right for them on their own, in their own way. Even if school friends, advertizers and strategically-placed shops and vending machines lure them into trying the alternatives, all is not lost. Even if they are hooked on junk foods for a while, don't despair. Feed them well when you can, build up

their health, reactivate their taste for wholesome foods. It may take a while. It may not happen before they leave home and become young adults fending for themselves, discovering all over again what eating is all about.

Young people today are most concerned about the future of the planet, about our fellow inhabitants, and about the way we treat both. They are amongst the most outspoken. They are making great changes. There is no reason why tomorrow's young adults—today's children—shouldn't also feel strongly about such issues, shouldn't campaign just as loudly and with just as much concern. If, however, enough people stop and think right now . . . maybe it won't be necessary.

Living Without Killing

And God said, Behold, I have given you every herb bearing seed,
which is upon the face of all the earth, and every tree,
in the which is the fruit of a tree yielding seed;
to you it shall be for meat.

Genesis 2:29

Living Without Killing

Vegetarians may be thought to be a cranky minority in the West, but they are very much in the majority world-wide. Whether because of the dictates of religion, preference, or force of circumstance, two-thirds of the people on this planet never—or very rarely—eat meat.

The main reason that flesh foods are consumed in such vast quantities in Europe and North America can be summed up in one word: habit. Habit also extends to what kind of flesh food is acceptable. In Britain it is acceptable to eat sheep, pigs, cows, poultry and fish. It is even better to eat partridge, pheasant, venison, frogs' legs, oysters and snails, which are all considered to be signs of prosperity, carrying with them prestige and sophistication. Most of us, though, would shudder at the idea of eating many of the flesh foods that are perfectly acceptable in other parts of the world. In the southern Mediterranean, tiny songbirds are considered a delicacy. In Australia it's kangaroo steak, in parts of Italy, fox. There are special butchers in France and Belgium selling only horseflesh. If the African habit of tucking into fried termites for dinner causes the British to wince, the Philippinos' preference for dog flesh is enough to have us up in arms!

One meat tastes much like another, especially when served with herbs and spices, or in a sauce. Yet as a nation of so-called animal-lovers we will campaign self-righteously against the slaughter of dogs and horses, whilst happily endorsing the equally cruel treatment of factory-farmed calves, chickens and nursing sows by buying their flesh to serve on our tables. It is illogical. Yet again it is based on habit, a way of eating with which we grew up, that we see all

around us, that advertizers and restaurants encourage us to continue. Better not to think about the animals, better not to know.

Since the early 1970s, though, more and more people have been stopping and thinking about the contradiction, about the rights and wrongs of killing to live, about how to manage without. The number of vegetarians has increased enormously. Many have been motivated by concern about the health hazards posed by meat in the form of saturated fats, too much protein, the hormones and antibiotics that are an inevitable part of today's farming methods. Or they have given up meat because of a desire to contribute to the easing of the world food shortage, aware that meat protein is one of the most wasteful of food production techniques.

Some make the decision for what are usually called 'moral reasons', a phrase that hints of superiority, of passing judgement on others. An alternative word might be 'love'. Love of animals, love of nature, love of life, and the realization that all creatures share the same will to live. We are all part of one ecosystem, breathe the same air, know the warmth of the sun, the joy of movement. Our lives are inextricably linked. How can we eat our brothers and sisters?

The history of vegetarianism

Many thinking people through the centuries have understood our affinity with nature and animals, a number of them becoming vegetarian. Of the ancient Greeks, Pythagoras came to be known as 'the father of vegetarianism', famed for his outspoken words on animals as well as his mathematical theories: 'O my fellow men, do not defile your bodies with sinful foods. We have corn, we have apples, bending down the branches with their weight, and grapes swelling on the vines. There are sweet-smelling herbs, and vegetables which can be cooked and softened over the fire, nor are you denied milk, or thyme-scented honey. The earth affords a lavish supply of riches, of innocent foods, and offers you banquets that involve no bloodshed or slaughter.'

He lived up to his beliefs, paying fishermen to return their catch to the sea. Though his words generally fell on unhearing ears, his principles impressed enough people for him to start a community, the effects of which were to be felt centuries afterwards.

Plutarch—one of the last of the classical Greek historians—took up his cause, his concern including the question of whether or not animals have souls. In an essay entitled 'On The Eating of Flesh' he could almost have been talking of today's farmers when he said, 'It is certainly not lions and wolves that we eat out of self-defence; on the contrary, we ignore these and slaughter harmless, tame creatures without stings or teeth to harm us, creatures that, I swear, nature appears to have produced for the sake of their beauty and grace. But nothing abashes us. No, for the sake of a little flesh we deprive them of sun, of light, of the duration of life to which they are entitled by birth and being.'

In Italy during the Renaissance there was a renewed interest in the philosophies of the ancient Greeks. About this time, Leonardo da Vinci was growing up on a Tuscan farm, surrounded by the plants and animals that he was to care passionately about for the rest of his life, drawing them again and again. All life was sacred to Leonardo. He loved to buy caged birds and set them free, and refused to eat even honey, claiming that it belonged not to him but to the bees. Like many intellectuals, he was a man of complex ideas, criticized and misunderstood by many who saw his vegetarianism as part of his eccentricity.

Percy Bysshe Shelley, the poet, believed in the Pythagorean ideal of a natural diet being the way to improved health, energy and mental powers. He argued for the laws of nature and the rights of animals, not just in conversation, but in poems such as *Queen Mab*. One of the principal reasons for his advocation was his belief that, if everyone ate this way, England could be self-sufficient and free of political links with other countries: his vegetarianism was as much political as anything else.

There have been many other famous vegetarians, their reasons for vegetarianism being diverse, yet all of them feeling a kinship with the world around them which persuaded them that it was wrong to eat meat. Louisa May Alcott, the author of *Little Women*, was brought up in a vegetarian family. Leo Tolstoy, after living a flamboyant, hedonistic life for many years, became vegetarian in his later years, his strong affinity for animals finally overcoming his habit of eating them. He also gave up hunting, alcohol, and much of his wealth—and was not backward in suggesting that others should do the same. George Bernard Shaw, a controversial man who was outspoken and witty about his ideals, was vegetarian for over eighty years, a philosophy that started in his teens when he read Shelley's poetry. He was also vociferous about his views on hunting, shooting, and the stupidity of war.

Though many people seem to have found that going without meat was not difficult at all, others spent their lives struggling to attain the high ideals they set themselves. Examples of such waverers include Richard Wagner, who adored animals, advocated sympathy with all life, and was especially appalled by vivisection. Henry David Thoreau, the author of *Walden*, believed in the simple life and in self-control, and rarely ate meat, though fish featured regularly in his

diet. H. G. Wells wrote pleading for sympathy for animals, and Upton Sinclair's book, *The Jungle*, set in Chicago's stockyards, did much to open people's eyes to the ugliness of meat production. Yet though both men felt strongly about the subject, neither managed to remain vegetarian for more than a short time.

Albert Schweitzer's simple plea for 'reverence for life' has become a catch-phrase, capturing the imagination of many thinking people and influencing them to follow it through in their lives. Schweitzer, however, was not a vegetarian himself. Many great thinkers have acted more as catalysts than as examples, unable to live the way that they would like, yet putting their ideals into such persuasive words that others have been influenced to take action on their behalf.

Religious vegetarianism

To many vegetarians, their diet is part of a philosophy which involves more than just a way of eating. Orthodox Hindus in India divide food into three categories, the third kind including meat, and to be eaten only by the lowest castes. Even more strict are the Jains, of whom there are about two million followers in India today. Their philosophy is based on non-violence, and they are so concerned about not harming other living beings that many of them wear masks to avoid breathing in insects, and brush the road in front of them to be sure they do not step on ants. As they are forbidden many professions they tend to go into business, and many of India's top businessmen are Jains.

Buddhism, which started in India and spread to Sri Lanka, China, Japan and Tibet, also teaches that all life is one, and many Buddhists are strict vegetarians. Some of the less conscientious follow the ruling that they can eat meat if it is given to them, and comes from an animal that has not been slaughtered on their behalf. Gautama Buddha, the historical founder of Buddhism, is said to have died from eating rancid pork.

At the opposite extreme was Mahatma Gandhi, born in 1869 to a Hindu family, a man who devoted most of his life to his belief in *ahimsa* (non-violence)—and was assassinated by a Hindu fanatic. Gandhi fasted to draw attention to the many issues about which he felt strongly, and was often successful in making his point, though physically he suffered enormously. Vegetarianism was one of the issues, and he was very much responsible for bringing the idea of the meatless diet to the rest of the world, though his emaciated state did little to recommend it. Yet his sincere beliefs, his kindness and his love of animals could not help but be impressive.

A very different kind of reasoning is behind the Seventh Day Adventists' philosophy of vegetarianism. They see the body as God's temple, not to be abused or violated in any way. The movement began in New England in the early nineteenth century, and still has followers both in the USA and in other parts of the world. The best-known member of the church is famous not so much for his religious beliefs as for his breakfast cereals. John Harvey Kellogg did much to promote healthier eating and a vegetarian diet, and began to market his cereals as part of his philosophy—though what he would think of many of the modern products sold under his name, over-refined and sweetened, is not hard to imagine.

The two principal Western religions seem to feel little affinity between animals and human beings. Orthodox Jews believe that *shehitah*, or kosher killing, is the least painful method of killing animals, and that the man who does the slaughtering is to be held in high regard. Animals are killed by having their throats cut, without previous stunning, and whether or not such a method is better or worse has been the subject of many debates. A short story by the Jewish writer Isaac Bashevis Singer—himself a vegetarian—is called *The Slaughterer*, and gives a vivid description not just of the religious implications of the job, but also of the effect it has on one man.

The Christian church is even less concerned, the Bible riddled with references to the slaughter of animals, and though some suggest that Jesus might have been vegetarian, the indications are that he ate both meat and fish. St David, the patron saint of Wales, may have abstained from meat, and it is almost certain that St Francis of Assisi was vegetarian, though his followers, the Franciscans, followed the Buddhist premise that they could eat meat if it was given to them. Certainly there are groups within both Judaism and Christianity which care about animals sufficiently to give up eating them—the Jewish Vegetarian Society and the Catholic Study Circle for Animal Welfare being just two of them. Yet in general the commandment 'Thou shalt not kill' is taken to refer only to fellow human beings.

Down on the farm

Many caring, thinking, animal-loving people continue to eat meat without feeling too much guilt by consoling themselves with the thought that this is a civilized country, that the animals are treated well, that there are laws to ensure that they suffer little if at all. As one owner of a broiler chicken unit said: 'These animals are luckier than those who live outside. They don't have to put up with excessive heat, or cold in the winter, nor do they have to scratch around for food. We even put the lights out for them when it's time to go to bed!'

The perfect life, you might think. And to help placate their customers, meat producers will not only give few of the true facts, but keep their factory farms well tucked away from the public eye. Transporters of animals now close in the side of the trucks so you rarely get a disconcerting sight of rows of panicky eyes peering at you as you drive close behind. Councils build their slaughterhouses in remote spots, and if they try to build one anywhere near habitation they are prevented by enraged meat-eaters who don't want such disgusting premises on *their* doorsteps—besides, it will upset the children.

In late 1984 the *Meat Traders Journal* discussed changing the image of the high street butcher, suggesting that shoppers—young housewives in particular—do not like to be reminded where meat comes from, intensive breeding systems, which mean they have at least two litters a year, giving birth to maybe ten piglets each time they farrow. It is a common practice to keep pregnant sows in stalls in which they cannot turn round for most of the gestation period, which is about four months. Before and after giving birth the sow may be put into a farrowing crate which restricts her movements even more, so preventing her laying on her young. The piglets—which used to be weaned at about eight weeks—are now more likely to be removed at three weeks and placed in a battery cage similar to those used to rear chickens. Later they may end up in a 'sweat box' where temperatures range between 75° and 85°F, the heat attained by a high density of stocking and the evaporation of moisture, much of it urine. Contrary to generally-held beliefs, pigs are naturally clean animals, and find such conditions distressing. They are also highly intelligent and become terrified when handled, especially at slaughterhouses, so they have to be injected with tranquillizers to calm them before killing.

Broiler chickens are one of the most popular meats eaten today; as the popularity of red meats has declined the interest in low-fat white meats has grown. Unfortunately they are one of the most intensively farmed of all meats, fed more additives than most animals, and reared under such unhygienic conditions that it has been estimated that some 79% of the 400 million chickens eaten in Britain each year contain salmonella. Kept in large windowless sheds, often several thousand in each shed, they can barely find room to stand. They take only 6-7 weeks to fatten up—their normal lifespan is 7-8 years—so are hardly more than chicks when they are packed into crates and sent off for slaughter.

A recent report told of a broiler chicken found by the roadside, presumably having fallen from a lorry on its way to slaughter. The bird was literally being eaten alive by maggots. The vet who saw the bird was shocked, commenting that there may be many chickens in such a condition inside broiler houses during hot summer weather.

Such conditions, such practices, such cruelties are the norm rather than the exception. At the end of 1981 the Farm Animal Welfare Council advised agricultural ministers that the following practices should be prohibited: short-tail docking of sheep, penis and tongue amputation, and cockerel de-voicing. Procedures the Council wished to see restricted to veterinary surgeons were vasectomy, electro-ejaculation (for the collection of semen), surgical de-horning, and the disbudding of sheep and goats. It is hard to believe such practices weren't stopped years ago; in the world of factory farming it seems that the methods are getting more archaic as time goes on.

A very small amount of meat is reared under natural conditions, without the use of hormones and growth-boosters, antibiotics and other drugs, and is sold in specialist shops. There are also, of course, still many people who obtain their own meat, shooting or trapping rabbits, grouse, pigeons, pheasants, and even deer if they live in one of the few areas where these animals still roam wild. They have the satisfaction of knowing that the creature probably had a reasonable life, and that it is unlikely to be contaminated with chemicals, though sadly, with such widespread use of fertilizers and pesticides, a growing number of wild animals have considerable build-ups of pollution within their bodies.

Many fishermen also take home their catch for dinner, though freshwater fish like carp tend to lack taste, and need to be cooked in imaginative ways if they are to be worth eating. Fish bought from fishmongers can be as contaminated as many meats, though for different reasons and in different ways. Shellfish are scavengers, and though they can accumulate bacteria and viruses without harm to themselves, it can be dangerous for the person who eats them. Problems have arisen, for example, on the Essex coast where shellfish are gathered near sewage outfalls. Though heating can destroy the toxins, it doesn't always do so. Fish caught in the open sea can be hazardous because of the pollution dumped both intentionally and unintentionally into the seawater. Large fish that eat smaller fish can build up considerable amounts of toxins in their bodies, including heavy metals and radioactive waste. A recent report in *The Times* told how the Mediterranean has now become so polluted by lead that people living round its shores are in danger of suffering brain damage from eating fish and shellfish.

Factory farming has, inevitably, reached the fish industry too. Trout and salmon are frequently produced in this way, with hormones and special feeds used to increase yields. Fish is frequently dyed—haddock coloured yellow looks like smoked haddock and costs far less to produce. Antibiotics are often sprayed on to fish to extend their shelf life, and putrefaction has already set in to much of the fish on display—the ammonia-like smell associated with fishmongers' shops is the giveaway.

The argument about whether or not fish have feelings has been going on for many years. It is hard to prove one way or the other, but watch a fish floundering and gasping on a river bank, and you will know that it has something in common with human beings, animals and birds—a will to live. Though some vegetarians eat fish quite happily, many feel that a fish's right to life is enough of a reason for not eating it.

Do animals have feelings?

We are brought up to care about animals: the family pet, the small cuddly toy we tuck into bed beside us at night, the lamb springing round the field in springtime. We are given books full of anthropomorphic characters wearing gingham skirts and checked trousers, furry creatures who can become as real as people, and even closer friends. We are told that it's cruel to tie things to the cat's tail, or pull the wings off butterflies. Yet at the same time we are told to eat up whatever meat dish is set before us, not to fuss, not to leave the fatty bits. A number of children put two and two together, decide that they feel bad about eating their pet rabbit, and refuse. Others are bullied into overcoming their natural sensitivity, the instinctive understanding that one vulnerable creature has for another.

But is their loyalty misplaced? Are animals here solely to serve and feed us? Or do they have feelings? It takes an extremely insensitive person not to be saddened by the sound of a cow crying for its calf, to feel the panic of an escaped and cornered bullock, not to be affected by the sight of lambs playing with each other as they trustfully follow the leader into the slaughterhouse. So we know that animals have maternal feelings, feel fear and playfulness. What else they feel is hard to say, how much they understand can only be supposition. But tales of the family pet reacting to the unspoken word are commonplace. Could this too not apply to farm animals? Do those that are left overnight outside a slaughterhouse, having heard the cries of other animals, being able to smell both blood and panic, not sense what is about to happen to them too? It doesn't take scientific tests to know the answer, to prove that animals have many feelings similar to our own, some maybe more heightened, their senses being sharpened where ours have often been dulled by lack of use.

The choice is ultimately ours. We can use animals as food-producing machines, treating them without feeling on the assumption that they are here on the planet for precisely that purpose. That in any case they have no feelings, and must therefore be undeserving of kindness or sympathy. We have the ability and the technology to do this. There is nothing to stop us. If, however, we have any affinity with the natural world around us, we must surely choose not to eat our fellow beings. There is little to compare with the elation of watching the cavorting of young animals, or looking into the innocent eyes of a fellow creature, and feeling no guilt—only the sense of completeness that comes with the knowledge that we are all one.

The Tradition
of Holistic Cookery

*Any history book with a description of the foods people ate,
whether Incas in Peru, Chinese of the Han dynasty, or Ancient Britons,
will reveal that their diet was entirely macrobiotic,
based on cereals and including other foods in season.*

Craig Sams
About Macrobiotics

The Tradition of Holistic Cookery

Despite a plethora of expert opinions, our knowledge of the origins of our species must to a certain extent be based on speculation rather than hard facts. Some say the first humans were vegetarian, that their bodies were designed to work most efficiently on foods of plant origin, and that it was only during the Ice Age that people were forced to start the unnatural practice of eating flesh. Others insist that the first people were hunter-gatherers, feeding on green leaves, nuts and fruits, and adding meat whenever it was possible, anything from easy-to-catch frogs, snails and grubs, to exotica such as beavers, orang-utans, leopards, rats, rhinoceros and even elephants.

Undoubtedly prehistoric people had to make do with whatever was available, and this depended very much on where they lived. In parts of the world where climatic conditions meant a lush growth of plants on which they and the animals they hunted could feed, there may even have been time for relaxation. In colder regions every waking hour was probably taken up with the search for food, the fight for survival.

It seems reasonably certain that planting and growing food from seeds became established at least ten thousand years ago, since when cereals have played a major role in the eating patterns of people throughout the world. This ability to grow food also meant a change in living habits, people now settling in communities rather than being continually on the move. Their living became more sedentary, though they still had to work hard on land that was sometimes very far from fertile and productive. In fact it was often the women, the children and the elderly who did such work, while the men went hunting for

meat to supplement the crops, and though it would seem that a supply of at least the basic food needed to support life would be assured, this was far from the case. Crops were vulnerable to attack from pests, to rust and a variety of other diseases, and, of course, to drought. At one time the Nile failed to flood the surrounding land for seven years, so nothing could be grown. In England there were more than two hundred famines between AD 10 and 1850, in China there were 1,800 between 100BC and AD 1910.

But the transition had been made and people had become farmers. Soon they would learn how to make tools such as the plough, the sickle and the hoe, using fire to smelt and forge them out of bronze, copper and tin. They learnt how to watch the seasons and the weather each one brought, working with them to ensure the best possible harvest. They learnt about pests and diseases, though it would take them much longer to conquer them. And when they did—with an army of chemicals rather than with good sense—that long understanding between human beings and the soil would be lost. In the end we became the masters, abusing rather than working with nature, and it is only now that we are beginning to understand the full implications of that shift of power.

One living whole

There hasn't always been such a conflict. Over the centuries many so-called 'primitive' peoples have shown great sensitivity and intelligence in their treatment of plants, animals, and the world around them, and as a direct result have lived long and healthy lives.

The North American native peoples are an oft-quoted example, and with good reason. Those who lived on the east coast when the early colonists arrived were already using quite sophisticated farming methods to produce beans, pumpkins, squash, and numerous varieties of the corn that was their staple, eaten every day. They were also well aware of the advantages of growing these crops together. Apart from the corn, a portion of which was dried to be kept for winter use, they ate the other crops they grew, nuts and berries, and fish and game whenever such luxuries were available. But it was corn upon which they depended, making it into bread, and also into a gruel to which they added whatever was available, especially vegetables and nuts, and sometimes fish or meat. Another dish, still popular, is *succotash*, a name derived from a native word meaning 'husked corn', and consisting of a mixture of corn and beans which is not only very tasty, but an excellent combination for increasing the protein content.

In Arizona, the Hopi were also skilled at growing foods from a soil that was not easy to cultivate, especially in the drier climate of the mid-west. Producing much the same foods, with an emphasis on corn, they also supplemented their diet with foods that grew wild in the desert, including seeds, berries and prickly pears.

The Iroquois added dried fruits and berries, nuts, and even maple syrup to their basic crops of corn, beans, squash and other vegetables. By soaking seeds in herbal concoctions before planting them, they managed to ensure even better harvests than their counterparts in other areas of the country.

If the success of the North American native peoples seems amazing, especially considering the limited tools, techniques and knowledge that were available to them, it can perhaps be explained by their shared attitude. They all had a deep and sincere belief in a mysterious force or dynamic energy, a spirit of life, which unites every entity in nature. Seeing themselves as a part of one living whole, they had a respect for the planet, using and taking only what they needed, being receptive to the needs of the soil and the plants.

Sadly, when Europeans discovered America, they looked upon it as a treasure-house existing solely to be exploited. As the effects of this irresponsible attitude spread across the country, forests were levelled, rivers dammed and drained, mountains gutted in the search for gold and silver, birds and animals exterminated—and the native peoples, nothing more than 'red savages' in the eyes of the whites, were virtually wiped out.

Even today, where in the few remaining reservations native North Americans eat refined foods and listen to the juke-box, many of the ancient ceremonies are still practised and revered, not just by the old, but by young people trying to re-establish their roots, to find their identities. The most important of these ceremonies is the corn dance.

Another excellent example of a race of people living in harmony with their environment, though in a very different way, is that of the nomadic Eskimo of Canada and Alaska, though there are now few of them living the way they did as recently as thirty years ago.

The Eskimo traditionally lived almost entirely on the raw flesh of sea mammals and fish. These included seal, whale and walrus, plus, when available, animals such as caribou, moose and bear. The most prized parts were organs such as heart, liver and kidneys; the tongue, ribs and vertebrae; and the fat, which was a favourite food, often chewed on like chewing gum. Though fire was difficult to make and use, food was occasionally cooked, or blood was heated to make a soup. Excess food, caught during the summer, would be dried and stored for the even harder months of winter.

Only very rarely was any other kind of food eaten: maybe a few berries or leaves, kelp or other seaweeds by those living near the sea. Some groups would eat the half-digested contents of caribou stomach, and so consume a little food of vegetable origin.

This diet, rich in fats and virtually devoid of many of the nutrients we consider vital to health, sounds extremely unhealthy. In fact, it is the diet on which the Eskimo thrive. Studies have been made of different groups, all living lives of extreme physical exertion and hardship, and have come to the conclusion that the Eskimo were, in general, a healthy people, with low cholesterol levels and little evidence of cancer, arthritis and heart problems, with clear skin and strong teeth. The main reason for the health of the Eskimo is that they have found a way of using their natural resources to provide as healthy a diet as possible; most of the fat they eat, though of animal origin, is polyunsaturated, and the absence of heart disease among the Eskimo is often quoted as evidence for the protective qualities of polyunsaturated fats.

The nutritional problems faced by the Eskimo started when their eating patterns changed dramatically. Since the 1950s, when many of the Eskimo of the Canadian Arctic were tempted to move into the settlements springing up around airports, their health has deteriorated dramatically. They have changed their diet to that of the settlers, become more sedentary, and taken up alcohol, cigarettes, candy and Coca Cola. And their bodies are unable to cope with the change.

Other Eskimo groups did not choose to leave their land, but were forced out. In his book *The Desperate People*, Farley Mowat tells the story of the Ihalmuit, who once numbered thousands, but are now virtually extinct. Traders in the skins of the white fox gave the Eskimo guns, which they used to kill their favourite meat animal, the caribou.

By 1925 so many caribou had been killed that there was no caribou migration that year, and this became the pattern for the following years. People starved and could do nothing about it. To make matters worse, forests to the south were frequently destroyed by fires started by prospectors, or settlers in a hurry to clear ground. Lichen is the main food of the caribou, and when spruce-lichen forests are destroyed by fire it can take up to a hundred years for them to regenerate. The ecological balance had been destroyed, and nothing could put it back together again. In 1942 one-third of the remaining Ihalmuit died. Relocated by government officials to an area that was not their homeland, which could not offer them the way of life to which they and their ancestors had been accustomed, they simply faded away.

The Eskimo diet is extreme. Most people would find it inedible. It suited the hard life and weather conditions under which the Eskimo lived, and made the best use of the available resources, though few nutritionists would recommend it under other conditions.

But there are other societies which, although they have very different eating patterns from ours, have been closely scrutinized and their diet highly recommended. One such group is the Hunza, who live in the Karakoram Mountains of Pakistan, who were first discovered in the early part of this century. Life in the region is not easy, the land being rocky and inhospitable, and conditions primitive. A few animals are kept—cows, goats or yaks—but only for their milk which is drunk as it is, or made into butter, yogurt, cheese, and a kind of cottage cheese. The Hunza take special pride in their gardens, which are terraced, watered by a unique system of irrigation from glaciers high above, and enriched with organic compost. Such attention produces excellent crops of a wide variety of vegetables, pulses and beans. These are supplemented with walnuts, cherries, apples, watermelons, and the apricots which are the Hunza's principal fruit, and come in as many as twenty varieties, many of them growing on trees that can be up to a hundred years old. The apricots are eaten either fresh or dried, and the kernels are cold-pressed to give oil—a particularly nutritious one—for use on salads and in cooking.

Meat is rarely eaten, and few of the foods are cooked, with the exception of chapatis, the small round loaves which are the mainstay of the Hunza diet. These are usually made from freshly-ground wheat, though other grains such as millet or buckwheat are sometimes added, as are ground beans.

The diet is simple, wholesome, and highly nutritious. It contains protein, vitamins, minerals and lots of fibre; no fatty foods, refined foods, empty foods. On such a diet, together with a good deal of exercise in fresh unpolluted air, the Hunza are a strong and healthy people, contented and playful, with no aggression or competitiveness, but possessing a sense of satisfaction and well-being. Nutritionists believe that their diet has much to do with their health and longevity; many of them live well over a hundred years, and remain active and alert for most of their lives.

It will be interesting to see whether the Hunza can continue with their unique way of life as the world grows smaller. Hunza society is already changing. An interest in simple living, ecology and natural foods has meant that the Hunza have received a good deal of publicity over recent years. If, in our desire to learn from them, we manage to destroy them, it will not only be sad, but will prove once again just how fragile is the link between people and their environment, how easily tipped the balance.

A healthy old age

Longevity is nothing out of the ordinary in the Caucasus area of the Georgian Republic of the USSR. These remote and isolated highlands can boast more centenarians than anywhere else in the world. The people have remained largely untouched by materialism and the tensions and turmoils of the times, and their basic lifestyle has remained unchanged for hundreds of years. Elderly people are an important part of the structure of society, having a valuable place and leading a useful life even when they pass a hundred, continuing to work a few hours each day in garden or orchard. As a result they remain fit, with good eyesight and teeth, excellent posture, and energy not just for working but also for walking and even swimming.

The Georgian diet varies slightly from one area to another, though the basics are the same: a mush made from cornmeal, cheese, buttermilk and yogurt (usually made from goat's milk), occasional meat, fruit, beans, and vegetables such as onions and asparagus, nettles, purslane, tomatoes, cucumber and cabbage. Together with many Asian peoples, the Georgians pickle many of their vegetables (a practice which has been connected with stomach cancer and hypertension all over the Far East), but their generous consumption of yogurt and buttermilk probably helps to protect them and thereby contribute to their fitness and longevity. It is interesting to note that overeating is seen as a dangerous practice, and that anyone who is overweight is considered to be sick and in need of help.

Nearby, in the Kazakh Soviet Republic, live a people who are now settled, but who not so long ago were nomads, and who at that time appear to have existed on milk and little else. For hundreds of years they moved across the plains and up into the mountains, their travels dictated by the seasons and by their continuous need for new pastures for their vast herds of goats, sheep, cattle and horses. Although some of the animals were slaughtered in the autumn, meat did not feature often in their diet. Instead they fed on milk, either as a drink, or making it into yogurt, cottage cheese, and a hard cheese that could be kept to supplement their winter diet. Presumably they collected and ate what foods they could along the way during their migrations, but apart from these luxuries they seem to have survived their hard lives eating the minimum of vegetables and fruits and no cereals.

It seems as though they must have suffered from deficiencies, yet there is no evidence to show this. The diet which had evolved over the years as right for their way of life was, presumably, also right for their bodies. In particular, the milk products derived from their herds provided more than enough protein, and (similarly to the animals eaten by the Eskimo) the free-ranging cattle produced milk with a very low saturated fat content. Their diet made the best use of what was available, it provided them with the nutrients they needed, and required the minimum of time and effort in preparation.

Longevity, contentment and remarkable powers of endurance seem to be synonymous with mountain dwelling. Mountain children who survive into adulthood do so because they are the strongest, and therefore have a better chance of living to a ripe old age. High altitude living automatically ensures lots of exercise in the open air, a hard but satisfying life, a simple diet based on foods best suited to the area, and little opportunity to be lured by refined foods, cigarettes and alcohol. There is often no excess fuel for light, so the people go to bed when it gets dark, rise with the sun, and live in attunement with the world around them.

Another such group is the people of Vilcabamba in Ecuador. Their life is hard, and their diet consists of little more than corn, beans, vegetables, milk—mostly consumed as cheese—and a little meat. It is low in calories and does not encourage obesity, yet it provides all the necessary nutrients in the most wholesome way. Like the Hunza and the Georgians, the people here frequently live to well over a hundred years of age, and even then are far from ready to give up their active lives.

In June 1969 the *Journal of the American Medical Association* reported the story of the Tarahumara, a group of people who live in the Sierra Madre mountains of Mexico. Their restricted diet is based on foods cultivated in their gardens—beans, corn and squash grown together—plus plants found in the wild, with occasional meat or fish. What was especially amazing was their athletic abilities and strong hearts, which enabled them to perform feats such as running a hundred miles without stopping, with no ill effects whatsoever. They were also found to be gentle, honest, polite people, with a strong sense of family.

The Tarahumara posed a problem. Their numbers were not large. Primitive conditions meant that 80% of children did not survive the first six years. As a result, the population remained stable, and the Tarahumara had sufficient space and food for everyone. Becoming aware of the horrific infant mortality rate, however, US physicians felt a responsibility to supply the vaccines and medicines necessary to lower it. The danger is now that within a very short time the increase in population will present new problems. Land and food will become scarce, people used to space and a large degree of solitude will find themselves cramped. Interference from the outside world, however well-intentioned, may again be the cause of the destruction of a society that has lasted for centuries.

The Chinese solution

Probably one of the most ecologically-aware nations today is China. In a land where the population is so huge that starvation is an ever-present threat, the Chinese have developed both an understanding of the soil, and of numerous techniques that have enabled them to make the maximum use of every bit of available space. For example, they often plant as many as three different crops in one field, each one chosen not only to benefit each other, but to ripen successively.

Neither is it only a select few who grow food for the masses. At present most of the country's 750 million peasants are still working their own plots of land, though the government aims to encourage more collective farming for greater efficiency.

Although Chinese meals traditionally include little meat, Chairman Mao's words, 'One man, one pig', are still respected and acted upon. The country's three hundred million pigs provide not just pork, but dispose of waste and give valuable fertilizer in return.

The Chinese, however, also realize the wisdom of eating plant foods direct rather than 'processing' them through animals, both to use land more efficiently and to promote good health. In the markets of thirteenth century Hancow fruits and vegetables abounded, including eighteen varieties of haricot bean, eleven of apricots and eight of pears, plus exotic items such as water chestnuts, lotus roots, lychees and bamboo shoots. The cooking of vegetables was already a subtle and highly-skilled art involving the minimum use of fuel and often just one utensil—the wok. Little has changed. The Chinese today cook the same ingredients in much the same way.

The Chinese reliance on grain as a staple has also changed little over the centuries, though that staple is not always rice. Rice grows best in the south of the country, where a third of the world's crop is produced. In other parts of the country, according to the terrain, cereal crops include millet, sorghum, buckwheat and oats. The main source of protein throughout the country is, however, the soya bean. Aware of its high protein content, plus the fact that it actually enriches the soil from which it grows, the Chinese have valued soya beans for more than four thousand years. During this time they have devised countless ways to use the bean, including making tofu, which, in a largely dairy-free country, could be called a Chinese version of cheese. Why the Chinese drink no milk is debateable. It is normally assumed that it is because they have no space for the luxury of cows, but it is also believed that many Chinese lack the digestive enzyme which helps the human body absorb milk, so it can make them feel quite ill. Bean sprouts are another way in which soya and other varieties of beans are eaten, a process that increases the protein and vitamin content of the bean.

The Chinese take seriously their responsibility to ensure the good health of their soil. Over the years they have become some of the most highly-skilled of all farmers. Waste is unknown, everything organic being returned to the soil including human waste, animal manure, soil from silted canals, and ashes. Crops are rotated. Pride is taken in keeping their gardens productive, and not just by one member of the family—it is a joint responsibility and a joint effort. More could undoubtedly be produced if, as the government wants, larger farms were formed and worked on by groups of people. But that is only a step or two away from the Western way of doing things, when people lose touch with the origins of the food they eat, and may not even know what it looks like as a plant. It seems sad that, after so many

thousands of years, the Chinese may be about to take a large step backwards.

Japan would appear to be very unlike China in many ways. Yet this small country, made up of four large islands and a sprinkling of smaller ones, has the sixth largest population in the world, which means that—like China—it is forever having to cope with the problem of producing a great deal of food from an often unpromising terrain. To a certain extent the Japanese are coping well. The fertile plains are generally used for growing rice, as they have been for centuries. With a long coastline and shallow inland waters, fishing is an obvious way of obtaining protein. Japan takes the largest share of the world's total catch, and the Japanese consume over 70lbs of fish per head annually. As in other countries, overfishing is depleting stocks, and pollution of the sea is giving rise to concern about the quality of some fish. The Japanese are already taking action. They have recently started farming oysters, shrimps and mussels, and can already supply most of the country's needs.

Japan, however, is becoming affluent. Producing a wide variety of products which are exported around the world, the Japanese can now afford to adopt a Western style of life, which many of them are doing with much enthusiasm. As a result they wear Western clothes, watch Western films, listen to Western music—and eat Western-style food in ever-increasing amounts.

Yet it was in the East that one of the original and possibly best-known holistic ways of eating was born. Over five thousand years ago the practical philosophy of yin and yang was very much part of everyday life. The kitchen and dining areas were considered sacred, meals were steeped in ceremony, and food was respected as the creator of human life and thought. This traditional way of eating and drinking, which survives now only in Zen Buddhist monasteries in Japan, has received growing attention in the West. There are similar philosophies of eating to be found all over the world, from the Far East to South America, differing widely in their details but all emphasising the importance of being aware of what is being eaten.

Though the philosophy is ancient, it is only in recent years that it has come to be called 'macrobiotics', a word taken from the Greek which conveys the art of selecting and preparing food so as to prolong life. Put simply, the concept is that all things are divided into two categories which are at the same time antagonistic and unifying. Day and night, black and white, good and evil, male and female, yin and yang. When applied to food, many systems have been tried, but the basic idea is that macrobiotics aims to balance each ingredient so that ultimately the eater too is balanced, and thus healthy and clear-minded, strong yet relaxed.

A macrobiotic regime can be followed in any part of the world providing the basic ideas are adhered to: that the bulk of the diet should be made up of cereals with vegetables and some pulses added, and that only locally-produced food should be eaten. Items to be avoided include coffee, tea, an excess of liquids, processed foods, foods grown in distant countries, animal foods and sugar. Three vegetables to be avoided by everyone are tomatoes, potatoes and aubergines, all members of the nightshade family.

Macrobiotics can be complicated or simple, but to be effective it must not only be followed but understood. Strangely, as it loses its appeal for the Japanese, it is becoming increasingly popular in countries such as the USA, France and Italy, particularly in cities, where people have maybe had enough of more sophisticated lifestyles and eating patterns, and feel a strong need for a holistic regime to get them back in touch with their

bodies and the world around them. A macrobiotic regime must, however, be flexible to be holistic. In Britain it is impossible to eat only home-produced grain, and many macrobiotic eaters end up eating imported foods at vast expense and cash crops from desperate Third World countries. All the philosophy and practice is futile without the health and happiness that come from a balanced way of eating.

Imitating the rich

The regular consumption of foods such as white flour, rice and sugar, of tinned and frozen foods, and of large amounts of meat and other animals products, tends to be restricted to the affluent. On the assumption that what the rich eat must be better, poorer people have been striving to imitate such eating habits for many years. Should their financial circumstances improve, such foods are one of the first things they spend their money on— partly for the pleasure of indulging their appetites, but also as a status symbol.

This attitude has, over the past twenty or thirty years, been the cause of a change for the worse in many Mediterranean countries. Tourism has flourished, bringing wealth to ordinary people in countries like Italy, Spain and Greece, people who in their own lifetimes have known what it is to till the soil, pick their own produce, make their own cheese. With tourism came the demand for the kind of foods to which tourists are accustomed, and which must be imported and supplied to ensure their satisfaction.

Now, surrounded by locally-grown fruit, the locals will prefer the more expensive, more sophisticated tinned variety. Too busy in hotels and bars to work on their land, they buy frozen vegetables instead, proud to be able to do so. Meat, which they used to eat only occasionally, and then only from animals caught in the wild, now features daily in their homes—veal from factory farms in Holland, beef from South America. Coarse breads, wholegrain pasta, unrefined rice—such things are considered foods fit only for peasants. In Italy most of the brown rice which is grown is exported for sale in 'health food shops', whilst the Italians refine what is left to eat themselves.

If being 'civilized' and affluent means being overweight and prone to cancer, heart disease and tooth decay, it seems preferable to remain a peasant, to live a simple but disease-free life. As the affluent world gradually comes to realize this, the appeal of a holistic lifestyle is growing. Amongst those still living a holistic life, however, the grass beyond the hill—be it processed, dyed and tinned—is still often the greenest.

And what of Britain? Most certainly our ancestors ate holistically; they had little choice. Interestingly, many of the peasants ate what we now know to be a healthier diet than the rich of those times who often gorged themselves on fowl, fish and game, and grew fat and gouty, suffering frequently from kidney-stones on a diet too rich in protein and fats, and virtually devoid of carbohydrates. Sugar too, though expensive, was available. Queen Elizabeth I, known to have had terrible teeth, was one of the earliest addicts, and suffered toothache for most of her life as a consequence.

Peasant fare would most likely have consisted of black bread, vegetable soup and eggs, with just a little butter, cheese and buttermilk, and occasionally some meat. Providing the harvest and hunting were good, people could live well on such a diet, though there was often a shortage of vitamin C which could affect health, especially at the end of a long hard winter.

Most country folk lived on similar foods up to the First World War, and even after that there were many people who continued to grow their own vegetables in the garden or on an allotment, to keep a few chickens or maybe a cow or goat for milk. But refined foods made an early appearance in Britain, and were eventually priced so low that they became a mainstay of less wealthy families. A diet of wholemeal bread and butter offers far more nourishment than one based on white bread, margarine and jam. Vegetables from the garden are preferable to the tinned or dried varieties, fresh-caught rabbit more nutritious than Spam. As eating habits changed, new health problems arose, though few people except for the occasional 'crank' connected the two. The newly-created National Health Service began to dish out pills and potions to alleviate some of the symptoms—and the trend was set.

It is now boasted that the British get more productivity from their soil than any other nation, and that despite one of the most crowded populations in the world, we could—if necessary—be virtually self-sufficient. Whether or not this is true is irrelevant. Plant foods are only as good as the soil in which they are grown, and much of our soil is dead, killed by irresponsible farming, overuse, and poisoning with chemicals. In the end the price we pay for food produced in this way is high. We end up with fields unable to be used unless artificially stimulated, wildlife destroyed, once-beautiful habitats changed beyond recognition, and the ill-health that must result from eating chemically-produced foods. Many now believe that this price is far too high.

The Holistic Meal

*There is something slightly pathetic about the ease
with which many of us are conned by habit and the advertizers
into believing that a portion of blanket-like factory-farmed chicken
set off against a small pile of frozen peas and some overboiled potatoes
is hitting the double top of* haute cuisine.

Jon Wynne-Tyson
Food for a Future

The Holistic Meal

Ask anyone in Britain what they consider to be a balanced meal, and nine times out of ten they'll say meat and two veg. Everyone should have a hot meal once a day, they'll add, implying that cooked food is somehow nutritionally superior to raw foods, over-boiled brussels better than bean sprouts. In keeping with this belief it is traditional for most families to eat a cooked meal each day, usually in the evenings during the week and at midday on Saturdays and Sundays. Increasingly often, in our affluent society, it is eaten in a restaurant. And if it doesn't consist of meat (or poultry or fish) and two vegetables . . . well, you can hardly call it a real meal, can you?

In many ways the theory is sound enough. Earlier this century, when the habit of eating such meals first took hold, the meat probably came from animals raised in your own back yard, or caught in the wilds. It was chemical-free, nowhere near as fatty as today's meat, and was often more like a garnish than the centrepiece of the meal, with plenty of vegetables, potatoes and cereals to fill you up. Nowadays the meat is likely to be factory-farmed, the vegetables tinned or frozen, dyed and sweetened with sugar, and overcooked. Because the meat tends to be

tasteless, all sorts of sauces are added to flavour it, and if those sauces are made with cheese, cream or eggs, as they often are, you have an overload of protein plus a dangerously high amount of saturated fats.

Another commonly-held attitude is that the dessert is not so much part of the meal as an extra, a treat, a reward for eating all your greens. Desserts tend to be devoid of nutrients, packed instead with white sugar, fats and flavourings, all the things we know to be bad for health, but which are somehow acceptable as part of the dessert. And so we leave the table feeling lethargic instead of energetic.

Balancing your meals

Eating holistically means a re-evaluation not only of the foods you eat, but the way you put them together. And the first thing to throw out is all those preconceived ideas about hot meals, meat and two veg, and so on.

Balanced eating means planning your meals around as wide a variety of natural ingredients as possible. Besides supplying protein, carbohydrate and fats (which will automatically include a good selection of minerals, trace elements and fibre), a meal should be interesting, appetizing and satisfying. Balance the ingredients you use in each dish to obtain a combination of textures and tastes. Choose colours carefully—we eat with our eyes as well as our mouths. An attractive-looking meal can whet our appetite, getting our tastebuds tingling with anticipation. Aim to make your meals easier to digest by adding—for example—herbs to a very creamy dish, or yogurt to a spicy one, by not overdoing the ingredients with very strong flavours, by letting the more subtle tastes come through. Too many highly-flavoured foods will actually dull your tastebuds, so that eventually you won't be able to detect the more delicate tastes of natural foods—the sweetness of young sweetcorn, the nuttiness of grains.

Forget, too, all the rules about what goes with what. Experiment with combinations that appeal to you. Be imaginative, be daring. Everyone knows that stir-fried vegetables are traditionally served with rice—why not have them with kasha for a change? Or over wholewheat noodles? Or as a filling for an omelette? Or on toast? Make a sauce by grinding any leftover pulses to a paste, mix with tomato purée and a little stock, add some herbs, and serve over pasta, or fill pancakes with it, or use it to moisten nut cutlets, cheese fritters or potato croquettes.

Fill a flan with any leftover vegetables, pour on a mixture of beaten eggs, milk or cream, and grated cheese, and make a quiche. Cookery used to be a creative art, the challenge being to make a limited number of fairly basic ingredients into something that looked, smelled and tasted delicious. Today's cook often follows recipes religiously, and if an ingredient is missing either rushes out to buy it, or abandons the whole project. Be old-fashioned. Use recipes as a starting-point, but then go on and adapt them as necessary, making use of the ingredients you have on hand, and those which you and your family like best.

Getting enough protein

The main thing to emphasize about protein is that we actually need very little. 35g of protein a day is all we need to keep healthy; most of us—vegetarians included—consume at least twice that amount, and often substantially more.

Until recently, two-thirds of the protein eaten in Britain came from animals and one third from plants; things are changing now for the better as the shift in protein consumption is now back to plant protein, but we are still eating far more protein than we really need.

By combining foods from different plants, or plant foods with other non-meat animal proteins, you can often increase the protein content so that the whole is greater than the sum of the parts. All proteins contain amino-acids, but in general only animal proteins contain the eight essential amino-acids without which our bodies cannot make the others we need. Soya beans are a complete protein, but most plant foods contain only some of the essential amino-acids, and are therefore considered to be incomplete. However, it is now agreed that by combining plant foods, any amino-acid deficiency in one can be complemented by the amino-acid content of another, so that when combined they can increase the protein quality of the dish by as much as 50% above the average of the items eaten separately. This means that you will be getting more protein from sources which make better ecological sense, put less of a strain on your digestive system, and cost nothing like as much as 'complete' proteins. Here are some examples of protein mixes:

> Muesli (grains, seeds)
> Rice and curried lentils (grain, pulse)
> Minestrone (grain, pulse)
> Beans on toast (grain, pulse)
> Wholemeal rolls and peanut butter (grain, nuts)
> Hummous and pita bread (grain, pulse)
> Stuffed cabbage leaves (grain, nuts)
> Cornbread and chili beans (grain, pulse)
> Gado gado (nuts, grain)

By adding small quantities of complete proteins—milk, cheese or eggs—a wide range of dishes can be made which combine complementary proteins and complete proteins. Such dishes include porridge, pancakes with spinach and cottage cheese, spaghetti with a cheese sauce, pizza, Spanish omelette, ploughman's lunch, potato salad with yogurt dressing, split pea soup made with milk, vegetable risotto with cheese, and quiche. These ways of mixing protein have been used in other countries for centuries, so foreign recipes are often excellent examples. Be imaginative: some of the most unlikely combinations go together not only to make good-quality protein, but to make delicious eating too.

It is important to see your meal as a whole, rather than as a series of courses. You may already have the habit of balancing the courses in a meal—you'd be unlikely to serve a thick, filling soup with a heavy rice dish, then follow it up with a stodgy pudding. In the same way, think of the meal as a nutritional balance. A low-protein starter such as sweet potatoes or a green salad can be followed by a cheese or egg dish, or vice versa. You can make up for a light, low-calorie, low-protein main course with a dessert such as apple crumble, making the topping with protein-rich oats and nuts, and serving it with yogurt, or a cheesecake made with ricotta cheese and dried fruit. The dessert should be part of the meal, chosen for its food value as well as its taste. There's no reason at all why it shouldn't be quite as delicious as the usual 'empty' endpieces—in fact it should be even more tasty. Empty foods have no place in a holistic way of eating.

Presentation

To make meals more enjoyable for everyone, don't forget the importance of presentation. This doesn't mean you have to serve food on bone china plates, eat with silver cutlery, or cover your table with a lace cloth—though you can if you like. What it means is that when the surroundings are pleasant, meals undoubtedly taste better and are better digested.

Choose crockery which sets off the food you'll be serving to its best advantage. Earthenware and stoneware pottery look attractive, and can be relatively inexpensive, though you'll pay more if you want it to be ovenproof. Unglazed pottery is cheapest, but it won't last as long. Stainless steel cutlery is good value for money, stays unblemished for years, is quick and easy to clean, and comes in an assortment of styles to suit most tastes. Tablecloths can be bold, pretty, subtle, lacy, whatever you like—non-existent of you have an interesting table. Instead you can use tablemats made of raffia, rush, cork or wood. It goes without saying that flowers and well-placed lights are indispensable for mood, that the table should be the right height, the chairs comfortable, and the glasses spotless.

Having said all that, there really is nothing to beat eating food outdoors. If you have a garden or patio, use it when the weather allows; if you live in a flat or a house without a garden, take an occasional picnic to the nearest open space. Eaten in the open air the most familiar foods take on a whole new meaning. Keep trays handy for when you want to indulge in breakfast in bed, or dinner in an armchair, or for when you're serving a buffet lunch—it's easier to balance a tray on your lap than a plate. Being set in the way you eat your meals is almost as bad as never varying what you serve. Both show a lack of imagination; both result in meals being boring.

Because it's pleasant to relax over a meal, inviting friends to eat with you has become an accepted way of socializing. If you eat wholefoods and the friends don't, you have a perfect opportunity to introduce them to a different way of eating without needing to say a word. Nowadays, though, entertaining has become synonymous with extravagance, splashing out, showing off, which puts off many people who like a simpler way of life, or can't afford any other kind. Don't let this stop you enjoying eating with your friends. Serve the foods you usually serve, with perhaps one or two luxury or exotic items to make the meal special. You could serve a simple and inexpensive main course such as a vegetable and bean casserole, or a soufflé, but start your meal with a few spears of fresh asparagus for each person, or half an avocado with your own home-made vinaigrette dressing, or cheese mousse with fingers of wholemeal toast. Or you could end the meal with a flourish instead: if pineapples are in season, use one as a shell to hold a fruit salad.

Pears can be made special by simmering them in a red wine. Many exotic dishes can be made from everyday ingredients, such as *hashmerim*, a Turkish sweet made with cottage cheese.

If your money won't stretch even this far, try to add just one or two less familiar ingredients to the meal itself. It's amazing the effect a few flaked almonds can have on cauliflower cheese, or a sliced yellow pepper on a salad, or a spoonful or two of tahini in a soup. Sprinkle walnuts over a potato salad; buy the smallest possible tin of artichoke hearts and add them sliced to a home-made pizza.

Those with more time than money to spare can spend it putting together dishes that few people make any more because they take so much time. Home-made vol-au-vents filled with vegetables in a white sauce are delicious and inexpensive, but very fiddly. And as a finale, there is nothing quite like home-made ice cream, preferably flavoured with strawberries or blackberries.

The important thing is always to eat holistically, not to see it as a way of eating to be thrown out on special occasions, high days and holidays. Refined and 'empty' foods, because they are best avoided, may have the glamour of forbidden fruits, but once your tastebuds have readjusted to wholefoods, you'll find that forbidden fruits aren't always as good as they appear to be from a distance.

Cooking for children

The good news is that many children have a natural distaste for meat, even more so for fish. So if you want to cut down on flesh foods, or cut them out completely, they're unlikely to raise many objections. The bad news is that they can easily become little 'junkies'. Junk food manufacturers have long been aware that children like sweet foods. Tinned beans, tomato ketchup, soft drinks—

all are sweetened to appeal to children. It used to be that baby foods were sweetened to make them more desirable, thus giving babies a sweet tooth before they even had any teeth, but this habit has been curbed in recent years as manufacturers have accepted that it is bad for babies' health. Unfortunately their sense of responsibility usually stops there. Any child who watches television is bombarded with advertisements for sweets, cakes, biscuits, munchy this, crunchy that—the majority of these 'goodies' made with refined ingredients and a selection of chemicals, and designed, flavoured, coloured and packaged to appeal directly to children. Vending machines are strategically placed so as not to be missed, school tuckshops perpetrate the trend by making junk foods even more accessible. The child who doesn't fit in and munch along with the rest is considered to be very odd.

If the manufacturers' morals are dubious, the resulting profits are undoubtedly worthwhile. And the habits of childhood linger on to become adult dependence, a craving for sweet things in times of stress or worry, a dulled appetite which means that only the strongest chemically-flavoured foods taste good, mood swings which are helped only by more junk foods. With sweet things on sale in the most unexpected places—petrol stations, off-licences, greengrocers, chemists, stationers, garden centres—you can pick up something to nibble all through the day. It isn't only the child that is at risk through eating this way, it's the adult she or he becomes. The effects of bad eating habits can easily be seen in children, partly becaause of their low body mass in relation to their food intake, partly because they tend to eat a much smaller range of foods than most adults, but the problems associated with adult obesity are often more far-reaching. Any child brought up on wholefoods has a

better start in life in every way. Even though when they are away from home the temptation is sometimes too much for a child to resist, the best thing any parent can do is ignore it. Just carry on at home as you did before—after all, home is where most habits are formed. Encourage your children to take an interest in food, get them to help in the kitchen, to make dishes they especially like. Explain why some foods are harmful; ask what they'd like instead, encouraging them to be aware of food as something important in their lives. Natural foods can be just as enjoyable as junk foods. It's worth making the effort to cultivate good eating habits in children, for their sake and for yours.

Snacks

Because they grow in fits and starts, use lots of physical and mental energy, and rarely like to sit still for long, children tend to prefer snacks to meals. So do a lot of adults, for many of the same reasons. Yet snacks, we are told, are bad for us. Picking between meals will ruin our appetites and make us fat. Snacks aren't 'real' food.

It all depends on how you define a snack. If it's a chocolate bar, or a packet of crisps, or a burger and a bottle of pop, you'd be better off without it. But you can snack on wholefoods and give yourself energy without putting on weight. Sneak a snack into a lunchbox or child's satchel, and eliminate the risk of hunger striking when only a vending machine is handy. It has even been shown that some people function far better if they eat little and often, that their bodies obtain more nutrients from the food and can digest it better, and that they are less prone to put on weight than if they sat down to one large meal a day.

For those who would like to be able to snack more often without feeling guilty, here are some good ideas:

Fruit and a piece of cheese
Banana
Sultanas and cashews
Trail mix (or any other fruit, nut and
    flaked coconut mixture)
Handful of granola
Yogurt-coated nuts
Oat bars (bought or home-made, though
    these are often high in fat)
Dried fruit bars (bought or home-made)
Crisps (the kind you buy in wholefood
    stores—less fat, less salt)
Biscuits, muffins, scones (home-made)
Plain yogurt with fruit added to it
Wholegrain crispbread and nut butter
Tamari-roasted seeds
Large dried fruits (peaches, pears,
    bananas)
Sesame bars (bought or home-made)
Popcorn
Toffee apples (made with molasses)
Dry-roasted soya beans
Carob bars

Look around your local wholefood or health food shop for more ideas. A number of them now also stock a selection of sweets made with natural ingredients—though be sure to read the labels. Some health food shops seem to confuse expensive continental confectionery with the more wholesome kind, so you may still end up buying a product made with quantities of sugar. It's always a good idea to keep sweet snacks to a minimum— there is no way round the fact that sweet things in large quantities aren't good for you! There are plenty of other things to eat that will give you energy, fill that gap, and not encourage a taste for sweet things.

Making up menus

On the following pages you will find suggestions for seven days of healthy eating. You will find recipes elsewhere in the book for dishes marked with an asterisk (*); ideas for accompaniments are also given under each day's menu. They can only, of course, be a rough guide. Lifestyles vary, and you may prefer your main meal at lunchtime, or may eat no lunch at all. It's up to you. Appetites also vary enormously from one person to another; what may seem too much for one person may leave someone else feeling decidedly hungry. Look through the ideas given here, notice the way in which each day's meals are balanced to use a wide range of ingredients and to supply as many nutrients as possible, then use the guide as an example on which to base your own menus.

MONDAY
Breakfast
An orange
Mixed grain granola*
Herb tea or coffee
Lunch
Cauliflower pâté*
Melba wholemeal toast
Watercress salad
Honey and wheatgerm flapjacks
Dinner
Vegetable hotpot including potatoes
Fresh fruit salad
Cashew cream

TUESDAY
Breakfast
Yogurt and fruit-juice drink
Wholemeal croissants
Herb tea or coffee
Lunch
Split pea soup
Red and white slaw*
Wholemeal baps
Dinner
Fresh corn on the cob
Ratatouille pancakes with cheese sauce
Lemon sorbet made with fresh lemons and
    raw sugar

WEDNESDAY
Breakfast
Dried apricot compôte
Grilled tomatoes on wholemeal toast
Herb tea or coffee
Lunch
Spinach salad (spinach, cucumber, celery,
    black olives)
Stuffed eggs
Wholemeal crispbread
Carton of plain yogurt
Dinner
Pea and peanut curry
Brown rice
Banana and tofu cream

THURSDAY
Breakfast
Fresh grapes
French toast with maple syrup*
Herb tea or coffee
Lunch
Spanish lentil soup*
Celery, raisin and apple salad with cashew
    nuts
Buckwheat biscuits
Dinner
Carrot quiche*
Steamed potatoes with chives
Chinese cabbage and tomato salad
Rhubarb flan made with wholemeal flour
    and raw sugar

FRIDAY
Breakfast
Orange and apricot juice
Porridge with honey, molasses or maple
    syrup
Herb tea or coffee
Lunch
Flageolet salad*
Wholemeal baps
Almond biscuits*
Dinner
Ricotta cheese and spinach pasties*

Baked tomatoes
Jacket potatoes
Fresh fruit salad with tahini and honey

SATURDAY
Breakfast
Fresh peach
Buttermilk muffins*
Herb tea or coffee
Lunch
Deep-fried tofu*
Raw cauliflower florets, watercress,
    tomatoes, a sprinkling of roasted
    flaked almonds
Rye crispbread
Dinner
Parsnip and cheese patties
Millet with mushrooms and onion
Broccoli
Honey cheesecake

SUNDAY
Breakfast
Half a grapefruit
Scrambled eggs and mushrooms on toast
Herb tea or coffee
Lunch
Stuffed peppers*
Creamed potatoes
Brussels sprouts
Blackcurrant fool made with fresh fruit, raw
    sugar and egg white
Tea
Sweetcorn and potato soup
Cold nut roast
California salad*
Bran and coconut cookies

The Holistic Kitchen

*The physical environment is important,
and creating a kitchen that is light and loving
is a joyful task.*

Kay Lynne Sherman
The Findhorn Family Cook Book

The Holistic Kitchen

Food is the key to a long and happy life, to physical health and spiritual wellbeing, a link with nature, our fellow human beings and with planet earth. So the place in which it is prepared should be, in a way, a shrine, a place not so much of worship as of love, a happy place.

Unfortunately, kitchens—in Britain especially—tend to be the last room in the house to receive attention. Often small and cramped, with few windows and a dismal view, a kitchen is little more than a utility room, a workroom in which you do what has to be done as quickly as possible, and then get out and get on with life. Much of this attitude stems back to the days when the servants were the ones who had to spend their time in the kitchen—so naturally no one was too bothered about the room itself, just as long as the cooking facilities were adequate. More recently, as women have emerged from the kitchen and begun to take their rightful place alongside men in the wider world, the convenience foods

that have helped set them free have eliminated much of the need for an attractive well-equipped kitchen. It takes very little space to open a tin or packet, to peel off the clingfilm.

Yet, as in nature, everything goes in cycles. After the apathy comes a renewed interest in food, a growing concern about the harm it does us, a demand for wholesome food. And at the same time, kitchens are coming back into popularity. This is partly due to the sudden interest of manufacturers who see a neglected market, an opportunity for profits. But if manufacturers are cashing in, it's because consumers want to rediscover

the kitchen, feel a need for the room that used to be considered the heart of a house; the place not only where food was prepared, but where the family gathered and lingered.

Is your kitchen the right kitchen for you?

Creating a mood

The mood you want to create depends very much on you, your family, your lifestyle, and the way in which you intend to use your kitchen. Anyone who lives alone, is out at work all day, or who cooks only occasionally, is going to want a different kitchen from the cook who loves inviting guests to dinner, or a household full of children who probably play and do their homework there as well as eat. The town dweller with a corner shop open until eight and at weekends will need less storage space than someone who lives far from the shops and needs to stock up when the opportunity arises.

Kitchens can be functional or fun, clinically neat or chaotic, a place designed to make it possible to prepare meals quickly and efficiently, or a room to live in, so that whoever cooks in it does so in a positive frame of mind, so that cooking is a good experience and not a chore.

The situation of the kitchen in the house, which way it faces, whether it is tucked away in a quiet corner or part of the main thoroughfare—all these things affect its mood. Good natural daylight is important. So is access to a garden or patio, especially if you like to grow your own herbs and vegetables. Such things are usually out of your control, but there are sometimes changes you can make. You could enlarge a small kitchen by knocking down a wall and making two rooms into one, maybe using the kitchen as a dining room as well. Or you could make a too-spacious kitchen cosier by putting up a wall and making it into two rooms. An easier way is to use a table, cupboards or hob unit

as a room-divider, which gives the illusion of reducing the room in size, yet means you are still part of whatever is going on on the other side. A high-tech kitchen could be divided with venetian blinds in dazzling colours—or black; in a rustic kitchen you could use a bank of lush green plants.

To improve daylight, consider having a window enlarged—this is often not as difficult as you might think, and well worth it. You could use mirrors to reflect what natural light there is, keeping the colour scheme pale and simple. Spotlights are useful too, and you can now buy adjustable clip-on lamps that can be moved as and when you need them. If you have ventilation problems, have an extractor fan fitted.

The choice of which colour to use in a kitchen is all-important—and so often overlooked. Colour affects us all the time, physically, emotionally and spiritually. We use it to describe our feelings: someone is green with envy, sees red, is in a blue mood. Because it affects us on so many levels, colour is used in healing; in hospitals, factories and schools; in dangerous situations to warn us of hazards. Contrary to what was once believed, it isn't only the sighted who can benefit from colour. American research has shown that blind children can also respond to it, a theory which opens up a whole new world. Colour consists of wavelengths of light that are interpreted by the human eye in an interaction of the optic nerves with the brain. It is thought that we can distinguish over a thousand different hues, each of us seeing them in a slightly different way, though the effects they can have on us are generally predictable. Red, for example, actually dilates blood vessels, making you alert and awake; it is also thought to stimulate appetite. Surround yourself with blue and your blood pressure drops, you are more likely to be calm and able to concentrate. Green is a soothing colour, bringing a reminder of nature into your home.

When choosing a colour scheme for a kitchen, there are a number of things to remember. Colours will seem more intense in a large room than in a small one, so it is often best to go for the shade lighter than the one that particularly appeals to you. Dark colours which seem dramatic during the day can be depressing at night, so choose carefully if you feel drawn to the darker shades, maybe adding accents of light, bright colours to break up the heavy mood. Remember too that although you can cheer up a cool room with peaches, rusts and autumn colours, or can add drama with purple or a warm glow with yellow, the colours must be right for you and your personality as well as for the room itself. Forcing yourself to live with a strong, dramatic colour when you are more drawn to soft, subtle shades will only make you feel uncomfortable in the kitchen. Compromise may be the answer. If you like things pale and pretty, but feel the room needs something stronger to do it justice, maybe paint or paper just one wall in a bright splash of colour. Too much white, incidentally, can cause glare, which constricts the pupil opening, making it bad for your eyes and nerves. Use it by all means, but break it up with other colours, or soften the white by adding just a touch of another colour—you can now buy a wide range of off-white paints ready-mixed.

One final point. The kitchen is potentially the most dangerous room in the house, so it is a good idea not to make it too bland, too soothing. You want to be calm, but also alert. Beige, for example, is gentle and easy to live with, but consider adding a dash of red or emerald green as part of the decor. Yellow, peach and pink are also thought to increase alertness.

Ways to use colour as an accent rather than on the walls include curtains, blinds, cushions on chairs, tablecloths, napkins, pictures and wall hangings. Flowers create a variety of moods: carnations are rather formal and elegant, roses speak of country gardens and summer, the simplest bunch of wild flowers adds charm as well as colour. If it's green you have chosen to brighten your kitchen, let plants do it for you—grow herbs in pots or a window box, and you have the added advantage of taste and fragrance as well as colour.

The cooker

For centuries the cooker has been far more than just a piece of equipment on which to cook a meal. The solid fuel stoves that were once found in every farmhouse kitchen and 'below stairs' in town houses also warmed the room itself, dried clothing, and heated water and the plates and dishes on which the meals were served. Such stoves are still occasionally found in old houses (or on sale—at inflated prices—in antique markets). Companies such as Aga, Rayburn and Jøtul are also making newer versions that retain many of the old features and advantages, yet are more streamlined to look at home in today's kitchens. They are beautiful pieces of equipment that cook foods in the time-honoured way—slowly and gently. You do, however, need to have access to a good supply of fuel if you intend to use this kind of cooker.

Most people in Britain cook with gas or electricity, the advantages of each being balanced by disadvantages. Both are cost-effective if used sensibly, so that ultimately it comes down to a matter of personal preference. Gas responds more quickly, and tends to bake more evenly. Electric heating elements have an increased efficiency over gas burners, and the electric oven—which is relatively airtight—lets out less waste heat than the gas oven. As manufacturers vie with each other to increase their share of the market, a whole new range of cookers is becoming available, many of them imported from Europe and Scandinavia, countries where kitchens have long been considered important enough to warrant the interest of top designers and technicians.

You can now get models of numerous shapes, sizes and styles, including fitted cookers, free-standing cookers, some with combinations of gas and elecricity, many with interchangeable parts. Some come topped with magnetic induction units which look like tiles but do not heat up, instead using magnetic energy to cook food by energizing molecules in both the food and the pan. There are cookers with built-in deep fryers and microwave ovens, self-cleaning ovens, eye-level ovens, timers that will switch everything on, judge when the food is cooked, and switch off. Some cookers look so unlike a cooker that you'd be hard-pressed to find it in an unfamiliar kitchen.

There is nothing wrong with high-technology cookers—except that they are unnecessary. Good natural foods need the minimum of cooking, can be served in the simplest dishes, and will taste all the better for it. They also need the minimum amount of energy to make them ready for the table. Ecologically it used to make sense to use a woodburning stove. Nowadays, with so many trees and woodlands being carelessly destroyed and so few being replaced, this is often no longer the case. The best course of action, then, is to make a careful list of the facilities you expect of a cooker, and of the ways in which you intend to use it. Then buy the best you can afford. Make a point of using it properly, never cooking just one item in the oven when you could be baking something else at the same time, maintaining it so that it works efficiently. Treat it as a luxury and a privilege—remember how many people in this world still have to cook over open fires.

The tools for the job

Complicated cooking techniques are rarely part of holistic eating. However, a certain number of basic kitchen tools are necessary, and good food deserves quality equipment. Though not strictly necessary, there are other items which either make the task that much easier, or give you the opportunity to widen your scope, maybe make certain ingredients at home, or become more creative without taking up cordon bleu cookery.

BASICS

A set of heavy pans

If you can't afford a set, at least invest in a couple, preferably of different sizes, plus if possible a frying pan. Make sure the lids fit well. Get the best quality you can afford, enamelled iron being preferable. Cast iron is also a good choice and you may be able to pick up seconds at a reasonable price (make sure the enamel inside isn't chipped). Stainless steel is a cheaper alternative. Plain glass pans and frying pans are now becoming available and are good to cook in. Don't buy aluminium—it leaves a poisonous deposit on food, and is usually too thin to cook evenly.

Knives

Though these often come in sets, two or three of different sizes will probably be enough. Look for heavy knives. Again it is best to pay as much as you possibly can. Higher quality knives are a good investment.

Chopping block

Hardwood is best.

Grater

Essential for grating cheese, breadcrumbs, apples for muesli, etc.

Steamer

A fold-up stainless steel steamer that can be slipped into saucepans of different sizes is ideal, and not expensive.

Whisk

Buy a rotary or wire whisk for making soufflés, muffins, pancake batter, salad dressings, etc.

Brush

A long-handled brush makes it quick and less messy to oil dishes and tins, also to coat pastry with milk or egg white. If you only intend to use it for oil, you can stand it in a small jar of oil ready for instant action.

Wooden spoon

Invaluable for making sauces, and gentle on both the food and your pots. A long handle will keep your hand clear of danger.

Wooden spatula

Should be flat, also with a long handle. Make sure you clean it well after use.

Measuring jug

Necessary until you can judge amounts for yourself.

Tablespoon

Also necessary for judging amounts, especially if you have no scales.

Rolling pin

Available in all sorts of materials from simple wood to decorated ceramics. One of the best is a hollow tube of glass that can be filled with ice cubes so that the pastry stays really cool.

Tins

For baking. These should include small cake or muffin tins, swiss roll tin, and a flat baking sheet. Get a couple of bread tins and start baking your own bread—kneading dough is wonderful therapy.

Oven-to-table casseroles

Perfect for winter stews.

Specialist dishes

Such as those made for flans and soufflés. At a pinch you could buy a flan ring and stand it on a baking sheet, and make the soufflé in any small heatproof dish.

Colander

Or any other kind of strainer, such as a sieve. Not strictly necessary, but a great help, and they're not expensive.

Empty screw-top jars

Invaluable for storing things; also for use as a seed sprouter (make holes in the top, or cover with muslin).

Mixing bowls

One would do; two would be better.

Grinder

A small grinder—whether it is one of the many inexpensive electrical ones made for coffee, or a hand grinder for use with grains —is well worth buying. Apart from coffee and grains, use it for grinding nuts (to make butters, rissoles, nut loaves), beans (to make patés, hummous, spreads), seeds (to add to biscuits and muesli), and so on. Some of them have a small blender unit which can be attached to the grinder, good for making soups and sauces.

Thermos flask

A wide-necked thermos flask is a great way to cook without using energy. It also means you can leave things to cook during the day so they are ready for you when you get home. Buy a large or small flask, depending on how many people you want it to cook for. Put in porridge oats and water or milk at night for the quickest hot breakfast ever. Cook beans, vegetables, soups and grains in it.

EXTRAS

Fridge

Not strictly necessary in our temperate climate, though summers *can* be hot, and ingredients that aren't packed full of preservatives go off quicker. Very small fridges are available for very small spaces.

Mortar and pestle

A nice old-fashioned way to grind herbs and spices without reducing them to dust. Can also be used for nuts, seeds, etc. if you don't have a grinder.

Garlic press

Quicker and easier than doing it without one.

Kitchen scissors

Good to have in the kitchen for all those times you need to cut something, also for trimming vegetables such as globe artichokes, for snipping chives, etc.

Wok

Excellent for quick, crisp stir-fried vegetables. It originated in China where cooking fuels were valuable, hence the wok is made in such a way that minimum heat is needed whilst maximum nutrients are preserved. There are a number of different sorts of wok now available, and it isn't necessary to buy the most expensive, as long as the one you choose is heavy and well-made.

Chopsticks

If you intend to eat the Chinese way.

Scales

Simple scales make mistakes less likely. Wall scales are neat and take up no space.

Sprouter

There are a number of special seed sprouters available, but the most common comes in the form of three round plastic tiers which fit together, allowing you to sprout three different kinds of seed at the same time.

Yogurt maker

There are a number of different kinds on the market at a range of prices. Having a yogurt maker means that you can have a continuous supply of home-made yogurt. (You could, of course, use the thermos flask instead.)

Juicer

For the luxury of home-made fruit and vegetable juices—and the fun of blending them.

Paper towels

Not really necessary, but useful if you like to fry things. Coloured dyes pollute: use white.

Water filter

Our water contains many additives, though what they are and in what amounts they are present varies enormously from one area to another. If you are concerned about your water supply, either fit a filter on to the tap (which will remove at least some of the chlorine, lead, mercury, etc.), or buy a filter that fits into the top of a jug, through which you pour water before using it. Simply boiling water helps a little.

Vegetable mill

These have a choice of discs so you can make finer or coarser purées, using cooked or some raw vegetables. All you do is turn the handle. Needs careful cleaning.

Pressure cooker

A more expensive piece of equipment, but worth it if you need to cook things quickly. Look for stainless steel or enamelled steel, which are more expensive but better. Cooks vegetables, beans and grains in the shortest possible time while sealing in the goodness.

Salt and pepper mills

More for the table than the kitchen, unless you like to season your food before you serve it. Freshly-ground salt and pepper have more taste. Such mills won't last forever as the grinding blades, once blunted, cannot be sharpened.

LUXURIES

Fridge/freezer

The larger the better if you are really cut off from the world, or if you have access to masses of fresh fruit and vegetables in season (though don't do what some people do and freeze the lot, never allowing yourself the pleasure of *fresh* ingredients!). Don't forget that a large freezer is a responsibility and can be quite expensive to run.

Slow cooker

Works on electricity; gives food the gentle treatment.

Fondue set

Fondues are an excellent idea for sharing a meal with friends and family, and this is one of the few occasions when it is hard to find alternative equipment.

Asparagus pan

If you like asparagus, it really does make it easier to cook.

Pasta-making machine

More of a pasta-shaping machine, so when you get tired of serving your home-made pasta as lasagne you can ring the changes. Most of these machines are imported from Italy. Using them can be as much fun as eating the results.

Toasted sandwich maker

The quick and easy way to make toasted sandwiches.

Ice cream scoop

If you're going to go to all the bother of making your own ice cream, doesn't it deserve to be served properly?

Skewers

Use them to make fruit and vegetable kebabs, or skewer baked potatoes to help them cook faster. Ideal for barbecue food.

Sugar thermometer

Helpful for anyone who likes to make their own wholesome sweets or jams.

Special dishes

These are cleverly-shaped to hold certain kinds of fruits and vegetables steady while you dig in. Look out for dishes shaped for grapefruit, avocados and corn-on-the-cob.

Washing up

When you don't use meat or rich sauces you'll find that dishes don't get anywhere near as dirty as they used to—neither does any remaining food stick as firmly. Very often you can clean a pan simply by soaking it in cold water, then scrubbing it with a brush. Plates may need no more than hot water. Any oil that remains on dishes, pans and knives will do more good than harm. Most washing-up liquids are synthetic detergents which are petroleum-based, depositing phosphates and mercury into our environment. Such detergents have been a recognized source of environmental pollution since the 1960s, being highly detrimental to freshwater ecosystems and killing plants and fish. There are one or two alternative washing-up liquids now coming on to the market, but if they are unobtainable in your area and you really need occasionally to use a little help, dilute a concentrated brand—then only use half as much as normal.

Order out of chaos

In a rambling country kitchen there is no problem providing you organize yourself. Go through all your cupboards and put the items you rarely use behind those you use more frequently, or on top of cupboards. If there are things you never use, throw them out or give them away. Arrange the items you need frequently where they can easily be reached—if you keep them to a minimum, you won't need more than a few shelves. Unless you continually entertain large numbers of people, it is wasteful to keep extensive sets of crockery, glasses and cooking pans—they will only crowd your life and your home.

The idea that all holistically-minded people live in the country is wrong. Many live in cities, some even in one-room bed-sitters where the kitchen is no more than a curtained-off corner of the room with a Baby Belling and just enough space to swing a lettuce. Under such conditions everything should obviously be kept to a minimum. Find a few basic pieces of equipment that you find comfortable to work with, and stick with them. To store them, make use of those places which are usually ignored, the ceiling, for example. Rails can be suspended from which you can hang saucepans, spoons and knives. A plate-drying rack can be suspended from the wall to hang over the sink; a chopping-board can be put over the sink when in use and slid between a cupboard and the wall when not wanted. Metal or wicker stacking baskets can be hung from a ceiling or a wall cupboard, and used for fruit or vegetables. Unused spaces on top of cupboards can be used to store things you rarely use. If you need scales, buy ones that fit on to the wall. A large sheet of pegboard or a metal grid can be fixed to a wall and used to hang all sorts of things on; glass shelves across a window provide storage space without cutting out too much light. Make a point, too, of buying things that stack inside each other—bowls, saucepans, crockery. Stacking plastic containers are a good way to store basic ingredients too, though don't pile things up too high—you'll be for ever picking them up.

Better safe than sorry

Accidents in the kitchen happen easily, so it's best to take precautions, especially if there are small children around. Cook on the rings at the back of the cooker whenever possible, and make sure you turn the handles away from little fingers. Keep the oven door firmly shut. Knives are best stored in a knife block, or held on a magnetic rack out of reach. Any sharp equipment should be washed with care, then dried and put away at once. Electric appliances should be switched off and unplugged when they are not in use. Curtains and other fabrics should be kept well away from live flames. Detergents and other toxic liquids should be kept out of reach—better still, don't use them. Any mess on the floor should be cleared up before someone slips on it, and if there are any items that cannot be reached without using a chair to stand on, consider buying a small solid stepladder—at least make sure your chairs are strong and firm. Climbing up to reach things is one of the main causes of accidents in kitchens.

Off you go

When everything is completed, your kitchen organized and equipped with the things you want to use, decorated to your satisfaction, safe and warm and pleasant, you are ready to start. Be aware of the life force in the ingredients you are handling, cook with care, cook with love. It is said that a meal cooked in temper, in haste, will tend to be indigestible, giving little sustenance. Through food you can show your love for yourself and for friends and family in a very tangible way. Sharing the task of preparing a meal with others can often create a closeness like no other. Eat together, and the circle is completed.

Producing Your Own Food

Now pause with yourselfe,
and view the end of all your Labours . . .
unspeakable Pleasure and infinite Commodity.

Gervase Markham
A New Orchard (1648)

Producing Your Own Food

Since the last war, people have been finding countless excuses as to why they cannot produce their own food. No time, no space, they don't have the right equipment, don't have the know-how. Why bother anyway when you can buy anything you need from the shops? Yet even as our society has become more technological, more removed from its important grass roots, there is a new swing back to doing it yourself. And the advantages make the effort more than worthwhile.

By producing your own food you can avoid many of the harmful substances with which commercially-produced foods are flavoured, coloured and preserved, so your health benefits. If you grow your own vegetables you get the added benefits of fresh air, exercise and the tranquillity and sense of purpose that come from working with your hands, from planting, growing and caring for living things.

Another advantage is a reduced dependence on shops and the outside world. When the threat of a bread strike has people queueing outside the bakers, you'll be looking forward to kneading the dough. When a recipe calls for soured cream, you'll make your own. When winter is at its worst and there are no salad ingredients to be had for love or money, you'll sprout your own grains and seeds. When friends arrive unexpectedly and the cupboard is almost bare, you'll make some pasta, serve it with a simple sauce, and surprise everyone as well as sending them on their way full of good food.

You'll generally save money by producing your own foods too, though not always. Some artificially-produced foods, bulked up with water, flavoured with inexpensive chemicals, made in cost-effective quantities, will work out cheaper. Your version, however, will contain many more nutrients and almost certainly taste better, and as the principle reasons for eating are to be nourished and to enjoy your food, you'll win.

There is one more reason for producing as much of your own food as possible. Far too many people today, especially those who live in cities, think of food as a commodity that comes ready for use in bottles or cellophane packs, or out of the freezer. Because they know little or nothing about how it is produced and where it comes from, they have no sense of awe or gratitude at what is little short of a miracle. Food is life—without it we cannot survive. It deserves to be consumed thoughtfully, to be understood and appreciated, never more so than when so many people in the world are going hungry. Learn how to produce your own food, do so whenever you can, and you will be nourished in many ways. Get your family and friends to help you as you work in the kitchen and in the garden, to pick fruit from the hedgerows with you, to share the happy and satisfying experience of total involvement.

On the following pages you will find many foods you can produce without complicated equipment, or taking too much time. Once you have discovered the pleasure of doing it yourself, go on and do more things. There are many books that will give you advice to get you started—some are listed at the end of this book. Once you have the habit, you'll find that nothing else compares with what you can produce with your own hands.

GHEE (CLARIFIED BUTTER)
What you'll need:
—A medium sized saucepan, preferably enamelled, cast iron, or stainless steel.
—A wooden spatula or slotted spoon.
—Muslin or a sieve lined with absorbent paper.
—A large screw-top jar.
—2lb (900g) butter, preferably unsalted.
Method:
Put the butter into the saucepan, melt gently, then bring to the boil, stirring continually. Lower heat and simmer for 30 minutes. Take the pan off the heat and use the spatula to remove the scum from the top. Set aside to cool for about 2 hours, then strain the liquid through the muslin into the jar. Cover and store in the fridge, where it should keep for up to a year.

SOURED CREAM
What you'll need:
—1 pint (570ml) single cream
—2 tablespoonsful lemon juice
Method:
Stir the lemon juice into the cream, mixing well. Cover and set aside. Let it stand overnight. The resulting cream will be thick and have the bite of soured cream—leave it longer still and it will become even thicker.

Soured cream can also be made with double cream, though obviously this will be much richer in saturated fats, and tastes much the same as sheeps' yogurt, which is only about 5% fat. To make an interesting topping for fresh fruit salads, stir a little fresh cream into your soured cream.

SOFT CHEESE
What you'll need:
—A medium-sized saucepan, preferably enamelled, cast iron or stainless steel.
—Muslin
—Plastic trays or cartons, such as those in
  which soft margarines are sold.
—2 pints (1140ml) milk (whole or skimmed,
  cows' or goats')
—juice of 1 lemon
plus your choice of seasonings:
—salt
—freshly-ground black pepper
—finely-chopped onion
—crushed garlic
—finely-chopped fresh herbs
—caraway seeds
—crushed pineapple
—grated Cheddar cheese
Method:
Make sure all your utensils are absolutely
clean, using a sterilizing solution if necessary. Put the milk into the pan and heat
gently until warm (approx. 100°F/
38°C). Add the lemon juice, stir well, then
set aside to cool. Put the mixture into a muslin cloth, tie the corners to make a bag, and
leave suspended so that the whey is drained
off (the whey can be used in baking). This
process can take anything from 12 to 24
hours.

Add flavouring, if you intend to use it,
mixing it evenly through the curds. Spoon
into the plastic trays or cartons (prick the
bases with a needle first, just in case there is
any excess moisture remaining). Cover and
store in the fridge. Best eaten within 3-4
days, though it can be kept for up to a week.
Makes approx. 8-10oz (225-285g).

When commercial cottage cheese is made,
a little single cream is stirred in before it is
stored. Try this for a smoother, creamier
version.

1. *Pour the milk into the clean pan.*

2. *Heat gently until warm.*

3. Collect the juice from a lemon.

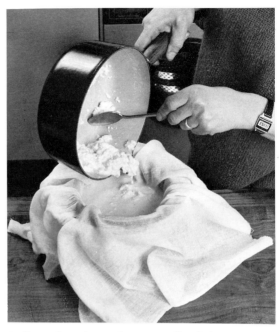

5. Pour the mixture into a muslin cloth.

4. Add the lemon juice to the milk in the pan and stir well.

6. Tie the corners to make a bag, and suspend it so that the whey is drained off.

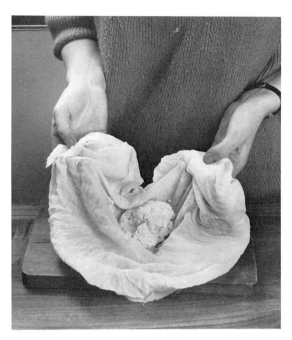

7. Carefully remove the cheese from the muslin.

8. Serve as it is, or flavoured. Though best eaten when fresh, it can also be covered and stored in the fridge for a few days.

YOGURT
What you'll need:
—A medium-sized saucepan, preferably en-amelled, cast iron or stainless steel
—Vacuum flask, glass jars, or an electric yogurt maker
—1 pint (570ml) milk (whole, skimmed, cows', ewes', goats', longlife, soya, or sterilized)
—1 tablespoonful natural yogurt or packet of yogurt culture
—1 tablespoonful single cream or skimmed milk powder
plus your choice of flavourings:
—honey
—maple syrup
—raw cane sugar
—lemon curd
—jam made with raw sugar
—fruit purée
Method:
Make sure all your utensils are absolutely clean, using a sterilizing solution if necessary. Put the milk into the pan and add the cream or skimmed milk powder if you are using it. Mix well, then bring to the boil, stirring to prevent a skin forming. Either cool the milk, or simmer uncovered for 10 minutes to help thicken the yogurt, then cool. When the milk reaches just above blood heat (approx. 110°F/43°C), whisk in the yogurt or culture. Pour at once into the warmed vacuum flask, seal and set aside. If using jars, make sure they are warm, add the milk, and seal, wrapping them in hot towels and storing them in a warm place such as an airing cupboard. If using a yogurt maker, seal it according to the instructions. The yogurt will set in anything from 3-8 hours (the average is 6-7 hours), depending on the milk, the starter, and where the container is kept. When ready, add flavouring if you are using one (you can add it when the

yogurt is served if you prefer). Store in a fridge, where it will thicken a little more. Eat within 4-5 days.

Although yogurt can be made by adding a spoonful of yogurt to the milk, setting aside a little of each new batch for this purpose, it is a good idea to use yogurt culture now and again. Bulgarian is best.

TOFU (SOYA BEAN CURD)
What you'll need:
—A small mixing bowl
—Wire whisk or fork
—A medium-sized saucepan
—A wooden spoon
—Muslin
—A colander
—4oz (115g) soya flour
—1¼ pints (700ml) water
—2 tablespoons lemon juice
plus your choice of flavourings:
—salt
—freshly-ground black pepper
—fresh or dried herbs
—chopped onion
Method:
Put the flour into a mixing bowl and gradually whisk in one third of the water, making sure the mixture is well blended and free from lumps. Put the remaining water into the saucepan, stir in the mixture, and bring to the boil. Lower the heat and cook gently for an hour. Stir in the lemon juice, then set aside to cool.

Lay the muslin across the colander, and spoon in the mixture. Tie up the corners to make a bag, then suspend it over a bowl and leave it long enough for the whey to drain. Add any flavourings at this stage. Store the tofu in a container and cover it with cold water. Change the water daily if the tofu is not to be used at once, though it is best to eat it fresh.

This recipe for tofu is easy and quick, but the tofu will not taste the same as the commercial variety. For fully-illustrated instructions on how to make a more authentic tofu, see *The Findhorn Family Cook Book*. If you'd like to know more about tofu, its history and uses, see the bibliography for more books on this fascinating subject.

SPROUTED BEANS, SEEDS AND GRAINS
What you'll need:
—A colander
—A small dish
—A large jam or kilner jar
—Muslin, cheesecloth or nylon net
—Elastic band
—1-2 tablespoonsful of the ingredient of your choice:
  Pulses: aduki beans, whole lentils, chick peas, mung beans, soya beans, whole peas, etc.
  Grains: wheat berries, barley, buckwheat, corn, oats, rice, triticale, rye, etc.
  Seeds: alfalfa, fenugreek, sunflower, sesame, etc.
Method:
Wash the beans, grains or seeds to remove all dust; this is easiest to do if you put them in a colander and let cold water run through them. Pick out any small stones, wild seeds or foreign objects, then put your chosen ingredient into the bowl, cover with tepid water, and leave overnight in a warm, dark place.

Now pour off the water and put the beans, grains or seeds into the jar. The water is rich in amino-acids and minerals, so use it in soups, drinks or sauces rather than throwing it away. Secure muslin across the top using the elastic band to hold it in place. Pour fresh water into the jar through the muslin, then gently tip it so the water drains away again. You can either return the jar to the warm, dark place, or leave it out in the light.

1. Put the well-washed beans, grains or seeds into bowls. Cover with tepid water and leave in a warm dark spot overnight.

3. Secure a piece of muslin across the top using an elastic band to hold it in place.

2. Pour off the the water. Tip the beans into a jar.

4. Pour fresh water into the jar through the muslin.

5. Tip gently so that the water drains away. Do this 2-3 times daily until the sprouts are the right length.

6. When using stacked sprouting trays you can grow different kinds of sprouts at the same time, rinsing them through in one go.

Sprouts grown in the light have more vitamin C and chlorophyll, but less vitamin B. Sprouts grown in a cooler place will take a little longer before they are ready to eat, but they too will have a higher vitamin C content.

Wherever you decide to grow the sprouts, they will need to be rinsed 2-3 times each day so they are always damp, yet they should not be left standing in water. In summer, or if you leave the jar in a warm place, make sure the sprouts do not dry out, or they will shrivel and die. Handle them carefully—they are fragile.

The shoots will begin to appear in a day or two, and will be ready to eat in anything from 3-5 days, when the shoots themselves will be between ¼″ and ½″ (6-12mm) in length. Eat the whole thing, though alfalfa should be put into cold water to release the small, hard husks, which will float to the top and can then be scooped off. All sprouts not intended for immediate use should be rinsed again, drained well, then stored in the fridge in a polythene bag or a container with a top. They will keep for a few days, though they are tastiest and most nutritious when eaten fresh.

Tips:

Buy only fresh, untreated seeds—shop at a wholefood or health food shop to be sure. Seeds intended for pets or for agricultural use may well have been treated with chemicals.

Choose the right size of jar. Some sprouts can increase in volume up to eight times, so you'll need to leave plenty of room. If they are filling the jar, but are not yet ready to eat, you can transfer some of them to another jar, but do so carefully to avoid damaging the tiny shoots.

Heavily-chlorinated water should be boiled and then left to cool before you use it to rinse your sprouts.

Although it is best to sprout each variety of bean, seed and grain separately, since they grow at different speeds, some can be grown together to make interesting salad mixtures. Ready-mixed seeds are available, chosen because they grow well together, or you can choose your own combinations once you have experimented with them separately. Good combinations are: mung beans, aduki beans and whole lentils; wheat, oats and aduki beans; alfalfa, cress and sesame seeds.

In theory all live beans, grains and seeds can be sprouted. In practice, though, many of the larger ones are very difficult to grow, especially if the temperature is uneven. The easiest are the smaller ones like alfalfa, mung, lentils, aduki and fenugreek.

You can buy specially-made sprouting trays. One of the most popular comes in three layers, which enables you to grow different kinds in each tray, or to start them on different days, thus ensuring a continuous supply of ready-to-eat sprouts.

WHOLEMEAL BREAD
What you'll need:
—Large pottery mixing bowl
—Small mixing bowl
—Wooden spoon
—Floured board or work surface
—Tea towel
—Two 2lb loaf tins
—3lb (1.4kg) 100% wholemeal flour
—Pinch of salt
—1oz (30g) fresh yeast, or ½oz (15g) dried yeast
—1 teaspoonful raw cane sugar, honey or molasses
—1¾ pints (1 litre) warm water
—2 tablespoonsful vegetable oil (optional)
Method:
Sift together the flour and salt into the large, warmed mixing bowl (pottery holds the heat better which is why it is ideal for bread

making). In the small bowl cream the yeast with just a little of the water and the sweetener (this feeds the yeast and so helps to activate it). When the yeast has dissolved completely, set it aside in a warm place for 5 minutes, or until it is frothy.

Make a well in the centre of the flour and use the wooden spoon to stir in the yeast, then add the rest of the water and mix well (you might need to add a drop more water if the dough seems dry). Transfer it to a floured board and knead for 5-10 minutes, at the same time working in the oil if you are using it. By kneading you are folding in air, so the longer you do it the better will be your bread. When the dough is supple and smooth return it to the bowl, cover with a tea towel, and put it in a warm place for about an hour, or until it has doubled in size.

1. Cream the yeast with a drop of the warm water and the sweetener of your choice.

2. Add the yeast mixture to the flour, then add the remaining water and mix well.

4. Return dough to warmed bowl, cover with a tea towel, and leave in a warm spot until dough has doubled in size.

3. Transfer the dough to a floured board and knead for 5-10 minutes.

5. Grease two large loaf tins.

6. *Divide and shape the dough. Place carefully in the tins, cover, and leave to rise to the top of the tins.*

7. *Bread is cooked when it sounds hollow if rapped with the knuckle. Cool on a wire rack.*

Turn the dough back on to the floured board and punch it down. Leave it in the warm for 10 minutes, then divide it in two and shape it into loaves. Put each loaf into a greased tin, cover them, and leave until the dough has risen to the top of the tins.

Bake in an oven preheated to 400°F/200°C (Gas Mark 6) for 10 minutes, then reduce the heat to 350°F/180°C (Gas Mark 4) and bake for another 30-40 minutes. The bread is ready when it sounds hollow when rapped with the knuckle. For a crisper loaf, remove the loaf from the tin and return it to the oven, standing it upside down, for a few more minutes.

Cool the loaves on a wire rack, covering them with a tea towel if you like them to be softer inside.

QUICK WHOLEMEAL BREAD

Follow the same procedure as above, but instead of placing the dough back in the bowl after the first kneading, shape it straight away, then put the loaves in the tins and leave them in a warm place to rise. When ready, bake them as described above. If you are using this method, it is very important to knead the dough really well the first time.

ROLLS OR BAPS

Follow the same procedure as for wholemeal bread up to the end of the first kneading. Then divide the dough into small portions and shape them into twists, cornets or rounds, weighing them if you want them to be exactly even in size. Place them on a greased baking sheet and cover them with a tea towel. Leave them in a warm draught-free place until they have doubled in size. Bake at 400°F/200°C (Gas Mark 6) for about 15 minutes, or until cooked.

This quantity of dough makes about 16 rolls. For a smaller amount, either half the ingredients, or use half of the dough to make a large loaf and make rolls with the rest. You can sprinkle the rolls with sesame or poppy seeds, crushed buckwheat or other grains.

BASIC UNYEASTED BREAD
What you'll need:
—Large pottery mixing bowl
—Wooden spoon
—Tea towel
—Floured board or work surface
—Two 2lb loaf tins
—3lb (1.4kg) 100% wholemeal flour
—Pinch of salt
—1½ pints (850ml) warm water
Method:
Sift one third of the flour together with the salt, put into a bowl, and very gradually pour in the water, stirring well to fold in the air. When well mixed, cover with a tea towel and leave in a warm place for a few hours.

Add the flour to make a soft but firm dough. Turn out on to a floured board and knead for 10 minutes. Put the dough back into the clean bowl, cover with a tea towel, and leave in a warm place for 8-12 hours (overnight is ideal).

Knead again for a few minutes, then divide it in two, shape each into a loaf and place it in a greased tin. Bake at 350°F/180°C (Gas Mark 4) for 1 hour, or until the crust is crisp.

The natural yeast present in fresh flour will make the bread rise, though this kind of bread is heavier and chewier than the more traditional wholemeal bread. If the water you use is heavily-chlorinated, boil it first. Add seeds, whole grains, dried fruit or herbs to the dough to make a more unusual loaf.

SODA BREAD
What you'll need:
—Large pottery mixing bowl
—Wooden spoon
—Greased baking sheet
—Knife
—1lb (455g) 100% wholemeal flour
—Pinch of salt
—2 teaspoonsful bicarbonate of soda
—½ pint (285ml) soured milk, buttermilk or natural yogurt
—¼ pint (140ml) warm water
—1 small egg
Method:
Sift the flour and salt into the warmed bowl, then use the spoon to stir in the bicarbonate of soda, mixing it well. Gradually stir in the milk, then add just enough warm water to make a moist but firm dough. Knead it briefly.

Shape the dough into a round loaf and place it on the baking sheet, flattening it slightly. Use the knife to cut a deep cross on the top of the loaf. Whisk the egg with a spoonful of water, and brush the loaf with the mixture.

Bake in a preheated oven, temperature 400°F/200°C (Gas Mark 6) for 15 minutes, then reduce the heat to 350°F/180°C (Gas Mark 4) and continue cooking for 15-25 minutes, or until firm to the touch.

This quick-to-make bread can be kept for a few days, but is much tastier if eaten when fresh.

WINE
What you'll need:
—1 gallon saucepan in which to boil the ingredients if necessary
—Campden tablets for sterilizing equipment
—Large plastic bucket or stone jar
—Muslin
—Polythene funnel
—Two 1-gallon demijohns
—Holed corks and a fermentation lock
—Thin plastic tubing
—6 bottles—dark for red wine, light for white

—6 corks
—Ingredients of your choice (see the list below)
—wine yeast
—1 dessertspoonful malt extract
—juice of 1 lemon
—raw cane sugar or white sugar—the darker the sugar the more golden the colour of the wine. Use 2½lbs for dry wines, 3lb for medium wines, 3½lbs for sweet wines.

Method:
First sterilize all your equipment.

Extract the juice from the fruit you are using. Softer varieties can be pressed by hand, or you can use a juice extractor or fruit press. Harder varieties will need to be boiled first to soften them. Trim, wash, then chop the fruit and put it into the saucepan, cover it with water and boil for as long as necessary, then strain off the juice.

Pour the juice into the bucket or jar and add a gallon of water. Stir in the wine yeast (made up according to the instructions on the packet), the malt extract (to feed and boost the yeast), the lemon juice, and ½lb of the sugar. Mix well, cover with muslin, then leave in a warm place to ferment, stirring occasionally.

Put a piece of muslin over the funnel and strain the liquid into the sterilized demijohn, filling up to the neck of the jar (add a drop of tepid water if necessary). Seal with the cork and airlock, pouring some sterilized solution into the lock to complete the air trap. Return the demijohn to a warm place for 10 days, then add ½lb of sugar, making sure it is well dissolved. After 5 days add more sugar. Continue to do this until you have added the required amount of sugar. Set the jar aside until fermentation ceases, which can take several weeks or even longer, depending on the temperature and the ingredients. If the fermentation seems to be stopping too soon, check that the spot in which the demijohn is

standing isn't too hot, or, which is more likely, too cold. Check that you've added enough sugar—too little or too much can affect fermentation. Stirring the wine can help reactivate it.

When fermentation has ceased altogether you can, if you want to, add another Campden tablet, then leave the wine to clear, the yeasts and solids sinking to the bottom. Remove the cork and the airlock, and use the thin plastic tubing to siphon off the clear wine into the second demijohn, sucking it gently to get it going. It helps if you place the empty jar at a lower level than the full one. Watch carefully as the first demijohn empties—you don't want to disturb any of the the sediment. Top up, if necessary, with a sterile solution of 2oz (55g) of sugar mixed with ½ pint (285ml) of water. Replace the cork and airlock and set aside for a few more months. You can repeat this process, especially if you intend to serve the wine straight from the demijohn. Alternatively, you can siphon the clear wine into sterilized bottles, filling them to the top. Sterilize the corks before putting them firmly into the bottle necks (soaking them for a few hours makes this process easier to do).

Wine should be left for at least six months and preferably longer, so that the flavour can mature.

Wine can be made from a variety of ingredients, including apples, apricots, barley, beetroot, carrots, cowslips, crabapples, currants, damsons, dandelions, elderberries, elderflowers, ginger, grapes, greengages, lemon, lime blossoms, mangolds, marigolds, parsley, parsnip, pears, plums, potatoes, quinces, raisins, rhubarb, rosehips, rose petals, soft fruits and wheat.

For inexpensive wine use whatever is in season—especially when there are bumper crops! Either buy in bulk, or pick your own, searching the fields and hedgerows, but keeping well away from roads where the plants will be laden with lead from exhausts. You can use damaged, overripe and bruised fruits for wine, and you can mix many types together to make unique wines that no-one will ever recognize. Although wine-making is essentially a simple process, there is much that can go wrong, so be prepared for a few disasters until you get the hang of it. Learn from your mistakes—and don't let them put you off trying again! Once you are more sure of your abilities and know what you like, make larger quantities at a time.

The above instructions have been deliberately simplified. A large number of books are available which give much more precise information—see the bibliography, or your local bookshop or library.

BEER

What you'll need:
—Large plastic bucket or stone jar
—Campden tablets for sterilizing equipment
—Muslin
—Saucepan
—Tea towel
—Thin plastic tubing
—Screw-top beer bottles, or bottles with press-on caps
—1lb (455g) malt extract
—¾oz (20g) hops (preferably Goldings)
—1 quart (1.14 litres) tepid water
—3 quarts (3.4 litres) boiling water
—1 teaspoonful granulated yeast
—honey

Method:
Sterilize all your equipment. Warm the malt slightly, then pour it into the bucket or jar, add the tepid water, and stir well to dissolve the malt.

Tie a small piece of the muslin to make a bag, putting ⅞ of the hops inside it, and drop this into a saucepan containing a quart of boiling water. Continue boiling for 10 minutes, strain the liquid on to the mixture in the bucket or jar, and then repeat this process twice more. Put the remaining unused hops into a muslin bag and add them to the bucket. Cover with a tea towel and leave to cool, then add the yeast, making sure it is well mixed. Set the bucket aside for the mixture to ferment, covering it again with the tea towel.

Leave for a day or two, then spoon off the froth that will have formed. Leave to ferment for at least a week, until there is no more activity. Use the thin plastic tubing to siphon off the beer, pouring it straight into clean bottles, allowing 2″ (50mm) space at the top. Add a teaspoonful of honey to each quart of beer. Screw or push the lids on tightly and set the bottles aside for ten days, by which time it should be ready to drink. Pour it carefully into a jug, trying not to disturb the sediment.

This simple recipe is from *Nature's Foods* by Peter Deadman and Karen Betteridge. There are many books giving more detailed instructions on making a variety of beers. See the bibliography for some suggestions to get you started.

GROWING VEGETABLES

Providing you have a small amount of garden space, some time to spare, and the desire to put them both to good use, you'll be able to grow a surprizingly large amount of the food that you and your family need. It is estimated that a 7′ square plot can produce up to 160lbs of food a year. Grow it organically and you'll be working with nature rather than exploiting it, contributing as well as benefiting.

To put it simply, organic gardening is based not so much on feeding your crops as on feeding your soil. When grown from healthy soil, your crops are likely to be excellent. It means understanding what kind of soil you have and treating it accordingly. It involves plenty of digging to provide air and good drainage, and enriching the soil with natural compost and manure rather than chemicals. It also means choosing and placing your crops with care, putting together plants that are mutually beneficial—marigolds with tomatoes, nettles with soft fruit, hyssop with cabbage, winter savory with beans. Because some crops need heavy feeding you will rotate your crops so as not to deplete the soil, a practice that will also reduce the incidence of pests and diseases, especially those that are soil-borne.

Organic growing means removing weeds by hand rather than spraying them with poisons, and doing the same with pests, or devising more natural ways of destroying them, such as using a spray of stinging nettle solution against black- and greenfly.

By putting you back in touch with nature and the world around you, gardening will also increase your awareness of the importance of soil, that same soil that is rapidly disappearing under roads, factories and housing estates, that is being ravaged by chemicals, depleted of any goodness it may have had by simply being overused. With your new awareness you can at least help to correct the balance by treating the soil with the reverence it deserves. In return you will be rewarded not just with a harvest of good things to eat, but with the improved health that comes from working with your own hands in the open air. And you'll save money!

What you'll need:

—A plot of land. This can be anything from a small plot in the back garden to a many-acred farm, a strip of land behind a garage or between the path and the fence. If you have no garden, consider renting an allotment, or persuade someone who doesn't use their garden to let you use it, maybe repaying them by sharing some of your harvest. Don't forget about tubs on patios, boxes on window ledges, hanging baskets (ideal for cherry tomatoes), basements (where mushrooms will grow if nothing else). If you have a garden but are not sure where to place your vegetable plot, pick an open spot rather than one shaded by trees or a building, though not too open, as winds can slow down growth in crops and even damage them.

—A compost bin. This provides an ecological way of getting rid of kitchen and garden waste, and in return gives you humus which is full of good things for both your soil and your plants. The simplest and least expensive kind of compost bin is little more than a compost heap, built in such a way as to allow a few inches beneath it so that air can circulate and encourage the layers of waste material to break down. There are various bins that can be built from kits, and ready-made bins too, all available at reasonable prices.

—Tools. Start with the basics: spade, trowel, hoe, fork, rake. Build up as you go along, buying only what you need—better still, share with a neighbour or friend and reduce your consumerism. It is wise to buy the best quality you can afford. Alternatively, look out for good-quality secondhand tools, which are often better value for money than cheap new ones. Look after them well and they'll last you a lifetime. Once you are used to growing your own vegetables, you might find it worth investing in a greenhouse (or maybe a half-wall greenhouse that fits against the outer wall of your house). This will enable you to expand your range and grow more exotic varieties, as well as help you get seedlings started earlier.

—Seeds. Growing from seeds is the cheapest way to grow your own produce—and probably the most satisfying. It is best to buy from the more reputable companies who now have an enormous variety of vegetables and salad crops to offer, many of them specially bred to provide large yields. Until you know exactly what will grow best in the space you have available, be prepared to experiment (ask local people what varieties grow best). Aim for variety, with some crops that will be ready early in the year, some in high summer and others later in the autumn. Don't start off too many seeds of one variety—if they all take you'll feel obliged to plant them all and have no space for anything else. And if you do only have limited space, it might be best to choose vegetables that are not widely available throughout the year—potatoes, for example, though delicious when home-grown, take up a good deal of space, yet are in the shops at a low price for most of the year.

For those who cannot be bothered with seeds, or when you start too late, or unexpected disaster strikes and your seeds fail, most garden centres will offer a selection of seedlings ready to be planted out.

Method:

First make a plan so that you know exactly what you want to grow and where you intend to grow it. If possible, plan the rows to go from north to south so each plant gets its share of the sun. Seeds can be sown directly into the ground, preferably under a cloche or frame, or they can be started off in an indoor propagator or in a greenhouse. Follow the instructions on the seed packet for the best results. The seedlings must later be thinned and planted out to allow space for growth, and any weak or diseased seedlings discarded.

From then on the job is simply a matter of caretaking. Keep an eye open for pests and diseases. If you catch such problems early they are easier to deal with. In hot weather vegetables will need watering—evening is the best time to water. Some plants benefit from being earthed up to help them stand in windy conditions, and climbing plants will need stakes to which they can cling.

Harvesting your crops is the best bit. Pick them when they are young for maximum taste and nutrients. Overgrown vegetables are never as flavourful, and in any case, removing the crop when young encourages a plant to yield more. Whatever you do don't make the mistake which has become prevalent with the sale of freezers—that of picking vegetables for freezing, and never getting the chance to taste the real thing fresh from the garden!

GROWING FRUIT

Especially suitable for smaller gardens and lazy people, a wide variety of fruits can be grown in Britain. They do require initially to be planted in the spot that is right for them—in the sun or in the shade, in the open or in a sheltered corner, depending on the variety. Many bushes, for example, make ideal dividers in your vegetable patch. They not only protect vegetables from the wind; they also help to stop pests from spreading and benefit from sharing the soil with the vegetables. Most fruit bushes and trees require occasional feeding, mulching (which cuts down on the need to water them so often), and pruning. Apart from that, you need do little except pick the crops when they are ready. Apple and pear trees, strawberries, gooseberries, blackcurrants, redcurrants, blackberries, raspberries—all will give crops year after year once they are established. When space is limited, try planting a gooseberry bush under an apple tree, strawberries under the gooseberry bush!

What you'll need:

—Plants. Young plants are best purchased

from a reputable nursery, where you will also receive advice on planting and care.

Method:

Plant carefully and water well, especially at first. Care depends on the individual plant; some, for example, will need watering more than others. Raspberries will need to be supported, and some soft fruits will need to be covered with a net to protect them from birds. Most trees and bushes benefit from occasional pruning, if only to remove dead wood and so strengthen the rest of the plant. In general, though, most fruits require little maintenance.

GROWING HERBS

Herbs are an essential part of cooking, adding all sorts of benefits, and even if you don't have a garden you can grow them. Ideally, though, they should be grown just outside the kitchen door, ready to be snipped and added to a dish. If little soil is available they can be grown in boxes or pots on a patio or balcony, or even indoors on a sunny window ledge.

What you'll need:

A patch of ground in a sunny, sheltered spot, or you can mix together a selection of small herbs in a large earthenware pot or well-drained trough. Herbs are usually either annuals or perennials, and are available in seed form; sometimes as seedlings.

Method:

Most herbs prefer an infertile and sandy soil. As they are often slow to germinate, it is a good idea to start them early, and they will do well in the warmth of a house or greenhouse. Move them outside only when the danger of frost is past.

When the plant is established, pick the tips or the leaves as needed. Snip the tops of chives, which will soon grow tall again. Fresh herbs have a sweeter yet less concentrated taste than the more familiar dried herbs, and in many ways are better, though as their growing season is short you may like to dry some too. To do this pick the top third of the plant, when the buds are just beginning to open and the weather is dry (if they are not dry they may become mildewed). To be sure they are dry, tie them into loose bunches and hang them in a warm airy spot out of the sunlight. When they are crisp and absolutely dry (which usually takes two to three weeks), rub them into a powder and store them in airtight jars, preferably in the dark. Bay leaves should be left whole. Even dried herbs soon lose their flavour, so use them fresh whenever possible.

PRESERVING YOUR HARVEST

Most vegetables and fruits are best eaten when fresh. The most obvious reason for preserving produce is if you have a glut, and no way of eating it all before it goes off (though do think of others—your glut may well help to fill someone else's food gap, and when *they* have a glut, you will no doubt be happy to help them reduce it!). Gluts can to some extent be avoided by careful planning. The other logical reason for storing food is that of convenience. If you live in an isolated place, or can get to the shops only occasionally, or are cut off for several months in the winter, it makes sense to prepare for difficult times by preserving what you can during times of plenty.

Even so, it is better to use excesses to create new foods. If your cow or goat is giving more milk than you and your friends can drink, make yogurt with the excess. Too many eggs? Make mayonnaise or lemon curd. Jams and chutneys are an ideal way to use a surplus of green tomatoes, apples, rhubarb, mushrooms, marrows and so on.

Still, though, there may be occasions when you would like to keep some vegetables and fruits without changing their taste too much and without losing too many nutrients. Here are some alternative ways to do so.

FREEZING

Freezing foods can be an excellent way of preserving them, as nothing needs to be added or subtracted, they can be frozen almost immediately after they are picked or dug up, and freezing helps to retain much of the original taste.

However, the multi-million pound freezing industry is an example of a good idea gone wrong. Vegetables are now developed and grown especially to be frozen, and though a reasonable variety of frozen vegetables is available, the one on which the industry concentrates is the pea, which now accounts for some 25% of all frozen food sales in Britain, and which has become the standard vegetable to be served day after day. Customers are encouraged to buy frozen foods rather than fresh, to buy large and expensive freezers in which to store them, to run these freezers on electricity, so wasting energy as well as more money. To make matters worse, many frozen foods have unnecessary colouring and sweetening added to make them more appealing. Though the industry may fare well, the customer often loses out by ending up with a nutritionally-inferior product that probably costs a lot more than its fresh equivalent, unless it is bought in bulk, which means even more of it has to be eaten simply because it is there. This is not always the case, however, and frozen peas are an interesting case in point. Since fresh peas quickly lose their nutritional value in storage, frozen peas can be nutritionally superior to fresh peas, even in season. The fact that they are available throughout the year means that a cheap and nutritional vegetable is constantly available, and many nutritionists believe that frozen peas

often protect poorer people from seasonal malnutrition. The best way of retaining the goodness in frozen peas is simply to drop them into boiling water for a few seconds rather than cooking them.

If you feel that you could make good use of a freezer, buy a small one. To run efficiently and economically a freezer should be full, so don't buy a large one unless you plan to keep it full most of the time. Use it for surplus vegetables and fruits, also for baked goods and simple dishes that you might have prepared when time was not a problem, all ready for use when you have no time to cook. Most foods can be frozen, though their taste and texture may well change.

Some guidelines:
—Only freeze good quality vegetables and fruits, putting aside for immediate use any that are blemished, damaged or over-ripe. Freeze them as soon as possible after picking.
—Some vegetables may need to be blanched briefly, then cooled at once in ice-cold water, though don't blanch unless you have to, since even a short blanch destroys up to 30% of the vitamin C content. Follow carefully the instructions that come with your freezer. Though most vegetables freeze reasonably well, some cannot be preserved in this way, especially watery vegetables such as cucumber, marrow and lettuces.
—Fruits are best frozen in a sweetened juice to prevent the growth of enzymes.
—Freeze in small quantities, or you may have to defrost a large amount when you only want one or two portions. Pack each item in moisture-proof bags or covered containers.
—When freezing cooked dishes choose them with care. Be sure to follow the instructions about setting the freezer temperature

control, packing it correctly, adjusting the thickness of the sauces, and thawing everything properly.

—Don't freeze food when you don't have to.

DRYING

One of the oldest methods of preservation, one of the simplest, and probably one of the best, drying has lost a lot of its popularity since the advent of the freezer. Even so, there are still some commercially-produced foods that are dried rather than processed—dried fruits, chestnuts, mushrooms, onions— though machines are often used instead of the sun. Obviously this method of food preservation is best suited to those areas where there is a good deal of sunshine, buteven in Britain many foods can be dried in this way in summer. It is also possible to dry some items indoors, in an airing cupboard for example, or in a cool oven, though care must be taken to keep the temperature high enough to remove the natural moisture of the food, yet not so high that it cooks it.

Method

Only use sound, ripe (but not overripe) fruits and vegetables, preferably freshly-picked. Wash the items to be dried, peel them if you prefer, then slice thinly or cut into rings.

Vegetables will need to be steamed until well-cooked before being dried. Fruit can be dried as it is, though it is a good idea to soak apple and pear rings briefly in salt water, then pat dry—this helps them to keep their colour.

The items to be dried should be laid out flat on a drying frame made of small mesh wire attached to a wooden surround. Take care that they do not touch.

Dry your harvest in a cool oven, an airing cupboard, or out in the sunshine (if left outdoors the trays should be covered with

muslin to protect the food from insects and dirt). Turn the fruit or vegetables over every now and again so that they dry right through.

Vegetable are ready when crisp. Fruit should be supple—squeeze it gently, and if your hand remains dry, the fruit is ready. Small fruit such as berries should rattle when the tray is shaken.

Store dried items in sealed containers or boxes lined with greaseproof paper, with paper between the layers of fruit or vegetables. Don't put different kinds together— onions, for example, can taint other foods. Store them in a cool, dark place.

Fruit can be eaten dry, or rehydrated by soaking it in water. Rehydrate vegetables in a vegetable stock for improved flavour.

BOTTLING

Bottling foods is another old-fashioned way of preserving them, though unlike drying it is quite complicated, requiring the right equipment plus a certain amount of time and patience in order to do the job properly. It is important that it *is* done properly as badly-bottled food can not only taste horrible, but can cause botulism, a form of food poisoning. For those who want to try it, here is the basic method. Before proceeding, though, you should read a book that goes more precisely into the details—look through secondhand bookshops for a cookery book grandma may have thrown out!

Method:

Collect together a number of preserving jars, plus lids and rubber bands or clips for each one, a large preserving pan in which the jars can stand, a rack to place inside the pan so the jars do not stand on the bottom, and a thermometer.

Choose undamaged fruit and vegetables. They can be slightly under-ripe. Peel, core and slice fruit such as apples and pears. Peel tomatoes, dropping them in boiling water first to make this easier. Vegetables should be peeled, sliced and partially cooked.

Fill the pan with water and bring it to the boil, then add the jars, lids and clips in order to sterilize them.

Pack the fruit or vegetable tightly into the jars, filling them right to the top. Pour a syrup of honey and water (plus spices if you like them) onto the fruits. Cover the vegetables with salted water. Seal the jars with the lids. If you are using screw-top jars turn the lids so they are tight, but not too tight, as the glass will probably expand.

Put the jars carefully into the boiling water, standing them on the rack. Make sure they are not touching each other. Simmer for the time advised, which will depend upon what fruits and vegetables you are bottling.

Remove the jars from the water and cool them in a warm room. Check that the lids are secure before storing the jars in a cool, dry, dark place such as a cupboard.

Though the above methods of preservation are far preferable to most of those used by commercial companies, they still reduce the nutrients in food which, when freshly harvested, is bouncing with vitamins and minerals. Use preserved foods by all means, but do not let them take the place of fresh foods on your table. Fresh foods are *live* foods, and it is only through them that you can hope to enjoy the taste of the real thing. Why settle for anything less unless you really have to?

A Wholefood Glossary

If we want the kind of food that sound economy and nutrition
suggest is necessary, then we must demonstrate both that we are
prepared to seek it out and pay for it, and that
we will not tolerate anything less.

Colin Tudge
Future Cook

A Wholefood Glossary

In this chapter you will find a list, in alphabetical order, of all the ingredients most likely to be incorporated into a wholefood diet. Some of them may be unfamiliar, but most of them will be foods you have known and enjoyed for many years.

In many cases, similar ingredients have been grouped together; thus sultanas, for instance, will be found under 'Dried Fruit'; chick peas under 'Pulses'; and broccoli under 'Vegetables'. If you cannot immediately find the ingredient you are looking for, consult the index at the back of the book.

Each description is divided into the following sections:

What it is: A simple explanation of what the product is and, in many cases, how it is produced.

Origins: Many wholefoods have been available for years, if not for centuries, and this section touches on their histories.

Principal nutrients: A brief resumé of the most important nutrients which can be obtained from the ingredient. This is in no way comprehensive, and in any case will vary enormously depending on the origins and growing and manufacturing conditions of the ingredient. Anybody who is particularly interested in the nutritional values of wholefoods should check more detailed sources (see the bibliography).

Buying and storing: Where to buy, what to look out for so you choose only the best ingredients, and how to store them to retain their goodness and taste.

Uses: Tips and ideas for using each ingredient in a variety of dishes, savoury and sweet, simple and impressive, familiar and exotic. Alongside many ingredients are complete recipes for specific dishes, with easy-to-follow instructions.

Quantities of ingredients are given in imperial, metric and US measures; use only one set of measurements in each recipe since equivalent amounts may not be exact. Where British and US terminologies for ingredients differ, both are given.

Where vegetable oil is mentioned as a recipe ingredient, use corn, sunflower, safflower or soya oil; blended vegetable oils are not a good idea because they often have a high degree of saturation.

As you will probably be aware, there is a wide range of opinion on the beneficial (or otherwise) effects of some wholefood ingredients, notably bran, honey, raw sugar, sea salt and vinegar. I have attempted to present the nutritional information as accurately as possible in the light of current knowledge, and also to incorporate the beliefs of advocates of certain ingredients even when these are not always scientifically substantiated. After all, how many times have 'old wives' tales' been later verified by scientific research? Holistic eating involves knowing the facts and not being frightened by them. Since the 'facts' are changing all the time and you have to go on eating, let common sense be your guide rather than fear or fanaticism.

AGAR AGAR

What it is: A powder made from the dried purified stems of kelp, which has exceptionally strong jelling properties. It is unbleached and therefore light grey in colour, though this does not affect the finished dish. A nutritious and vegetarian alternative to gelatine.

Origins: Has long been used in Japan, where there is a tradition of cooking with seaweed. As gelatine beomes more expensive, agar agar is now being used increasingly by sweet manufacturers.

Principal nutrients: Rich in iodine and other minerals.

Buying and storing: Buy in packets from wholefood and health food shops. Store in a cool, dry place.

Uses: Can be used to make sweet and savory jellies. Add two teaspoonful of agar agar to one pint of liquid (or follow the amounts given on the pack). Bring the liquid almost to the boil, then simmer for 3 minutes. The liquid can be water, stock, vegetable or fruit juice—agar agar is especially good with acid fruits.

MOULDED SALAD

1 pint/570ml/2½ cups water
3-4 tablespoonful lemon juice
1 tablespoonful raw cane sugar, or to taste
2 teaspoonful agar agar
2oz/55g/½ cup walnuts (English walnuts)
1 small cucumber
2 sticks celery
2 dessert apples

Bring the water to the boil and add the lemon juice, then stir in the agar agar until it dissolves. Simmer briefly. Leave to cool slightly. Coarsely chop the nuts, slice the cucumber and celery, chop the apples. Add them to the lemon mixture.

Rinse the mould with cold water, shake off any excess, pour in the mixture. Leave to cool, then stir to distribute the salad ingredients evenly. Put in a cold place to set. When ready to serve, dip the mould quickly into hot water, then invert over a plate. Surround with lettuce, watercress, or other greenery.

BRAN

What it is: The tough outer coating of a grain, usually wheat. This is removed during the processing of white flour. Very bland in taste, crunchy in texture, it can be added to most dishes.

Origins: When Dr T. R. Allinson discovered, in London in the 1880s, how bran helped his patients, he campaigned to stop it being removed from flour, but he was considered to be a crank and was ignored. Eventually he was even struck off the medical register. In the early 1900s, the Kellogg Company in the USA sponsored research into the effects of their product *All-Bran*, and came to many of the same conclusions as Dr Allinson. But it has only been in the last decade that fibre has come to be considered as an important and necessary part of our daily diet, and not, as was formerly the case, as an irritant which was devoid of nutrients and therefore best avoided.

Principal nutrients: Bran on its own is not a good source of nutrients. In fact, unprocessed bran prevents minerals such as iron, calcium and zinc being absorbed in the small intestine. When eaten in bread or baked goods, however, bran is a good source of B vitamins, phosphorus and iron. Keeping the bran in grains, or adding bran to flours which have had the bran removed, is believed to help such conditions as constipation, diverticular disease, varicose veins, obesity, piles, hiatus hernia, and possibly some more serious conditions. It is filling, yet contains only about 117 Calories per ounce, so it is also a help for those wanting to lose weight.

Buying and storing: Available coarse or fine milled— for those unused to bran it might be best to start with the easier-to-digest fine. Now available from wholefood and health food shops, plus chemists and many supermarkets. Make sure it is unprocessed natural bran.

Uses: It is recommended that two tablespoonful a day should be added to each person's food, usually in baked goods, though additional bran is not necessary if you are already eating wholegrain breads and other wholegrain products. Bran should not be eaten raw, but added to bread, pastry or hot breakfast cereals, or added to stews and casseroles. When using bran in baking you may need to add extra water to the recipe as bran absorbs more than flour alone. Use it as a coating for fritters, and add it to sauces.

BUTTER

What it is: A fat made by agitating cream so that the fat globules coalesce into progressively larger grains of butter fat. It takes the cream from ten pints of milk to make ½lb of butter. Salt and colourings are frequently added.

Origins: Dairying is a traditional farming practice in temperate climates. Most of the butter consumed in Britain today comes from northern Europe, though some still comes from New Zealand.

Principal nutrients: Butter is approximately 80% fat and 20% water. It also contains vitamins A, D and E. As the fat is highly saturated—the kind suspected of building up in the arteries—butter should be used sparingly. It need not be dropped completely, however, especially by people who do not eat meat. Unsalted and undyed butter is best.

Buying and storing: Best bought frequently and in small amounts. Store in a cool place, preferably in a fridge.

Uses: Keep butter for use only when you are going to appreciate its flavour. Delicious spread on fresh bread or muffins, or on young vegetables, especially sweetcorn. Some baked goods, shortbread for example, taste far better when made with butter.

BREWERS' YEAST

What it is: A by-product of the brewing process, and very nutritious, so well worth adding to your food. It is available in pill form, but the powder is the kind you need for kitchen use.

Origins: The earliest recorded use of yeast as a medicine was in Egypt in 1550 BC. Most brewers' yeast on sale in Britain is produced in this country.

Principal nutrients: Contains sixteen of the twenty amino-acids, and is a very good source of the B complex vitamins. Also contains large amounts of iron, calcium, phosphorus, and two important trace elements: chromium and selenium. As it is easy to destroy the water-soluble B vitamins, brewers' yeast is an excellent way to replace them.

Buying and storing: Available from health foods and wholefood shops, also from many chemists. It must be fresh, so shop where there is a quick turnover. Store in an airtight container in a cool, dry place.

Uses: Start by adding 1 teaspoonful a day and work up. The easiest way is to add it to soups, gravies, casseroles and fruit juices. A quick breakfast drink can be made by whisking together milk, fruit juice, a little vegetable oil, and a spoonful or two of brewers' yeast.

BUTTERMILK MUFFINS

¾lb/340g/3 cups wholemeal (wholewheat) flour
4 good teaspoonful baking powder
Pinch of salt
2oz/55g/⅓ cup raw cane sugar
2 eggs
½ pint/285ml/1⅓ cups buttermilk
3oz/85g/½ cup sultanas (golden seedless raisins) approx. 4 tablespoonful vegetable oil

Sift together the flour, baking powder and salt, then add the sugar. Whisk the eggs lightly, make a well in the centre of the dry ingredients, and add the eggs. Lightly whisk the buttermilk and add it to the mixture, stirring well. Mix in the sultanas. Add enough oil to make the batter fairly liquid, taking care not to overmix.

Grease a tray of muffin tins and fill each one ¾ full with the batter. Bake at 400°F/200°C (Gas Mark 6) for about 20 minutes, or until well risen. Test by inserting a fine knife into one or two of the muffins, which should come out clean. Cool on a wire rack.

BUTTERMILK

What it is: A by-product of the butter-making process, buttermilk is the residue left after churning. It has a slightly acid flavour.

Origins: Buttermilk is not widely used in Britain, but is popular in many other countries including Germany and Scandinavia, America, India and the Middle East.

Principal nutrients: Buttermilk is low in fat and calories, high in protein. It is especially easy to digest.

Buying and storing: Like most dairy products, it is best bought in small amounts, and should be kept in the cool. Available from some health food and wholefood shops, also delicatessens. It can easily be made at home.

Uses: Use buttermilk in baking cakes and pies. Blend it with fruit juice or fresh fruit and ice for a summertime drink. Add it to sauces to serve with vegetables, or curry sauce.

CAROB

What it is: A dark brown powder used as a substitute for chocolate. It is made from the beans of a tall evergreen tree (sometimes called locust bean trees), which are dried and then ground.

Origins: St John the Baptist is said to have lived in the wilderness on honey and locusts (not, as is often indicated, the insects!), so it has obviously been valued for thousands of years. It is often used as food for animals as well as humans, and at one time the seeds were used as currency in the Middle East.

Principal nutrients: Contains protein, carbohydrate, calcium and phosphorus, also pectin (a type of dietary fibre), which it is thought may help to calm upset stomachs. Unlike chocolate, it contains no caffeine, and is unlikely to cause allergic reactions.

Buying and storing: You can buy it from most health food and wholefood shops. Transfer the powder to an airtight container and keep it in a cool place.

Uses: Can be used as a substitute for chocolate. Especially good in milk shakes, also cakes and confectionery. You can also buy carob bars (like chocolate bars) which, when melted, make an ideal coating for biscuits.

CAROB CAKE

4oz/115g/½ cup margarine or butter
4oz/115g/⅔ cup raw cane sugar
2 eggs, lightly beaten
4oz/115g/1 cup wholemeal self-raising flour
2oz/55g/½ cup carob powder
2 teaspoonsful mixed spice
grated rind of ½ an orange

Blend together the softened fat and sugar. Add the eggs. Sift together the flour, carob powder and spice, and stir in the other ingredients. Add the orange peel, distributing it evenly.

Spoon the mixture into a shallow greased and floured tin, smoothing the top. Bake at 350°F/ 180°C (Gas Mark 4) for 20-25 minutes or until firm when pressed lightly. Leave to cool slightly, then cut into squares and transfer to a wire rack.

CHEESE

What it is: A versatile high-fat and high-protein food made from the milk of cows, goats and sheep. Regulations demand that it must contain not less than 40% fat on a dry weight basis, which must be milk fat. Cheese other than soft cheeses are cured by being left to mature with salt under a variety of conditions, each producing an individual flavour. There are about four hundred different types of cheese.

Origins: Cheese was probably first produced by the nomadic tribes of eastern Europe and western Asia, who might have put milk into pouches, slung them over their camels, and let the movement do the rest. Cheese is now one of the most popular foods of all, and is produced all over the world.

Principal nutrients: These depend on the exact composition of the milk or cream from which the cheese was made, though most cheeses are protein-rich, and contain calcium plus the eight essential amino-acids. Hard-pressed cheese, such as Cheddar, contain nearly twice as much protein, weight for weight, as prime beef, but remember that most of us eat far more protein than we need anyway, so getting enough protein is not a valid reason for eating quantities of cheese! Cottage cheese, the dieters' favourite, can be up to 80% water. Dutch cheeses are usually lower in fat than British cheeses, and some recently-introduced cheeses, like Ferndale and Shape, have only half the fat of their traditional counterparts. Cheeses to avoid include the processed variety, which often contains flavourings and emulsifiers, and any highly-coloured cheese (some colourings are natural, but many are chemical). Many cheeses have a high salt content, another reason for not eating too much. Vegetarians will want to avoid cheeses made with animal rennet (the inner stomach lining of a calf); there are an increasing number of cheeses now being made with rennet of vegetable origin. Look out for cheeses made from goats' or sheeps' milk, these are less likely to contain additives than cheeses made from cows' milk.

Buying and storing: Buy only a week's supply at a time, wrap it in foil or greaseproof paper, and store it in the lowest part of the fridge. Take it out of the fridge for an hour before serving, so it can regain its flavour. Hard cheeses can be frozen, though may be crumbly when defrosted. Stale cheese can be grated and kept in an airtight jar in the fridge, ready to use in cooked dishes.

Uses: Cheese is a familiar and widely-used food, popular because of its versatility as much as anything. Being a very high-protein product, it can be sprinkled over grain and vegetable dishes to make a completely balanced meal. Try it with sweet things too: cottage cheese instead of cream with fruit salad; a chunk of hard cheese with an apple pie or crumble.

RICOTTA CHEESE AND SPINACH PASTIES

For the pastry:
½lb/225g/2 cups wholemeal (wholewheat) flour
4oz/115g/½ cup polyunsaturated margarine
Pinch of salt
Cold water to mix

For the filling:
½lb/225g/1 cup ricotta cheese
½lb/225g/8 ounces fresh spinach
1 large egg
Good pinch of nutmeg
Seasoning to taste
1oz/30g/3 tablespoonsful walnuts (English walnuts)
1 tablespoonful sesame seeds

Put the flour into a bowl, rub in the fat to make a crumb-like mixture. Add salt, then enough water to make a firm dough. Wrap in clingfilm and chill.

Meanwhile, mash the ricotta cheese. Steam the shredded spinach, then drain and chop as finely as possible. Stir it into the cheese with most of the lightly-beaten egg, nutmeg, seasoning and chopped nuts.

Roll out the pastry and cut into large circles. Put a little of the filling on one side of each, fold into a pasty, and press to seal the edges. Brush the tops lightly with the remaining egg and sprinkle with seeds. Arrange on a baking sheet and bake at 375°F/190°C (Gas Mark 5) for 20-30 minutes, or until pastry is cooked.

CREAM

What it is: Cream consists of the fat of milk together with a decreased proportion of water and the other constituents of milk. It is separated from milk by heating and then rotating. Whipped cream may contain sugar and stabilizers. Ultra-heat treated cream and sterilized cream may contain emulsifiers. In Britain, regulations state that single cream must contain not less than 18% fat, whipping cream not less than 35% fat, and double cream not less than 48% fat.

Origins: Cream is most widely used in northern countries, as it has always been. Its poor keeping qualities make it unpopular in hot climates. Most of the cream on sale in Britain is home-produced, though tinned creams are sometimes imported from other parts of Europe.

Nutrients: The same as in milk, but cream is especially rich in saturated fats, so should be used sparingly. Single cream has approximately 60 Calories per ounce, double cream about 128. Soured cream, a single cream that has bacterial culture added, has a fresh taste, is easy to digest, and is less fatty. Worth looking out for too is the relatively small amount of double and clotted cream that is sold direct from farms, which is less likely to be processed. Being a high-fat product, cream—especially double and clotted cream—should definitely only be a special occasion ingredient.

Buying and storing: Keep cream in the cool. Make sure it is covered and well away from strongly-flavoured foods, as it can easily become tainted.

Uses: As with butter, use cream only when you intend to taste it. Two ways to lower the fat content without ruining the flavour are to mix cream with yogurt, or to add a stiffly-beaten egg white.

MINCEMEAT

1lb/455g/3 cups mixed dried fruit
1 large cooking apple
4oz/115g/⅔ cup raw cane sugar
Grated rind of 1 orange
Grated rind of 1 lemon
2 teaspoonful mixed spice
4oz/115g/¾ cup brazil nuts
4oz/115g/½ cup vegetable fat
2-4 tablespoonful brandy

Mince the dried fruit, grate the apple, and combine with the rind and spice. Coarsely chop or grate the nuts, grate the fat, and stir into the other ingredients together with the brandy. Keep mixing until everything is thoroughly blended. Spoon into clean, dry jars and seal well. Keep in a cool place (preferably in a fridge) until needed.

DRIED FRUIT

What it is: A wide variety of fruits both from the vine and from trees can be dried in order to concentrate the goodness into a form that will keep. The simplest and best way to do this is to lay them in the sun, but nowadays many fruits are dried artificially. Some, especially the pale varieties such as apple rings and sultanas, are treated with sulphur dioxide; others are sprayed with food grade mineral oil (usually liquid paraffin) in order to stop them sticking together as well as improve their appearance. As such additives may be harmful to health, and as oil certainly prevents the body absorbing the fruit's fat-soluble vitamins, it is a good idea to wash fruit in hot water before using it.

Origins: Drying foods was one of the original ways of preserving them for when there were few fresh ingredients about, and because fruits can so easily be treated in this way, people have been doing it for centuries. Nowadays most countries produce dried fruits of one kind or another.

Nutrients: Apart from being an excellent source of fibre, dried fruits contain many minerals, iron in particular, and vitamins, the exact content depending on the fruit and where it was grown. Though better for us than refined sugar in many ways, the sugar content of dried fruits is not beneficial to our health—a recent trial on dental caries showed raisins to be a worse culprit, weight for weight, than a Mars Bar (though one would rarely eat that weight of raisins at a time!).

Buying and storing: To get them in the most natural condition, dried fruits are best bought in health food or wholefood shops. When buying from supermarkets, check to see if oil or anything else has been added. Fruits from California and Australia are usually sun-dried. Store in an airtight jar in a cool, dry place.

Uses: Though mostly used in sweet dishes such as muesli, mincemeat, mixed compôtes, Dundee cakes, jams and chutneys, dried fruits can also be added to a number of savoury dishes. Try them with salads, in curries, on pizzas, or with vegetables.

DRIED APRICOTS

First cultivated in China, apricots are now grown on a large scale in Australia, Iran, Turkey and California. Apricots are one of the most nutritious dried fruits, containing more protein than any other, and a good source of vitamin A (the vitamin C in fresh apricots is lost in the drying process). Tests have shown that the iron content is especially well-assimilated. Available as whole fruits, or in halves or pieces.

Uses: Make into a purée and use as a dessert, adding whipped egg white, yogurt or cream to thicken, or add extra liquid (orange juice, for example) and mint to make a summer drink. Chop coarsely and mix into coleslaw or Waldorf salad, or use with rice, celery and herbs as a stuffing. Wild (sometimes called Hunza) apricots are best lightly-cooked with lemon juice and maybe some honey, and served whilst warm, sprinkled with walnuts. Dried apricots make a very tasty nibble as they are.

DRIED APPLES

Many of the dried apples on sale in Britain are home-produced, and come in the form of rings. Contrary to popular opinion they are not rich in vitamin C (even fresh apples contain only about 2mg/100g), and are not as rich in nutrients as most dried fruits.

Uses: Nice cooked with lots of lemon and spices. Can also be chopped and baked in biscuits (they go well with sunflower seeds), added to muesli, or mixed with other dried fruit in a compôte. Eaten straight from the pack, they make a good substitute for sweets.

DRIED BANANAS

Bananas are split lengthways, sun-dried, then packed together in cellophane. Dark and sticky, they are sometimes called banana figs. They are popular with children as an alternative to the more usual kinds of confectionery, and are packed with energy because of their high sugar and starch content. Banana chips are now widely available, though these are usually processed with white sugar and deep-fried. Look out for those sweetened with honey.

Uses: Dried bananas can make an easy dessert if heated in the oven in a lemon and honey sauce, then topped with nuts, yogurt or cream; or chop them and add them to a curried rice salad or green salad. Banana chips are often added to fruit and nut mixes to give sweetness as well as a crisp texture. Try them over your breakfast cereal (good with granola), or crushed lightly and added to a crumble topping, or sprinkled over a chocolate (or carob) sponge.

CURRANTS

These are a vine fruit, usually made from the tiny seedless purple Corinth grape grown in Greece. Though the smallest of all, they are rich in minerals—potassium in particular. Buy currants with a good dark colour, and avoid very small ones.

Uses: Currants are traditionally used in a variety of recipes including Spotted Dick pudding, Easter Biscuits, and Eccles Cakes. They are especially suitable for biscuits and cakes because of their size.

DATES

Dates are one of the oldest cultivated fruits, known to have been eaten in the Arab world more than 7,000 years ago. They are still as important to the Bedouin today as they were then, since they will tolerate desert conditions in which no other tree will grow. Date palms may live for a century, and many trees produce more than 100lb of dates every year. Date palms are now also grown widely in California. Apart from having the highest natural sugar content of all dried fruit, dates provide a substantial amount of potassium and calcium. The best are packed whole in long boxes, the poorer quality being stoned and compressed into slabs to be sold for baking. Loose dates are also available at many wholefood stores. Whichever kind you choose, use them sparingly as their Calorie content, at 70 per ounce, is fairly high.

Uses: An excellent fruit to use in baking as it allows you to reduce or even cut out sugar altogether. Try making a purée of dates, a little water, and lemon juice, and spreading over pastry to make date slices, or using with bread instead of jam. Such a purée can also be used to sweeten dishes liked cooked apples. Use dates to make a healthy 'fudge', or add them to vegetables and salads. Walnuts are traditionally used with dates, and nutritionally they make a well-balanced partnership.

FIGS

Figs are usually sun-dried. Sugar forms a natural deposit on the skins which can be eaten, or washed off if you prefer. Figs originated in Asia, but are now produced in many countries around the world. As they are particularly difficult to transport in their fresh state, most figs are dried.

Uses: Figs go well with the taste of aniseed—combine the two in a fruit slice. Soak figs in fruit juice, then chop them and add them to a fruit salad—this is very nice with melon and oranges. Add to muesli for a change, or use with apples in a crumble. As they are famed for their laxative properties, try them lightly-cooked, flavoured with lemon peel, and topped with yogurt and maybe some wheatgerm for an especially healthy breakfast.

DRIED PEACHES

One of the largest dried fruits, and not widely available. The flavour is rather like that of dried apricots. Dried peaches are a good source of potassium, phosphorus and vitamin B3.

Uses: Because dried peaches usually come in halves, they look particularly attractive when added to fruit salads or used in flans. Try them in chutney, or make a sweet and sour sauce with peaches and almonds and serve it with a grain dish such as rice.

DRIED PEARS

These too are not widely available, but are worth trying if you can find them. They have a sweet and delicate flavour, and are a good source of fibre. They are usually sold in halves.

Uses: Dried pears make an unusual flan filling, delicious topped with grated chocolate or carob and dabs of whipped cream. Try chopping dried pears and adding them to plain yogurt with small pieces of crystallized ginger. Also good mixed with nuts and raisins and used to fill pancakes. Dried pears combine well with prunes.

PRUNES

One of the most widely-used dried fruits, prunes are made from specially-grown plums. Most of the prunes sold in Britain come from the USA, where they are dried with blasts of hot air (though Californian prunes may be sun-dried). The fruits are sold whole, usually with the stone inside. Prunes contain substantial amounts of vitamin A and iron. Everyone knows about their laxative properties! What is less well-known is that, with only 35 Calories per ounce, they contain only half the calories found in most other dried fruits.
Uses: Add to a salad of Chinese leaves, cucumber and tomato. Make a purée of cooked prunes (or chop them finely) and stir into plain yogurt. Prune juice is delicious, especially with a little lemon or orange juice added. Soak prunes in molasses and serve with yogurt or cream. Stuff lightly-cooked (or well-soaked) prunes with nuts (whole or chopped, mixed perhaps with a little honey), or with marzipan, cream or curd cheese.

RAISINS

These are also very popular and widely-used. Large and sweet, chewy in texture, they are made from various varieties of grapes, the best coming from Muscat grapes. Raisins are produced for export in the eastern Mediterranean, Australia, South Africa and the USA. They are a good source of calcium, phosphorus, potassium, and some contain vitamin B6 and iron.
Uses: Raisins are one of the most versatile of dried fruits, and can be added to many dishes as well as eaten raw. Try them in curry sauces, as part of a stuffing mixture for vegetables such as peppers or aubergine, and they go well with cheeses. Also nice with root vegetables as they both sweeten and moisten. A few spoonsful of raisins soaked in fruit juice, with wheatgerm and yogurt added, make a quick and nutritious breakfast.

SULTANAS

Made from white seedless grapes, sultanas are soft and sweet. They are widely grown in the eastern Mediterranean, Australia and South Africa, though the best come from Turkey. Sultanas contain calcium and vitamin B6.
Uses: Add to apple strudel, or with cashews in a muffin batter. Sultanas are good in tomato chutney and nice in curry sauces, especially when served with eggs. Eaten in small quantities (remember those teeth!) they make a healthy treat for children to nibble.

DRINKS

What they are: We all need to consume a certain amount of liquid each day, the amount depending on the climate, our lifestyle, and so on. Ideally this should be water from an unpolluted mountain stream, but few of us have access to this kind of supply! Instead, we tend to drink huge amounts of coffee and tea, both of which contain unhealthy substances, put a strain on our bodies and nervous systems, and can even be addictive. Many people, especially children, drink pops and sodas and cokes which contain even more harmful ingredients (flavourings, colourings, etc.). To many people, 'drink' means alcoholic drink—if you were invited to visit someone 'for drinks' you might be disappointed if you were served only spring water. A small quantity of beer or wine can be beneficial to the body, easing stress and raising the levels of the blood fats which help protect against heart disease. The excessive drinking of alcohol, however, has become a social institution our bodies can well do without. The following are alternative drinks that are thirst-quenching, refreshing, and in no way harmful.

COFFEE SUBSTITUTES

These are not as popular as they deserve to be because people often expect them to taste like coffee—which they don't. Made from such ingredients as dandelion root, malt, barley, chicory and figs, these drinks are available from health food and wholefood shops, and most come in powder form so you can make them up in the way you would a cup of instant coffee. Buying these alternatives to coffee will not only improve your health; you will also not be supporting multinational companies who make their profits from a crop which removes millions of acres from the production of necessary staples, and which has been responsible for the disastrous deforestation of vast areas of the South American continent. Try these alternatives, but think of them as drinks in their own right rather than as coffee which tastes rather strange—you may well find that you prefer them.

HERB TEAS

Herb teas, unlike ordinary tea, do not contain tannic acid or caffeine, and are not dyed. Many have medicinal properties too. Make them with fresh leaves when they are available, or buy dried herbs instead. You can also now buy a large range of herbs in tea bags, either singly or in delicious mixes, often with spices added. Don't forget that herbs are powerful—it is best not to drink the same kind all the time, but to vary them. Some favourites to try are:

Chamomile   Antiseptic, soothing; a good nightcap.
Dandelion   Make it from fresh, young leaves.
Elderflower   A purifying herb; tastes a little like lemonade.
Fennel   Especially good after a meal, or for stomach cramps.
Hibiscus   A delicious fruity taste.
Lemon Balm   A fresh summery taste. Helps balance the system.
Lemon Verbena (Vervain)   An excellent relaxant.
Mu Tea   A classic mixture containing ginseng and other exotic oriental herbs.
Nettle   Not as strange as it sounds: a good source of iron and vitamin C.
Orange Blossom   Soporific qualities, so good at night.
Peppermint   A favourite with everyone; a good tonic.
Raspberry Leaves   Considered to be strengthening.
Rosehip   Another favourite, sweeter than most.
Sage   Excellent for nervous exhaustion.
Spearmint   Helps the digestion.

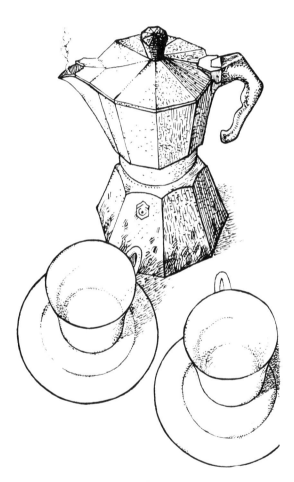

DECAFFEINATED COFFEES

These are becoming very popular, and are available both as a ready-ground powder or in bean form. They are actually the original coffee bean from which the caffeine has been removed by treating the aqueous extract with boiling ethylene dichloride or methylene dichloride, and then drying. Many nutritionists believe that the use of chemicals in this way, with their possible residues, may make decaffeinated coffee just as bad for you as the original kind, though this has so far not been proven.

JUICES

Fruit and vegetable juices contain the concentrated goodness of the ingredients from which they are made, and should be considered a food rather than a drink. They can, of course, be diluted to taste, adding a little lemon juice and some crushed ice if you like it. Juices are best made at home with an extractor or juicer, and should be drunk right away while still full of goodness. Such juices are also useful for children who refuse to eat their fruit and vegetables, or for older people whose teeth may not be able to cope with them.

If you want to try frozen and tinned juices, check the labels. Many of those imported from Europe, though much inferior to the fresh variety, do not contain dyes or additives, and are therefore a good alternative. Watch for added sugar: the words to look out for are 'fruit drink' (or worse, 'fruit-flavoured drink') rather than 'fruit juice'. Most fruit juices sold in cartons are reconstituted from concentrated fruit juice, but look out for cartons of pressed English apple juice.

WATER

Tap water in Britain is a highly-processed liquid; it is filtered, chlorinated and adjusted for hardness in order to provide a safe supply. In some areas fluoride is added, though in many places water naturally contains fluoride, often in excess of levels which are added artificially. It may also contain harmful nitrate levels as a result of land fertilization or inadequate sewage treatment. If there is any doubt about the quality of the water supply it is a good idea to boil it, though this will not be necessary with mains water supplies. If you are interested, your local water authority will provide you with an analysis of your local water. Mineral waters are an excellent but expensive alternative. Several home-bottled waters are now available in Britain, and these and imported mineral waters are available not only in health food and wholefood shops but in supermarkets too. They are worth buying for their taste as well as their therapeutic properties. Incidentally, iced water is a shock to your system and should be avoided; very hot drinks are not particularly good for you either.

EGGS

What they are: Eggs are the ova of certain species of birds and animals, usually contained in a shell shaped like an elongated sphere. In the West we generally only eat birds' eggs, and then only of a very few species. Eggs are one of the most perfect foods of all, containing all the nutrients a chick embryo needs in order to develop. They are also inexpensive and very versatile.

Origins: Eggs have been used as food for centuries almost everywhere in the world. The eggs of almost any bird can be eaten, but for most people in the West 'eggs' are synonymous with chickens' eggs. Duck and goose eggs are sometimes available from farms, which are worth trying, having a stronger taste than chickens' eggs.

It is only in recent years that the majority of eggs have been produced in factory farms, a practice that has turned eggs from a natural food into a processed one. Chickens in factory farms are often cramped together so they can hardly move and rarely see daylight. These conditions tend to make them aggressive, so they are often tranquillized; because they are prone to disease, they are frequently given antibiotics as a matter of course. To make the yolks the bright yellow that customers expect, dye is added to their feed (though this is a natural dye, beta carotene). Thus in order to supply eggs at a lower price, a great deal of the nutritional value of this important food has been lost.

Deep litter eggs are a better choice, though better still is to track down your local supplier of free-range eggs—as demand grows, more and more small-scale farmers are producing eggs from birds which are allowed to move freely, and feed on a natural diet. Free-range eggs are more expensive, but still a bargain compared with most animal products.

Principal nutrients: Eggs contain a balance of amino-acids: 95% of the protein can be used by the human body, and egg white is almost a complete protein. Eggs are also a good source of vitamins and minerals, and at only 70 Calories per egg are good for anyone watching their weight. Free-range eggs not only contain fewer chemicals than factory-farmed eggs; they contain more vitamin B12, folic acid, calcium and iron. What makes eggs a particular cause for concern is the habit of frying them in animal fats or in highly-saturated vegetable oils.

Brown eggs are no different from white ones, except for the colour of their shell. Eggs which contain a tiny red speck have been fertilized, so contain more natural hormones.

Buying and storing: Buy eggs frequently—they are best when fresh. Store them in the cool (not necessarily in a fridge), with the pointed ends down, and well away from strongly-flavoured foods. Fresh eggs should keep up to 12 days at room temperature, 3 weeks in a fridge. To tell if an egg is fresh, put it into a deep bowl of water. If it sinks it is fresh. A not-so-fresh egg will stand on its end; a stale egg will float.

Uses: Eggs can be used to make dishes in their own right, such as omelettes, soufflés and egg custards. They are also useful as an addition to sauces, or you can hard-boil them and sprinkle them over stews, pancakes, pizzas and soups as a garnish. Whisked egg white can be added to fruit to make a light dessert dish. Because eggs are easy to digest, they are especially important in childrens' diets, and for anyone who has problems with heavier food.

CARROT QUICHE

For the base:
4oz/115g/1 cup rolled oats
2oz/55g/½ cup wholemeal (wholewheat) flour
2 tablespoonsful vegetable oil
Seasoning to taste

For the filling:
½lb/225g/8 ounces carrots
4oz/115g/1 cup grated Cheddar cheese
2 eggs, beaten
⅛ pint/70ml/⅓ cup single (light) cream
Seasoning to taste
Parsley to garnish
2 large carrots for topping
½oz/15g/good tablespoonful butter

Mix together the oats and flour, stir in the oil, add seasoning. Moisten with just enough cold water to make a dough, and press it against the sides and base of a flan dish.

Slice and then boil or steam the carrots until soft. Drain and purée them by hand or in a blender. Stir in the grated cheese, eggs, cream and seasoning.

Pour the mixture into the prepared flan case and cook for 20 minutes at 375°F/190°C (Gas Mark 5). Cover the top with rings of finely-sliced carrot and brush the top with melted butter. Bake at the same temperature for 10-15 minutes or until the pastry is crisp and the filling set. Garnish with parsley sprigs.

FRESH FRUIT

What it is: Fruit is the fleshy seed-bearing part of certain plants.

Origins: Fruit must have been a very important part of the diet of the first human beings. In Asia Minor, where it is believed the ancestors of the human race first stood on two feet, they would have found an ample variety of fruits within easy reach, just waiting to be picked.

Nutrients: Most fruits contain little protein or fat, but are excellent sources of the mineral salts needed for the correct functioning of the human body, together with vitamins, especially vitamin C, natural sugars, and fibre, which is found mostly in their skins (so eat the skins, but wash them well first).

Buying and storing: Organically-grown fruit is well worth looking out for—this is produced without chemical fertilizers and without spraying, which means that it contains no dangerous additives. If you find a worm in your apple, think of it as a good sign! Many fruits can be kept in the fridge. When you take them out to eat, make sure you leave them at room temperature for at least an hour before eating them.

Uses: Though fruit is becoming more popular in Britain, we have one of the lowest fruit consumptions in the EEC. What's more, we have developed a habit that very few other nationalities follow to such an extent, that of cooking most of our fruit. It's fine to cook fruit occasionally, but do try to eat some fresh fruit every day. Nowadays there is an excellent variety to choose from, but remember that variety in the fruit shop is often only possible because of relative or absolute poverty elsewhere in the world. Think about where your fruit comes from and try to eat local fruit whenever possible, keeping the more exotic varieties for occasional consumption.

CALIFORNIA SALAD

1 small melon
1 large peach
1 banana
Squeeze of lemon juice
2 sticks celery
½ cucumber
2 large tomatoes
16 grapes
2oz/55g/½ cup pecan nuts
Endive lettuce to serve
Watercress to garnish
For the dressing:
4oz/115g/½ cup cottage cheese
2 tablespoonsful desiccated coconut
1 tablespoonful honey
Milk to mix

Peel and chop the melon, slice the peach and banana. Toss the fruit in lemon juice. Slice the celery and cucumber, quarter the tomatoes. Mix with the fruit plus the grapes and nuts.

Sieve the cottage cheese, stir in the coconut and honey, and add enough milk to make a pouring consistency. Pile the fruit and vegetables on to a base of endive lettuce and spoon on the dressing. Garnish with watercress.

APPLES

One of the most popular fruits in Britain, and grown widely too. Apart from numerous varieties of succulent dessert apples there are a number of different kinds of cooking apples. Store both kinds in the bottom of the fridge.

Uses: Chop raw apples and add to salads. Mix with cheese and use to fill an omelette. Cook apple with red cabbage, or put it in a curry sauce. Make apple sauce for a quick topping, to mix into yogurt, or to spread on bread or gingerbread. Crabapples can be used for jams and jellies.

APRICOTS

Choose apricots that are firm but not hard, with a good colour and no blemishes. If ripe, eat at once as they don't keep well. If unripe, leave at room temperature for a few days. Store in a cool place.

Uses: Nice raw with celery and walnuts. If cooking to make a purée, add vanilla. Halves can make a French style flan, maybe topped with almonds and whipped cream. Fresh apricots make a tasty crumble.

BANANAS

An ancient food originating in the tropics, yet not known in Britain until the 1890s. Bananas are usually picked when green and allowed to ripen *en route* for their destination. The pulp is ready when brown spots appear on the skin; even a completely brown banana may be edible providing that the skin has not been damaged (the riper the fruit, the easier it will be to digest). Always leave bananas to ripen in the room— do not put them in a fridge. As bananas are a good source of natural carbohydrate (containing about 94 Calories each), they are an ideal snack food, especially for children. They are also a good source of potassium.

Uses: Chop and add to salads; bananas are especially good with rice salads. Mash and add to yogurt, or use in a milk shake (bananas are just as good with soya milk, and are nice with tofu). Hot bananas in honey sauce make a quick dessert. Serve them with curry, or fry them and serve them American-style with sweetcorn. Plantains (another variety of banana, green in colour) are much used in West Indian cookery, and are ideal for savoury dishes. Look out for them in speciality shops.

BERRIES

Berries come in numerous different colours and sizes, and many are grown in Britain, where the temperate climate suits them particularly well. They are all fragile fruits, best eaten within 24 hours of being bought or picked. They can be kept in the fridge, and shouldn't be washed until just before using them.

BLACKBERRIES

The larger ones are usually cultivated, the smaller ones picked in the wild (these have a better flavour). Blackberries are traditionally teamed with apples in pies, crumbles, flans and jams. Try lightly-cooked blackberries with soured cream on blintzes or pancakes.

CRANBERRIES

A sharp red berry that grows mainly in New England (USA), and has a unique taste. Used both for sweet sauces (to serve with ice cream or cheesecake) or for more savoury sauces (traditionally served with turkey, but good too with nut roasts).

GOOSEBERRIES

A green hairy berry that can be small and sharp, or larger and sweeter in taste. Use to make pies, fools and crumbles. A gooseberry sauce makes an unusual topping for an ice cream sundae.

MULBERRIES

No longer very well known, but grown in Britain on a small scale. A large firm red berry something like a raspberry, but with a spicier taste. Best eaten raw with yogurt or cream and maybe a little sugar.

RASPBERRIES

An expensive fruit that is less sweet than most berries, though with a good flavour. Again, best served as they are with cream and yogurt and maybe a little sugar. Use raspberries to top a flan or ice cream, or make delicious sorbet, or, if you have masses, beautiful jam.

STRAWBERRIES

The large strawberries, often light in colour, are cultivated, but nothing beats the small dark red wild strawberry for taste. Both kinds only have a very short season, though some may be imported at other times of the year. Best used in tarts, flans and gateaux. If you have a surplus, try making them into a purée to use as a sauce, to stir into yogurt, or to mix with milk to make a shake (this sauce will freeze well).

CHERRIES

The name is taken from Cerasus, a city in Asia Minor where cherries were discovered by Europeans, though they had been eaten in China and Japan for many centuries. The Romans brought them to Britain, but they are still not widely grown in this country. The large sweet black variety is usually imported from Italy. Cherries can be dark red or pale peach in colour. Keep them in the cool, and eat immediately once they are ripe.

Uses: Add to fruit salads, use to fill crêpes or to top a flan. For a splendid dessert, cook cherries in sauce, pour on a drop of cognac and set fire to it!

ORANGES
Available in many varieties. Blood oranges are the sweetest. Bitter Seville oranges can be made into marmalade.

SATSUMAS
A smaller, easier-to-peel type of orange, especially popular with children.

TANGERINES
Traditionally eaten at Christmas; another small, sweet variety of orange. Makes an interesting sorbet.

CITRUS FRUITS

Most citrus fruits are grown abroad, since the British climate is not hot enough to grow them well. Yet oranges have been known in Britain since the thirteenth century, and have been imported ever since. Citrus fruits (so called because they contain citric acid) are a good source of vitamin C. Nowadays the skins are often sprayed to give them a shine, and may even be dyed. Organically-grown citrus fruits are best, and fairly widely available—ask to be sure. Buy only firm fruit. The heavier it feels in the hand, the juicier it is likely to be.

GRAPEFRUIT
Usually yellow, but look out for the pink-tinged Texan
grapefruit which are sweeter. Serve hot grapefruit topped with a knob of butter and some cinnamon. Grapefruit flesh, coarsely-chopped, is delicious stirred into yogurt. Try grapefruit with avocado.

LEMONS
Used for its juice. You can add grated peel to many dishes to add interest, but use only organically-grown lemons for this since the wax sprayed on commercial lemons is toxic.

LIMES
Use in the same way as lemon.

CURRANTS

Blackcurrants and redcurrants are very small, delicate fruits; blackcurrants have a very strong flavour and are the better known of the two. They should be eaten within 24 hours of buying or picking, and can be stored in the fridge. Do not wash them until just before using. They are a good source of vitamin C if eaten fresh and raw.

Uses: Both types can be used in jams, jellies, sauces, ice creams, sorbets and fools. They are used together in Summer Pudding.

DATES

Usually imported from Middle Eastern countries, fresh dates are finding their way into more and more shops. They are moist, plump, and very sweet. If necessary they can be kept in the fridge for several days. Do not buy damaged or shrivelled dates.

Uses: They are really too expensive to cook (dried dates, which are cheaper, are the ones to use for cooking). Wash and chop fresh dates and add them to fruit or savoury salads, or split them, remove the stones, and stuff them with cream or curd cheese, marzipan, or walnut halves, and serve them as a party nibble.

FIGS

Although some fresh figs are imported to Britain from Mediterranean countries, they are expensive and hard to find. This is because they travel badly, and really should be eaten very soon after being picked. If you can buy them, or can obtain them locally (they do grow well in Britain in some locations), eat them as they are, or maybe topped with honey, nuts and cream.

GRAPES

Grapes are widely grown, and many countries export part of their crop to Britain. Whether they are white or black they should have a bloom on them, be firm and not over-ripe, and preferably still on their branch. Can be kept in the salad drawer of a fridge for a few days if not required for immediate consumption.

Uses: Add a few grapes to a salad or a bowl of muesli. Mix tiny seedless grapes with cream or yogurt and use to stuff crêpes. Top a cheesecake with grape halves.

LYCHEES

This small brown brittle-skinned fruit comes from the Orient. It is often tinned and exported, but as the syrup is usually made from white sugar, the delicate taste of the fruit is swamped, so buy the fresh fruit if you can get it. Each lychee contains a large stone, and the pinky flesh is crisp and sweet and best eaten just as it is. They can be stored at room temperature for up to 4 days.

MANGOES

A large fruit from India, where it is considered to be the king of fruits! Should be heavy and unblemished, and is ready to eat when still firm, but yields slightly to pressure. Rich in vitamin A, and a good source of vitamin C.

Uses: Best eaten in slices, but for something really exotic try making ice cream or sorbet with mangoes.

MELON

There are a number of varieties, all crisp and sweet. Most of them contain up to 95% water, so are excellent for slimmers. To check if a melon is ready to eat, press your thumb into the end opposite the calyx, which should give slightly. Ripe melons can be kept in a cool spot for a few days before you are ready to eat them, and will probably develop a sweeter taste as they continue to ripen. Watermelons, with their pinkish flesh, are particularly thirst-quenching.

Uses: Melon cubes go well in both fruit salads and savoury mixtures. The flesh can be made into a sorbet. Cream cheese goes well with melon. For a quick and attractive starter or dessert, slice off the top of a large melon, scoop out the flesh and shape it into balls, mix with juice, orange segments and grapes, and pile everything back into the shell to serve.

PEACHES

These are mostly imported from Mediterranean countries, where they are picked before they are ripe and left to ripen en route. The result is that they taste nothing like peaches eaten fresh from the tree. To choose a peach, look for a firm unblemished skin and a heavy fruit. Can be kept at room temperature for a few days to ripen. A nectarine is similar to a peach in taste, and looks the same except that it has a smooth skin.

Uses: Mix chopped peach with sugar and nuts to fill a crêpe. Mash and mix with whipped egg white to make a fool. Make a purée and use as a natural sauce, or add mineral water or another fruit juice for a long drink. Stuff halves with a sweet crumb mixture and bake to make a hot dessert. Fill a sweet omelette with peaches.

PEARS

Another very popular and widely grown fruit in Britain, available in many varieties. Can be kept in the fridge for up to 2 weeks. Pears are ready for eating when soft around the stalk, and as they begin to deteriorate more quickly than most fruits, should be eaten at once.

Uses: Crisp pears can be cut up and added to salad, but pears tend to work better in sweet combinations. Try them in a chilled soup, or cooked in red wine with cinnamon and served with cream. Layer pear halves in a flan and, when cooked, top with flaked chocolate. Also nice with sweet rice dishes.

PERSIMMON (SHARON FRUIT)

An unusual fruit, not widely available, but well worth buying if you can find it. Like a large peach-coloured tomato to look at, persimmons must be eaten when they are ripe—not before or the taste is bitter. Slice off the top and spoon out the exotic-flavoured flesh. They do not always ripen, though if you find some that are almost ready to eat they can be left at room temperature for a few days, and will probably be delicious. They are usually imported from Italy or Israel.

PINEAPPLE

Imported from a variety of hot countries, pineapples are now easy to find in the shops, especially during the winter. They are rich in vitamin C, and have a delicious acid yet sweet taste that bears little comparison with the tinned and sweetened variety. A pineapple is ready to eat when it is soft at the opposite end from the leaves, or when the leaves pull out easily. An under-ripe fruit can be kept at room temperature for a few days until it is ready.

Uses: Nice eaten just as it is. Try adding pineapple pieces to a beetroot salad, or to cream cheese, or thread them on to kebabs with vegetables and cheese. Pineapple upside-down cake is a traditional way to bake with the fruit, but try crushed pineapple in biscuits too, maybe with some walnut pieces. Pineapple jelly is another idea.

PLUMS

These are grown in Britain in a number of shapes and colours—look out for red, golden and purple ones. Many plums are imported too. They vary in sweetness, some being good to eat as they are, others better for cooking. Plums are quite a good source of vitamin A. Damsons are the smallest, sharpest plums. Greengages are green and can be sweet or rather sour. All are best eaten fairly quickly once ripe, though they can be kept in the cool for a few days.

Uses: Usually cooked and used in pies, crumbles, flans and other dessert dishes. They make excellent jams. A plum sauce can be made to serve with stir-fried vegetables Chinese-style. Try a sweet chilled plum soup.

RHUBARB

This has been grown in Britain for centuries, but was originally valued for the appearance of its large leaves and the herbal qualities of its roots rather than as a fruit. For a long time people were nervous of eating it, and although it is an ingredient in many traditional dishes, it is still used in very few countries other than Britain, and is one of the least popular fruits here. Stems should be bought or picked when firm and easy to snap. Can be kept in the bottom of the fridge for a few days, or cooked and then frozen for later use. Rhubarb is not usually eaten raw.

Uses: Cook chopped rhubarb until soft but still holding its shape. You will need to add a good amount of sugar or honey—sweeten it according to your taste. Use the fruit in a crumble or pie. Rhubarb Brown Betty is made by layering fruit with spices, raisins and breadcrumbs. Can also be used to make an unusual marmalade, for chutneys and jams—and, of course, rhubarb wine.

GHEE

What it is: Ghee is butter which has been heated and then skimmed.

Origins: The home of ghee is the Indian subcontinent, where its ability to keep well in a hot climate makes it especially useful.

Principal nutrients: Ghee is not as high in fats as butter because the unstable fats have been removed during the clarifying process—it is still, however, a high-fat ingredient. It does not burn as butter does, so can be heated to higher temperatures, making it less likely to be absorbed by the food being cooked in it.

Buying and storing: Keep ghee covered in the fridge. It will last up to a year.

Uses: Use in cooking as you would use butter.

GRAINS

What they are: Grains are the seeds of certain species of grass. Though small and uninteresting to look at, grains are actually tiny food stores and are packed with nutrients. Their food values are roughly similar and they contain protein, carbohydrates, minerals such as calcium, phosphorus, iron and potassium, B vitamins, and sometimes fats. Most important of all, especially as far as people in the affluent West are concerned, is their high fibre content.

Origins: Since grains were first cultivated some 15,000 years ago, they have been a staple food for the majority of the world's population. They still are, particularly in non-industrialized countries. Not only are they highly nutritious, containing everything needed for the growth of a new plant, but their tough coats make them easy to store. They are also versatile in use, and can be eaten as whole grains, in flakes, or made into flours. In the past the choice of grains available in any part of the world was dictated by climatic conditions, though with the development of new varieties and bulk transport this is less the case today.

Buying and storing: Look out for unrefined whole grains in health food and wholefood shops—the few that are sold through supermarkets are usually the processed variety. They can be bought in large amounts, as they will keep well in a cool, dry place. When buying flours, do not get too much at once as they can go off quite quickly. Store flours in an airtight jar, in the fridge if you have room.

BARLEY

This small whole grain was used by the Egyptians 5,000 years ago for the brewing of beer. It is still used for this purpose, especially in Scotland, where it is also used to make whisky and vinegar, and to feed livestock. In fact it is a highly nutritious grain for humans too, and ideal for slimmers since it has the lowest calorie count of all grains. Be sure to buy pot barley, which is the whole grain, and still contains the bran and germ. Pearl barley has the two outer layers removed, which makes it quicker to cook but less nutritious.

Uses: Barley is very easy to digest, so use it when cooking for invalids or for adding to baby foods. Use barley in soups, stews, scotch broth, bean hotpot, or to make barley water. Use quick-cooking barley flakes to make milk puddings or to add to muesli. Barley flour is fine and sweet when made from pearl barley, darker and coarser when made from the whole grain. Add it to bread dough.

BUCKWHEAT

Buckwheat is technically not a grain, but is related botanically to dock and rhubarb. It comes from a plant that has heart-shaped leaves and attractive pink flowers. It is, however, used as a grain, and has much the same nutrients. Buckwheat was brought to Europe from Asia by the Crusaders—hence its other name, Saracen Corn. It is now grown in many countries, but especially in Russia, where it is used in a variety of ways. Buckwheat honey is also very popular there. Buckwheat groats are the crushed, hulled grain, and kasha is ready-roasted buckwheat.

Uses: You can make kasha yourself by putting grain in a dry pan and cooking over a medium heat, shaking it often, until it begins to colour. Add water or stock to kasha and cook until thick. Use it to make pilaffs, as a base for vegetables, or add egg and make it into a loaf or burgers. Cook buckwheat groats like rice and use in the same way. Buckwheat flour can be used to make Russian-style blinis, also muffins and biscuits (mix with wheat flour for the best results). Buckwheat spaghetti can now be bought in many shops, or you can make your own.

BULGUR (BURGHUL)

This is actually cracked wheat. It was much used in eastern Europe at one time, and it is said that Ghengis Khan celebrated his victories by loading the tables with bulgur dishes, including a fermented version to drink! It is especially high in protein, and quick cooking.

Uses: This delicate-flavoured grain can be used as a base for pilaffs and risottos, and is especially good with stir-fried vegetables. Try it also in Bazargan, an Eastern salad where the grain is not cooked but soaked. Bulgur flour is interesting but rather heavy.

BAZARGAN

½lb/225g/1 cup bulgur
Soya sauce
½ small onion
Fresh parsley
Fresh mint
2 tablespoonful olive oil
2 tablespoonful lemon juice
Pinch of mustard powder
Seasoning to taste
2oz/55g/½ cup walnuts (English walnuts)
4 tomatoes
Lettuce to serve

Put the bulgur in a bowl and cover with boiling water. Add soy sauce, cover, and leave until cool, by which time the bulgur should be cooked.

Meanwhile, finely chop the onion, parsley and mint, and add to the bulgur. Mix the oil, lemon juice, mustard powder and seasoning, and pour over the bulgur. Stir well, add the chopped nuts and quartered tomatoes. Cover the mixture and chill overnight for the flavours to mingle. Serve on a lettuce base.

MAIZE (CORN)

This popular yellow grain was first used in South America some 10,000 years ago, during the great Inca and Aztec civilizations. The native peoples of both North and South America worshipped it, performing fertility dances in its honour. Though the corn used today is very different from the wild corn of those times, it still forms a staple for many people in South and Central America, as well as parts of southern and eastern Africa. The USA is one of the biggest producers of corn today, but it is mostly used for cattle feed, which is also the case in Britain. When buying cornflour, make sure you get the stoneground variety from which the germ has not been removed. Processed cornflour is pure, white and nutritionally dead.

Uses: Apart from using the flour to thicken sauces, it can be used to make tortillas (Mexican pancakes), flatbreads and corn muffins. Polenta is Italian cornmeal. Maize flakes can be added to stews, casseroles and soups. Popcorn is an inferior grade, but it still makes a nutritious snack, popular with children—pop it, then flavour it with honey or a little salt.

POLENTA

1½ pints/850ml/3¾ cups water
Pinch of salt
½lb/225g/1½ cups polenta (cornmeal)
2oz/55g/¼ cup margarine
1oz/30g/¼ cup wholemeal flour
1 pint/570ml/2½ cups milk
Seasoning to taste
Pinch of nutmeg
1 large carrot
6oz/170g/3 cups mushrooms
2oz/55g/½ cup grated Parmesan cheese

Bring the water to a boil, add salt and sprinkle in the polenta, stirring continuously, until thick. Pour into a shallow, lightly-greased tin and leave to cool.

Melt 1½oz (45g) of the margarine and add the flour. Cook briefly, then stir in the milk and flavouring. Heat the remaining fat in another pan and gentle sauté the grated carrot for a few minutes, add the chopped mushrooms, and cook until just soft. Stir into the white sauce.

Use a cutter or glass to cut the polenta into small circles, and layer half of them in the base of a greased ovenproof dish. Cover with half the sauce. Repeat this to use up the rest of the ingredients, and top with the grated cheese. Bake at 350°F/180°C (Gas Mark 4) for 20-30 minutes.

MILLET

A very small, beige-coloured grain that has been hulled as the outer casing is extremely tough. Millet was a staple food in China before rice was introduced, and is still eaten in parts of Africa, Asia and India, and in Russia, where athletes are said to train on a diet of millet. It is also a staple for the Hunza, the long-lived Himalayan people whose diet is thought to be responsible for their excellent health. Millet is a balanced source of the essential amino-acids, and contains more iron than any other cereal. As it is gluten-free, it can be used by anyone who wants to avoid gluten in their diet.

Uses: Dry-roast millet first to give it more flavour. Cook with 4 parts water to 1 part millet—a small amount expands to feed many! Use as a base with bean or vegetable dishes, or make into croquettes. Shape into balls and deep fry. Millet is also nice with fresh or stewed fruit, nuts and yogurt as a dessert.

OATS

An easy-to-grow cereal, even in colder climates. Once very widely used in Scotland, where it grows well, but now less popular. It is an exceptionally nutritious grain, rich in minerals, vitamins including E, and polyunsaturated fats. It has one of the highest protein content of all grains, and has by far the highest fat content of any grain. Oats are sold in the form of the whole grain, as rolled oats, or as unrefined cut oats, also known as pinhead oats. Instant or quick-cooking oats have usually been partially cooked. Jumbo oats are slower-cooking but have a better texture.

Uses: Muesli, granola (try mixing with other flaked grains), cakes, bread, porridge. Sweet and savoury biscuits such as oatcakes and flapjacks. Use oats to make a delicious crumble topping. Stir into a vegetable casserole or soup to thicken it.

MILLET CROQUETTES

1 tablespoonful vegetable oil
1 small onion
6oz/170g/¾ cup millet
¾ pint/425ml/2 cups vegetable stock
1 tablespoonful fresh chopped herbs
Seasoning to taste
3oz/85g/¾ cup grated Cheddar cheese
Sesame seeds to coat
Vegetable oil for frying

Heat the tablespoonful of oil and sauté the finely-chopped onion for a few minutes to colour. Add the millet, cook briefly, stir in the stock. Bring it to a boil then cover the pan, lower the heat, and simmer for 20 minutes, or until the millet is soft and sticky and the stock has evaporated. Add the herbs, seasoning and grated cheese. With floured hands, divide the mixture into 8 pieces and shape into croquettes. Roll in sesame seeds, pressing them firmly against the croquettes, then shallow-fry in hot oil, turning them frequently, until golden. Drain on paper towels.

FINNISH FLATBREAD

½lb/225g/¾ cup rye flour
Good pinch of salt
2 teaspoonsful baking powder
1oz/30g/2 tablespoonsful raw cane sugar
⅓ pint/200ml/¾ cup milk
1oz/30g/2½ tablespoonsful melted butter

Sift together the flour, salt and baking powder. Add the sugar. Stir in the milk and knead briefly to make a smooth dough. Grease a large baking sheet. Use floured hands to shape the dough into a large circle about ½″ (12mm) thick, and lay it on a baking sheet. Prick with a fork. Bake at 425°F/220°C (Gas Mark 7) for 10 minutes or until lightly browned. This very heavy, traditional type of bread is best eaten whilst fresh. Cut into wedges to serve.

To make a lighter version, replace some of the rye flour with wholemeal.

RICE

Probably the most widely used of all the grains, rice has been a staple in Asia, China, Africa, South America, Spain and Italy for thousands of years. This small grain with a similar structure to wheat can be bought in a variety of forms including long-grain, short-grain, and sweet, the latter being white and especially glutinous, but not necessarily refined. All rice has had the outermost husk removed (it is inedible), but in addition most of the rice now sold in the West is refined white rice which has had the next layer removed. This isn't vitally important when a wide variety of other foods is available, and for its valuable starch alone the eating of white rice rather than no rice at all should be encouraged, but those who survive on rice and very little else would not be able to do so on the processed variety. The unrefined variety is usually called brown rice. Compared with other grains, rice is very low in fibre, brown rice containing about 1.5%, white rice about 0.5%. Rice flakes contain fewer nutrients than the whole grain, but are quicker to use. Rice flour is rich in B vitamins. Wild rice has been eaten by native Americans for centuries, and was especially nutritious—it is now being grown commercially with the aid of chemicals, which may make it cheaper and more widely available, but decreases its food value too.

Uses: Use the whole grain as a base for Indian and Chinese food, to make risottos, pilaffs and rice loaves. Stuff balls of rice with cubes of cheese and fry them. Use rice for sweet dishes too. Rice flakes can be added to soups and stews to thicken them. To make wild rice go further, mix it with brown rice.

RYE

Rye will grow even under the most difficult conditions, and so was grown widely throughout much of Europe. As well as providing a basic food, rye may well have been responsible in the Middle Ages for what were at the time thought to be a series of plagues. This is because rye is subject to attack by a fungus called ergot, which can affect the central nervous system and produce hallucinations and trances. It is now less widely grown than it was, and is only popular in Germany, Scandinavia and Russia, although it is used in the USA to make rye whisky.

Uses: Cook the chewy grains like rice and use as a base for vegetable or bean dishes (you can speed up the cooking process by cracking the grains first with a rolling pin). Rye can be combined with other grains including barley and wheatberries. Pumpernickel and other black breads are made with rye flour, sometimes combined with other flours such as barley—because rye flour is low in gluten it makes a heavy bread. To use rye flour in other baked foods look out for 'light' rye flour which has had more bran removed. If you can find rye flakes in the shops, try them in soups and vegetable hotpots.

SORGHUM

This large, hard grain is actually a variety of millet. It survives with only the minimum of water, so is widely used in hot dry countries. In many parts of Africa it is still an important staple, the white grain being eaten as meal, a bitter red grain being used to make beer, and sweet sorghum supplying syrup when the stems are crushed. Although it is the third most important cereal in the world (after wheat and rice), it is little known in Britain, though more shops are now stocking it.
Uses: The grain can be cooked like rice, or can be added to stews, soups and casseroles. It can also be ground to make a flour which will produce a heavy bread, or can be used in both sweet and savoury porridge-type dishes. Sorghum contains no gluten, so is suitable for a gluten-free diet.

TRITICALE

This is a grain first produced in the 1930s, when wheat and rye, two crops that grow well together, were crossbred. The result is a grain that contains 2% more protein than either wheat or rye, and an improved amino-acid balance. It is now being grown in North America and Russia, and on a small scale in Britain
Uses: Can be used as a whole grain, or ground into a flour to use in bread (where it is best combined with wheat flour). It is a very good sprouting grain, and gives a delicious harvest that can be added to salads, vegetables and soups.

WHEAT

Half the population of the world relies on wheat as a staple, and it is the most widely-used grain in Britain, supplying about a quarter of our protein intake. It is a hardy plant that grows well in most climates in one variety or another—hence its popularity. Wheat is usually made into bread, a technique that was first used around 4,000 BC, when the Egyptians discovered how yeast could lighten the end-product. To get the right balance, most of our bread is made with a combination of the soft wheat which grows best in the British climate, plus hard wheat imported from the USA, Canada or Russia. When buying flour always ask for stoneground wholemeal flour, which contains all the goodness of the complete grain, and has been ground in the gentlest way to ensure that nutrients are not destroyed. Wholemeal flour is usually available in 100%, which gives heavier results but contains all the original grain, 85% or 81%, which have had some bran removed to give lighter results. Wheat has the highest fibre content of any grain—around 10%. Kibbled wheat is the cracked grain. Semolina is ground wheat.
Uses: Wheat grain (also known as wheatberries) is tough, chewy, and takes a long time to cook. It goes well with eggs, and vegetables of all kinds, especially peppers. Try draining the cooked grains and then frying them for an interesting texture. Frumenty is a sweet recipe introduced by the Romans, and is wheat boiled in milk with cinnamon and honey (or raw sugar) added. Kibbled wheat is best used in cereals and breads, while wheat flakes go well in muesli or other breakfast cereals. Semolina is used in desserts, and also makes good cheese fritters. For basic bread recipes, see 'Producing Your Own Food', an earlier chapter of this book.

MIXED GRAIN GRANOLA

4oz/115g/1 cup rolled oats
4oz/115g/1 cup barley flakes
4oz/115g/1 cup wheat flakes
4oz/115g/1 cup rye flakes
⅛ pint/70ml/¼ cup honey
3 tablespoonsful vegetable oil
2oz/55g/½ cup flaked coconut
4oz/115g/1 cup chopped nuts, one kind or mixed
4oz/115g/1 cup chopped dates

Mix together the flaked grains. Gently heat the honey and oil in a large pan, stir so that they are well-mixed, then add the grains and stir again. Cook over a very low heat for about 30 minutes, stirring frequently. Add the coconut and nuts and continue cooking for 15 minutes, or until the grains and nuts begin to colour (some people like them well-roasted, in which case cook them for longer). Remove from the heat and mix in the chopped dates. Set aside to cool, then transfer to a large screw-top jar. Can be eaten as a breakfast cereal with milk or fruit juice, or used to top fruit purées, ice cream or yogurt.

HONEY

What it is: A sweet heavy liquid produced by bees from the nectar of flowers. A wide variety of honeys can be bought, from pale cream to very dark, from very sweet to fairly bland, and from liquid to hard-set.

Origins: Honey has been used for at least fifteen thousand years, and not only as food. The Prophet Mohammed recommended honey as a remedy for every illness, and the ancient Egyptians used its antiseptic and antibiotic qualities for treating wounds and burns. Many naturopaths nowadays advise the use of honey for these and many other ailments, especially for sore throats, which also encourages people to swallow it and get the benefit of its nutrients.

Principal nutrients: These vary considerably depending on the flowers from which the bees fed, the weather and the season. However, all honeys consist of about 25% water, the rest being divided between glucose and fructose about 4:1, which is only very slightly more fructose than is contained in refined sugar. Thus although honey is better for you than sugar weight for weight, there isn't much in it from a nutritional point of view, and it isn't a good idea to add more than very small amounts of honey to your diet. Most honeys contain vitamins B and C, as well as traces of minerals. Many people talk about the important enzymes to be found in honey, but unless parts of the bees themselves have been left in the honey this is not the case. Although the nutritional evidence does not show honey to be a particularly health-enhancing food, many people swear by its beneficial qualities, so be aware of the range of opinion! At the very least a switch from sugar to honey will reduce your dependence on a land-hungry cash crop, and thus help the planet in a small way.

Buying and storing: It is worth paying for the more expensive brands of honey as these will tend to be the tastiest. Many of the cheaper brands contain honey from bees which have been fed on white sugar. Keep honey in a screw-top jar in a dry spot at room temperature. Crystallization does not affect the quality of the honey, but if you want to make crystallized honey run freely again, stand the pot in a pan of warm water.

Uses: As honey is very concentrated, use it in small amounts, and only if you intend to taste it. Don't overheat it if you are using it in cooking. Honey can be used wherever a recipe asks for sugar—use ¾ the amount of honey as is asked for in sugar, and adjust the liquid accordingly. To make honey more nutritious as a spread, try mixing it with wheatgerm, peanut butter, tahini or ground nuts.

FRUIT AND HONEY SPREAD

1lb/455g/3 cups dried pears, soaked overnight
1lb/455g/1⅓ cups honey
1 lemon

Drain the pears and then purée them in a blender. Stir in the honey and mix very well. Add lemon juice and some of the peel of the lemon, finely grated. Store in a screw-top jar in the fridge, and use within a few weeks. Good on bread, stirred into yogurt, or as a topping for ice cream. Try whisking in an egg white, spooning it into glasses, and topping with nuts for a dessert.

If you like you can add spices to this spread, or you can make it in exactly the same way using other dried fruits such as apricots and peaches.

JAMS AND PRESERVES

What they are: Jams and preserves are usually made from fruit and sugar, sometimes with pectin added. Pectin occurs naturally in ripening fruit and reacts with the sugar to set the jam, though different fruits contain different amounts, so that sometimes more pectin needs to be added.

Origins: Jams and preserves have been popular for centuries in many parts of the world, and were originally devised as a way of using surplus stocks of over-ripe fruit, as well as preserving fruits to be eaten when fresh supplies were not available.

Principal nutrients: Mass-produced jams are made from overcooked fruits and white sugar, with colourings and preservatives added. A wide variety of more wholesome jams is now becoming available, so look out for those which say 'reduced sugar'. Remember that jams made with raw sugar or honey may taste nicer, but are not necessarily better for you. Some spreads made just with fruit are also available. Though jams and preserves are not particularly nutritious and are not a necessary part of our diet, they are a pleasant luxury. What is important is to avoid those that contain harmful additives.

Buying and storing: Naturally-produced jams and preserves are available at most health food and wholefood shops; low sugar jams (though still made with white sugar) are available at supermarkets. All these jams should be kept in a sealed jar in the fridge.

Uses: Apart from the obvious one of spreading on bread, muffins and scones, jams can also be stirred into yogurt and rice puddings (try lemon curd this way), spooned over ice creams, used to sweeten stewed fruits, to decorate flans and fill pasties, and to flavour cream, ricotta or cottage cheese.

MARGARINE

What it is: Nowadays there are a large number of margarines on the market from which to choose. These can be hard or soft, come in a tub or in block form, and be made from animal fats, a blend of animal and vegetable fats, or from vegetable oil only. Soft margarines which say on the packet that they are made from oils like soya or sunflower are a fairly recent innovation; these are often, but not always, low in cholesterol and high in polyunsaturates.

Origins: Margarine was invented by a Frenchman, Mège-Mouries, in 1869, as an alternative to butter. It was made from animal fats, and though it proved reasonably acceptable, especially in Holland where the product was developed, margarine still retained its reputation as an inferior product to butter.

Principal nutrients: Most margarines contain salt, some colouring, and added vitamins A and D, which are insisted on by law. Margarines high in polunsaturates are preferable to others, since instead of clogging the arteries as saturated fats tend to do, they may actually help clear cholesterol. However, all margarines still contain saturated fats, and replacing butter with margarine will not automatically protect you from an overdose of saturated fats. Go easy on both! Margarines can be used for both cooking and spreading.

Buying and storing: Buy small amounts frequently from a retailer who has a fast turnover. Keep margarines in the cool, preferably in a fridge.

Uses: Use as a spread, especially in sandwiches when taste is not of primary importance. Soft margarines can also be used for frying and baking, and on vegetables and baked potatoes instead of butter.

MAPLE SYRUP

What it is: A natural syrup taken from various species of maple tree. The trees are tapped in the spring, and the fluid is either allowed to evaporate, or is boiled away, leaving a concentrated syrup 30 to 50 times stronger than the sap.

Origins: Maple syrup is produced only in North America. It has long been a popular food in New England, where it has been collected in much the same way for hundreds of years.

Principal nutrients: Maple syrup contains natural sugars and some minerals, but it is used not so much as a food as a very special sweetener with a distinctive mellow taste and smooth quality. As with honey, maple syrup is better for you than refined sugar, but it is still a sugar, and not for consumption in large quantities (not that you'll be able to afford large quantities of maple syrup).

Buying and storing: Look out for 100% pure maple syrup. It is expensive, but far superior to the artificially-produced varieties that are now available. Keep in a sealed bottle in the cool.

Uses: Use on pancakes, French toast and ice cream, stir into yogurt, mash with bananas, or use as a sweetener when baking. Goes well with rice dishes. Use instead of sugar on pancakes or waffles. Trickle over fresh fruit (blackberries, for example) and top with whipped cream. Can make an interesting sauce for carrots.

FRENCH TOAST WITH MAPLE SYRUP

6 slices wholemeal (wholewheat) bread
2 eggs
3 tablespoonsful milk
Vegetable oil for frying
Maple syrup

Halve the bread slices. Whisk together the eggs and milk and pour into a wide, shallow dish. Dip the slices of bread briefly into the mixture, making sure that both sides are covered with the egg mixture. Heat the oil and fry the bread until it begins to colour, then cook the other side. Serve while still hot with maple syrup poured over the top.

MILK

What it is: Milk is a highly-concentrated liquid produced by animals for their young, and is very rich in nutrients. It comes from a wide variety of animals, and until recently was usually drunk while still fresh.

Origins: Milk has always been used as part of the human diet, starting of course with the breast milk that traditionally sustained the newborn baby. In many parts of the world, milk is still the chief source of protein, supplemented by cereals and vegetables.

Principal nutrients: Milk is very high in protein, and is a good source of calcium. It is also rich in saturated fats, which are the kind suspected of contributing to many illnesses prevalent in the Western world. Many nutritionists believe that we drink too much milk, using it as a drink when it should really be considered as a highly-concentrated food. On average, British people each drink ⅔ of a pint of milk a day, most of it a highly-processed product. It is true that pasteurization kills most bacteria and prolongs the life of milk, but it also destroys some of the nutrients. At the same time the use of drugs and artificial feed supplements increase the amount of additives present in milk, with added risks to health.

Buying and storing: Cows' milk is delivered daily to most homes in Britain, and is now available as full-cream milk, or as semi-skimmed or skimmed milk with some or most of the fat content removed. Long-life milk has been heat-treated so that it will stay fresh until it is opened. In some country areas raw milk is still available, and is worth trying. A growing number of health food, wholefood and speciality shops now sell goats' and ewes' milk, which is usually produced on a small scale and therefore a more natural product. These milks are also easier to digest, and unlikely to cause the allergic reactions often suffered by some people when they drink cows' milk. All milk should be drunk as soon as possibly after purchase, and should be kept meanwhile in a cool place, preferably in a fridge.

Uses: Think of milk as a food. Make a white sauce to go with vegetables and rice and you have a completely balanced meal. Use milk to make egg custards or sweet puddings. Give milk to children, invalids and old people—anyone who is reluctant to eat. Instead of drinking surplus milk simply because it will go off if you don't, turn it into yogurt which will keep longer and is easier to digest. Most importantly, remember that you don't need a lot of milk in anything.

MOLASSES

What it is: This thick, dark treacle is a by-product of the sugar-refining industry. When the sugar cane is crushed and processed it loses all its valuable minerals and vitamins, and it is these that make molasses such a highly nutritious sweetener.

Origins: The introduction of molasses dates from the beginning of commercial sugar refining some 200 years ago. The popularity of molasses waned as white sugar became cheaper, and molasses are sometimes considered to be the poor relation of sugar. It is still widely used in the sugar-plantation area of the USA, where many of the traditional molasses-based dishes come from.

Principal nutrients: Molasses is an extremely nutritious product, with the darker varieties being the best. After yeast, molasses is the richest source of the B vitamins, especially vitamin B6. Weight-for-weight it contains more iron than liver, together with considerable amounts of copper, calcium, phosphorus and potassium. Molasses has fewer Calories than other natural sweeteners—59 per ounce for blackstrap molasses compared with 80-90 for honey and 112 for sugar.

Buying and storing: If kept lidded in a cool dry place, molasses keeps well for a long time.

Uses: In savoury dishes molasses goes well with beans (as in Boston Baked Beans), and sweet and sour sauces. Can also be used on bread, stirred into drinks, or used to flavour chutney. Use in baking for such favourites as flapjacks and gingerbread. As it has a strong and distinctive flavour, go slowly until you are used to it, adding quantities to suit your own taste.

BANANA MILK SHAKE

1½ pints/850ml/3¾ cups milk (animal or soya)
3 large ripe bananas
Squeeze of lemon juice
3 tablespoonful molasses, or to taste

Blend or whisk together the milk, bananas and lemon juice. When thick and creamy add the molasses to taste. Chill briefly before serving.

NUTS

What they are: Nuts are the dried fruit, encased in a protective shell, of various trees.

Origins: Like fresh fruit, nuts were among the first foods eaten by human beings. Nuts of one variety or another grow in most countries, whether the climate is hot or cold, wet or dry, and as they are easy to collect and store they are a perfect food.

Principal nutrients: Nuts are one of the most concentrated sources of protein available, some offering considerably more protein than meat at a much lower price. Apart from protein, nuts are rich in other nutrients, including vitamins B1, B2 and B6, nicotinic acid, vitamin E, and several important minerals. Their fibre content is high. Nuts are a fatty food, but apart from coconuts and brazil nuts the fat is mostly polyunsaturated and thus not a danger to health. Unfortunately, mass production has resulted in many nuts being treated with preservatives and dyes, and the biggest-selling nuts in Britain are those that have been salted and fried (usually in saturated fats), making them unhealthy, and stripping them of most of their nutrients.

Buying and storing: All nuts are best bought as fresh as possible, preferably still in their shells. To avoid additives, shop from a reputable outlet, and ask to be sure. When buying ready-shelled nuts, do so only in small quantities, and store them in an airtight jar, preferably in the dark. It is best not to grind or chop nuts until just before you intend to use them.

ALMONDS

The attractive almond tree with its pink flowers grows in Britain, but the nuts it produces are usually of the bitter variety and therefore not edible, though the oil can be extracted to use as a flavouring agent. Sweet almonds are grown in Spain, India, North Africa and America. Almonds have one of the highest protein contents of all nuts, and are also an excellent source of calcium. Yogis are said to breakfast on a few almonds soaked overnight in milk.

Uses: You can buy almonds whole, blanched or flaked. Use them in cakes, biscuits and dessert dishes. Add roasted chopped almonds to ice cream. Sprinkle whole almonds over salads and vegetable dishes, or stir them into chop suey.

ALMOND BISCUITS

3oz/85g/¾ cup ground almonds
1oz/30g/1good tablespoonful sesame seeds
4oz/115g/¾ cup rice flour
Few drops natural vanilla essence
2 egg whites
Pinch of salt
4oz/115g/⅔ cup raw cane sugar
Blanched almonds (optional)

In a bowl mix together the ground almonds, sesame seeds, rice flour and vanilla essence. Whisk the egg whites lightly with the salt, stir in the sugar, and add to the dry ingredients, stirring well.

Drop by spoonful on to a greased tray (or, better still, rice paper). Press lightly. Top each biscuit with a nut if liked. Bake at 350°F/180°C (Gas Mark 4) for 20 minutes or until golden. Leave to cool before removing carefully from tray. If using rice paper, tear round each biscuit.

CASHEW NUT BUTTER

½lb/225g/2 cups raw cashew nuts
2-3 tablespoonsful vegetable oil
Pinch of salt (optional)
Honey (optional)

In a grinder, reduce the cashew nuts to a fine powder. Mix in just enough oil to make a creamy butter, making sure it is well mixed. Cashew butter has a sweet, very delicate flavour. If you prefer a more savoury taste, add salt, or make it sweeter by adding a little honey.

Other nut butters can be made in the same way, using just one kind of nut or different kinds in combination. Try using roasted nuts too. A peanut butter made of half raw and half roasted nuts is delicious.

BRAZILS

This large white nut comes in a tough angular shell, and these in turn are clustered together in larger shells rather like coconuts in appearance, the clusters each weighing up to 4lbs. Originating in the Amazon forests of Brazil, they grow on trees that can reach 150ft in height. Nowadays, brazil nuts are grown in other parts of South America and in Africa.

Though a good source of protein, and rich in zinc and vitamin B1, brazil nuts are one of the few varieties that contain saturated fats. They are still worth eating regularly for their smooth, creamy taste, but go sparingly.

Uses: Use them in a brazil nut roast. Grind them to make sweets, or to add to pastries or biscuits. Chop them coarsely and sprinkle them over fruit salads, muesli or a fruit flan.

CASHEWS

This soft, pale, kidney-shaped nut is not strictly a nut, but a legume that grows at the end of a pear-shaped fruit. It originated in Brazil, but is now grown in other countries including India, which is one of the largest exporters. They are expensive, but well worth buying for their sweet, delicate flavour.

Uses: Cashews can be roasted and salted to make a delicious snack. They also go well in mixes with dried fruit, seeds and flaked coconut. Add cashews to curry, or make cashew fritters. Grind them to make a butter, or add water to make a cream-like liquid to pour over fruit salad.

CHESTNUTS

These large brown nuts of the *Castenea* tree grow in Britain, but are usually hard to peel and have little flesh. Most of the chestnuts on sale in Britain during the winter are imported from France or Italy. Chestnuts, unlike most nuts, are low in fat and low in Calories (only 48 per ounce), with only 3% protein, yet they are very high in carbohydrate. Chestnuts can be stored in the fridge in a ventilated container for up to two months, whilst whole shelled nuts can also be blanched and frozen.

Uses: To peel chestnuts, slit them at the pointed end, then cook in boiling water for approximately ten minutes, or until the thin shell can be peeled away (the time will depend on how fresh the nuts are). They are sweet and floury when cooked, making them a good choice for stuffings, or to add to other nuts for a roast. Whole chestnuts go well with brussels sprouts—try a hotpot with cheese on top. Purée chestnuts and use them in sweet dishes.

CHESTNUT SOUP

¾lb/340g/12 ounces chestnuts
2 tablespoonsful vegetable oil
1 large leek
1 large green pepper
1 stick celery
1¾ pints/1 litre vegetable stock
Seasoning to taste
Good pinch of mace
¼ pint/140ml/⅔ cup soured cream

Cut across the top of the nuts, put into a saucepan with water, and bring to the boil. After about 10 minutes, remove from heat and leave to cool slightly, then use a sharp knife to remove peel and inner skin.

Heat the oil and sauté the chopped leek, pepper and celery until they begin to colour. Add the stock and halved chestnuts. Cook for 10 minutes or until all the ingredients are tender. Purée in a blender and return to the pan, add seasoning and mace to taste. Reheat gently, then stir in the soured cream and leave on a low heat for literally a minute or two more. Garnish with chopped celery leaves or a few rings of raw leek.

COCONUTS

Coconuts originated in Malaya, but are now grown throughout the tropics. The fruit of the tall coconut palm, the actual flesh is protected by a tough fibrous shell, and the hollow fruit usually contains a milky liquid. Coconuts are low in protein, the highest of all nuts in fibre. They contain saturated fats, which makes it a good idea to restrict their use, though a small amount of coconut gives a delicious flavouring. Store fresh coconut in the fridge, covered in water, and change the water frequently. Once it has been cut open, a coconut should keep for up to four days.

Uses: Coconut milk is excellent in curries, or as a substitute for water or milk in savoury sauces or sweet dishes, especially with rice. Fresh grated coconut can be added to fruit salads or muesli, or used when making granola. Roasted flaked coconut makes a tasty nibble, or can be sprinkled over dishes. When coconut is dried and grated it is called desiccated coconut—make sure you buy the unsweetened kind. Use it in cakes, biscuits, coconut bread and Indian-style sweets.

HAZELNUTS (COB NUTS)

Hazelnuts are one of the few varieties of nut that grow well in Britain. *Hæsil* is the Anglo-Saxon word for 'head-dress', which describes the way the nuts fit into their cap of leaves. Hazelnuts are now grown widely throughout the world. They are a particularly good source of vitamin E, and, having a very low Calorie count—just 110 per ounce—are an ideal choice for dieters.

Uses: Hazelnuts are one of the most popular varieties of nut with chocolate manufacturers—make your own sweets using raw cane sugar and carob instead of chocolate. As they go so well with sweet foods, try them in cakes and biscuits, sprinkled over ice cream, stirred into yogurt or chopped over fruit salad. To bring out the flavour, roast them in a moderate oven for 10-15 minutes (this also makes it easier to remove the skin). Ground roasted hazelnuts mixed with a little oil make a tasty butter.

PEANUTS

Probably the best-known nut in the world, though peanuts are in fact not nuts at all, but the pod of a leguminous plant which grows underground on long tendrils. Records of the use of peanuts as early as 950 BC have been found in South American tombs. The USA is now one of the largest producers of peanuts.

Peanuts rate with almonds as the nuts richest in protein. They also contain the eight essential amino-acids, and are rich in linoleic acid. Fairly high in calories, they should be eaten sparingly, though if used in main dishes rather than as a between-meals snack, they are no more fattening than meat, and equally nutritious.

Uses: Peanuts are available whole, flaked, and ground into a flour. Do not buy the fried variety. Mix equal quantities of raw and roasted ground peanuts to make a tasty butter. Use with curries, Chinese dishes and salads. Make into patties, or mix with spinach and egg to make a loaf. Peanuts are good with sweet dishes too.

PECANS

These nuts, from the southern part of North America, were once the staple diet of many native peoples. They are a smooth, creamy nut that comes in a brittle pink or red shell, and are only just finding their way into British shops. You can also usually buy them ready-shelled from health food and wholefood shops.

Uses: Pecans are especially good with sweet dishes. Try them in biscuits, fruit cakes, flans, or layered with cream between two rounds of sponge cake. In the USA, two popular ways of using pecans are Pecan Pie (the filling made with eggs, syrup and nuts) and Maple Pecan Fondants (sweets made with maple syrup). Try them too with savoury salads and vegetable dishes.

PESTO SAUCE

1-2 cloves garlic, peeled and chopped
1 good tablespoonful fresh basil leaves
Salt to taste
4oz/115g/1 cup grated Parmesan cheese
4oz/115g/1 cup pine nuts
1 tablespoonful lemon juice
¼ pint/140ml/⅔ cup olive oil

Use a mortar and pestle to grind together the garlic, basil and salt so that you have a smooth paste. Gradually add the cheese and pine nuts, stir in the lemon juice. The mixture should be thick and smooth. Now add the olive oil drop by drop, stirring well, so that the sauce is the consistency of a thin cream. Adjust seasoning to taste. Serve with pasta, or stir into a vegetable soup. Also makes an unusual alternative to soured cream as a filling for jacket potatoes.

PINE NUTS (PIGNOLIAS)

A tiny white oily nut that is taken from the cone of certain species of pine trees. Most of those on sale in Britain are imported from Italy. As the nut is hard to remove from the tough casing, they are expensive. They are a good source of protein, and add a distinctive taste and texture to dishes, even when used only in small amounts.
Uses: Excellent with Middle Eastern dishes, especially those containing aubergines and tomatoes. Use in sweet and sour sauces and rice stuffings, and to make Italian pesto sauce. Sprinkle a few lightly-roasted pine nuts over fruit salads or use them to make sweets.

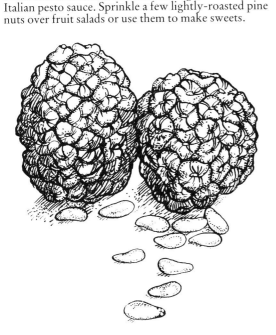

PISTACHIOS

A small green nut that comes originally from a tree native to Syria, though it is now grown in Turkey, Israel, Greece and Italy, and on a large scale in California and Texas. Pistachios are not widely used in Britain because of their high price, though they are becoming more popular.

Uses: Pistachios combine well with sweet ingredients, and are used traditionally in such foods as halva, Turkish Delight, and pistachio ice cream. Sprinkle them over any fruit salad or sorbet, or add honey and pistachios to low-calorie ricotta cheese and top with grated chocolate for a quick dessert. Pistachios make a very special nut roast. Roasted salted pistachios make a good accompaniment for drinks.

WALNUTS (ENGLISH WALNUTS)

Walnuts probably originated in ancient Persia, though numerous varieties of walnut tree now grow throughout the northern hemisphere. Fresh (wet) walnuts are available only for a limited time each year, and are creamy and sweet. Most walnuts are imported already dried. They are the highest of all nuts in polyunsaturated fats.

Uses: Walnuts have a dry, rather savoury taste, and can be used in many ways. Try them in Waldorf Salad or add them to vegetable dishes. Mix them with lightly-fried onions and mushrooms to make a pancake filling, or add them to cheese sauce. Try them with Middle Eastern dishes instead of the more expensive pine or pistachio nuts. Good with sweet dishes, and very popular in cakes, especially when combined with dates or bananas.

OILS

What they are: Smooth and viscous substances which are lighter than and insoluble in water, and are generally liquid at room temperature. Oils used to cook with are usually of vegetable origin, most animal products which are oils at high temperatures being fats at room temperature. Although some vegetable oils are fairly highly saturated, several pure vegetable oils are high in polyunsaturates, which tend to help clear the arteries of fats rather than clog them.

Oil is extracted from plants in one of three ways:
COLD-PRESSED OILS The seeds are pressed in hydraulic presses, no heat or chemicals being used.
SEMI-REFINED OILS   The seeds are heated and pressed at the same time.
REFINED OILS   Various processes are used to refine vegetable oils. The most common is to dissolve the seeds in a petroleum-based material, then to purify the oil with caustic soda and fullers earth. This process gets the most oil from the seeds and is therefore the most profitable.

Principal nutrients: As well as the fat content, vegetable oils also contain vitamins, particularly A, D and E, and minerals.

Buying and storing: If you can afford the higher price, buy cold-pressed oils which contain far more nutrients. All oils should be stored in a cool, dark place in a sealed bottle.

Uses: All vegetable oils can be used in salad dressings, and for shallow or deep frying. Add a drop of oil to water when cooking pasta or rice to prevent it sticking.

CORN OIL

This is extracted from the relatively soft corn grain, and as this is not difficult to do, it is a less expensive oil than most. It is rich in phosphorus and a good source of vitamins A, D and E. Corn oil is easy to digest.

OLIVE OIL

This is imported from Mediterranean countries where olives are a staple. It is a monosaturated oil, which does not clog the arteries, though does not have the ability to lower cholesterol levels as do polyunsaturated oils. Virgin oil, from the very first pressing, is the best and most expensive—excellent on salads. All olive oils make good salad dressings. To cook with it, try mixing it with another oil such as safflower.

PEANUT OIL (ARACHIDE OR GROUNDNUT OIL)

Usually imported from the USA, and made in various ways including cold-pressing—check the bottle. This oil does not cloud like others, so can be clarified and used again, though this reduces the antioxidants in the oil so is not to be recommended as common practice.

SAFFLOWER OIL

Made from the very oily seeds of a tall thistle-like flower that grows in hot climates. It has the highest linoleic acid content of all oils—up to 80%.

SESAME OIL

Made from the tiny sesame seed, this oil has been used for cooking in Africa and the Far East for centuries. It is especially popular because, unlike other oils, it does not turn rancid in heat. It contains considerable amounts of both lecithin and linoleic acids.

SOYA OIL

Made from the highly nutritious soya bean, this is a cheap and healthy oil to use, being high in polyunsaturates, and containing most of the nutrients found in soya beans.

SUNFLOWER OIL

An oil extracted from the seeds of the popular flower, and rich in itamins A, D and E. It is mostly imported, and its linoleic acid content varies depending upon where the flowers grew, this being higher in cold countries such as Russia, lower when made from African or American flowers. Sunflower oil is thought to have diuretic qualities, and is being used to help treat kidney complaints.

MAYONNAISE

2 egg yolks
Good pinch of dry mustard
Seasoning to taste
½ teaspoonful raw cane sugar
Approx. ⅓ pint/200ml/¾ cup sunflower oil
Approx. 2 tablespoonsful vinegar or lemon juice

The egg yolks should be at room temperature. Put them into a bowl with the mustard and seasoning, and whisk well. Add the sugar. Very gradually add the oil, whisking continually, until the mixture begins to thicken. You can then add the oil more quickly to make a thick, smooth mayonnaise. Stir in the vinegar or lemon juice, mixing well. Adjust seasoning and consistency if necessary to suit your own taste. If it is too thick, add a spoonful or two of boiling water and whisk well—this will also improve its keeping qualities. Keep in a cool place and it should stay fresh for up to a week. Mayonnaise can be made in a blender.

PASTA

What it is: Pasta is a paste made from durum wheat, an especially hard wheat grown mainly in Italy and North America. The wheat is finely ground, sometimes spinach or egg are added, and the resulting paste is shaped into some 150 varieties of pasta, the most popular being spaghetti and macaroni. Most dried pasta on sale in supermarkets is made from refined white flour, though a growing demand for wholewheat varieties means that more are being introduced, and they are in any case available at health food and wholefood shops. Freshly-made pasta is also sold through speciality shops—and you can make your own with far less effort than is usually imagined!

Origins: No one quite knows where pasta originated, though Marco Polo is said to have introduced it to Italy after visiting China. By the Middle Ages, Italian cooks were already making a variety of shapes, and even now pasta is a mainstay of the Italian diet, especially in the south, where it is usually eaten at least once a day.

Principal nutrients: Wholewheat pasta is an excellent source of fibre (containing three times as much as white pasta). It also offers a substantial amount of protein, various minerals and B vitamins, and with less than 100 Calories per dry ounce, it is far from fattening, providing of course that the sauces that are served with it are chosen carefully!

Buying and storing: Freshly-made pasta should be eaten the same day. Dried pasta will keep for ages if stored in a cool, dry spot. There are special jars available for spaghetti.

Uses: Pasta cooks very quickly and is filling, so makes an excellent food. It can be served in countless ways, both in savoury and sweet recipes. Be adventurous and make up sauces of your own. For a change, serve noodles instead of rice with Chinese food. Allow 2-3 ounces (55–80g) of pasta per person.

HOMEMADE PASTA

½lb/225g/2 cups wholemeal (wholewheat) flour
Pinch of salt
2 eggs
1 tablespoonful vegetable oil
Cold water to mix

Sift together the flour and salt. Make a well in the centre and add the eggs lightly beaten with the oil. Mix, adding just enough water to bind. Knead lightly until the dough is smooth and glossy. Wrap in clingfilm and set aside in the cool for 30 minutes.

Divide into two and roll out on a floured board. The pastry should be as fine as possible. Cut into thin strips to make tagliatelle, into oblongs for lasagne, or to be rolled up to make cannelloni.

Homemade pasta is best used the same day, but if put in an airtight container and put in the fridge will keep for a day or two.

When cooking it in boiling water, test after literally two or three minutes—it is ready when tender but still firm.

PULSES

What they are: Pulses are dried vegetables. They come in many different varieties, and form one of the staple foods of the world. For many people they are the most important staple, though they are vastly underrated in the West. They are not only highly nutritious, very versatile and easy to store; they also cost considerably less than most foods because they are easy to grow. Indeed, it may well be their low price that has induced people into thinking of them as an inferior ingredient!

Origins: Pulses have been keeping people alive for thousands of years. Broad beans can be traced back to the Bronze Age; chick peas grew in Egypt in the time of the Pharaohs. In Britain in the Middle Ages, beans were ground to a powder and mixed with wheat, rye or barley to make a kind of bread. Although there was no scientific knowledge of food values, people soon discovered that pulses contained a good deal of nourishment, and as such were to be consumed regularly. In the absence of any other protein foods, many Third World countries rely heavily on pulses, and with growing concern about both the wastefulness and dangers of eating too much meat protein, pulses are gradually becoming popular in the affluent West too.

Principal nutrients: Exact nutritional breakdowns vary from one pulse to another, depending on where it was grown and how old it is. In general, though, all pulses are a good source of protein, though only soya beans are a complete protein. Serving pulses with cereals, nuts or dairy products does, however, make up any deficiencies, so the meal as a whole is perfectly balanced. Pulses also contain good amounts of iron and mineral salts, plus the B vitamins riboflavin and niacin. They contain approximately 25 Calories per ounce when cooked.

Buying and storing: Even though pulses will keep indefinitely if stored in a sealed container in a cool place, it is a good idea to buy from a retailer who has a fast turnover, and aim to use them within a reasonable time. Younger pulses cook in less time, and retain more goodness. Because cooking beans takes a long time, make a habit of preparing more than you need, and keeping the extra to use at a later date. They will last for up to a week in the fridge, several months in the freezer. Soak beans overnight, or bring them to the boil, simmer briefly, and set aside for an hour. Boil them for ten minutes, then simmer until tender, which can take anything from one to three hours. When cooking beans, do not add salt until the end, as this slows down the cooking process.

ADUKI (ADZUKI) BEANS

A small red-brown bean which is the seed of a bushy plant native to Japan. It has a sweet taste, and is easier to digest than most beans. It is thought that drinking the juice may help in kidney complaints. Aduki beans frequently feature in macrobiotic cooking, and are considered to be the king of beans by those who follow this way of eating.

Uses: Allow approximately 1 hour to cook. Add to soups, stews, salads and rice dishes. Do as they do in China and Japan, and mash cooked beans to a purée, then make into cakes. Fry as burgers. Use in sweet dishes—aduki are particularly good with apples.

BLACK BEANS

These are a member of the kidney bean family, much used in the cookery of the Caribbean, South America and Africa; a bigger, 'meatier' bean that makes more of a meal.

Uses: Allow approximately 1½-2 hours to cook. Use in stews and winter savouries. Make into a loaf, or combine with onions and rice. Black beans go especially well with spiced and curry sauces. Can be refried Mexican-style.

BLACK EYED PEAS (BLACK EYED BEANS, KAFFIR BEANS, COW PEAS)

This medium-sized white bean has a distinctive black mark that gives it its name. It originated in Africa, where it is still a staple, the dried seeds being ground to make a coffee substitute and the shoots eaten as a green vegetable. Black eyed peas are also grown in the USA (one variety has pods which reach up to 3 feet in length), and feature in a number of the traditional dishes of the southern states.

Uses: Allow approximately 45 minutes-1 hour to cook. Cook with onion, garlic and spices. Add cold to a salad. Mix with vegetables and other pulses for a hearty stew.

HOPPIN' JOHN

6oz/170g/1 cup black eyed peas, soaked overnight
2 tablespoonsful vegetable oil
1 onion
2 tablespoonsful fresh parsley
6oz/170g/¾ cup brown rice
1½ pints/850ml/3¾ cups vegetable stock
3 firm tomatoes
Seasoning to taste
Parsley to garnish

Put the black eyed peas in fresh water, bring to the boil and cook for ten minutes. Lower heat, cover pan, and cook for 30 minutes.

Heat the oil and sauté the sliced onion. Add the parsley and cook a minute longer, then stir in the drained black eyed peas together with the rice and stock. Bring to the boil, then simmer for 30 minutes, or until peas and rice are cooked. Drain off any excess liquid, stir in the quartered tomatoes and seasoning to taste. Serve topped with sprigs of parsley.

BORLOTTI BEANS (PINTO BEANS)

An unusual bean with a pinky flecked skin, another member of the kidney bean family. It has rather a bland taste, and goes floury when cooked. Borlotti beans are popular in Italy, where they are added to a variety of dishes.

Uses: Allow approximately 45 minutes-1 hour to cook. Borlotti beans go well with pasta, or in casseroles. As they can easily be mashed to a purée, try borlotti beans in loaves and croquettes. Make a soup and sprinkle with grated Parmesan cheese.

BROAD (WINDSOR) BEANS

Large flat beans which, when dried, are a brownish colour. They were a staple food for the Egyptians, Greeks and Romans, and are still widely grown in many areas including South America, where they are roasted and ground into a flour.

Uses: Allow approximately 1½ hours to cook. The skins can be tough, and may need to be rubbed off after cooking. A good choice for winter casseroles and stews. Broad beans can also be served in a white sauce as a vegetable, or cooked with tomatoes, onions and garlic.

BUTTER (LIMA) BEANS

One of Britain's most popular beans, the butter bean originated in Peru. It is now grown in many tropical areas including Florida, and in Africa, where it is an important source of protein. A large flat white bean, it is a member of the kidney bean family, though is much more subtle in taste, and goes floury when cooked.

Uses: Allow approximately 45 minutes-1 hour to cook. Add to soups, stews and vegetable casseroles. Can be used in salads, or served in a white or cheese sauce, adding lots of herbs. Mash, add egg, and make into burgers, or stir mashed beans into a tomato sauce to make it thick and creamy, and serve with pasta. Make a butter bean pâté.

CHICK PEAS (GARBANZOS, CHANA, CECI, BENGAL GRAM)

A beige-coloured pea the size and shape of a hazelnut. It grows in a small twisted pod, and because it is easy to cultivate it is used in many parts of the world including America, Africa, Australia, India, and around the Mediterranean.

Uses: Allow approximately 45 minutes-1 hour to cook. A very versatile pulse, and one that features in the cuisines of many different cultures. Try falafels, deep-fried balls of ground peas, or make the peas into hummous by mashing and mixing with tahini, garlic and lemon juice. Serve with African couscous. Grind it into a flour (called gram in India) and make into a batter for deep-fried vegetables, or serve chick peas in a white creamy sauce. Good in soups and stews too, or with onions and garlic in a tomato sauce.

PAKORA (DEEP-FRIED VEGETABLES)

½lb/225g/2 cups gram (chickpea/garbanzo) flour
1 teaspoonful ground coriander
½ teaspoonful ground cumin
½ teaspoonful ground allspice
Seasoning to taste
Cold water to mix
Approx. 1½lbs/680g mixed fresh vegetables
Ghee or vegetable oil for frying
Soya sauce to serve

Mix together the flour, spices and seasoning. Add enough water to give the consistency of a thin white sauce, beat well, then chill for 1 hour.

Meanwhile, prepare the vegetables. Cut parsnips, carrots and courgettes into strips. Slice onions thinly. Break cauliflowers and broccoli into bite-size clusters of florets. Mushrooms should be halved unless they are the button variety.

When ready to cook, heat a pan of oil until it spits when batter is dropped into it. Dip the vegetables into the batter one at a time, making sure they are coated completely, then drop them into the deep oil and cook until crisp and brown, giving tougher vegetables such as carrots a minute or two longer. Drain at once, and keep them warm while using up the remaining ingredients in the same way. Arrange on a serving dish, sprinkle with soya sauce, and serve with rice and Indian-style side-dishes such as yogurt and cucumber, and chutneys.

If you prefer, you can finely chop the vegetables, mix into a spoonful or two of the batter, and drop into the hot oil by the spoonful. Onion is particularly nice this way—maybe you could combine both methods and serve them together.

FIELD BEANS (TIC)

A small brown bean that is one of the few grown in Britain, and therefore very cheap. They have a rather bland taste which needs livening up, but this also means that the beans are versatile and can be used in countless ways.

Uses: Allow approximately 1 hour to cook. Add to stews, slow-cooking casseroles. Mash and make into a pâté, or combine with nuts to make a roast. Add to minestrone soup for a change.

FLAGEOLET SALAD

6oz/170g/¾ cup flageolet beans, soaked overnight
½ small cauliflower
½ red pepper
2 spring onions
4oz/115g/2 cups small mushrooms
Lettuce
Watercress
For dressing:
    1 small carton natural yogurt
    Squeeze of lemon juice
    Seasoning to taste
    Watercress

Drain the beans, put in a saucepan with fresh water, and boil for 10 minutes. Lower heat and cook for about 30 minutes more, or until just tender—do not overcook. Rinse, then drain well.

Wash and trim the cauliflower into florets, and mix with strips of pepper and the finely-chopped onions. Slice the cleaned mushrooms and add.

Make up the dressing by mixing together all the ingredients. Add a little finely-chopped watercress. Mix enough of the dressing with the beans and prepared vegetables to moisten but not drown them—any extra can be served at the table. Arrange the salad on a lettuce base and garnish with a few more sprigs of watercress.

FLAGEOLETS

A very pretty pale green bean that grows in long slender pods shaped like flutes, which is where the name comes from. The beans are picked when young, and therefore have a delicate taste not unlike the fresh bean. They are expensive. A popular bean in France.

Uses: Allow approximately 45 minutes-1 hour to cook. Can be added to soups, hotpots and casseroles, but do not use with strongly-flavoured ingredients or their effect will be lost. Probably best served as a vegetable on their own, or in salads.

HARICOT (NAVY) BEANS

A small white bean used throughout much of the world, but best known as the tinned bean in tomato sauce—baked beans!

Uses: Allow 1-1½ hours to cook. Good with barbecue and spicy sauces, or make your own homemade version of the tinned variety. Add to stews and casseroles. Nice in salads.

KIDNEY BEANS

A large, fat, shiny bean with a distinctive red colour and a full flavour. Records indicate that it was used in Mexico seven thousand years ago, and it is still very popular in that part of the world, and throughout Central and South America.

Uses: Allow approximately 1-1¼ hours to cook. Kidney beans are excellent in chili dishes and thick soups and stews. They go well with rice, and make a good filling for stuffed pancakes. Try them in a sweet and sour sauce, or use them in a salad to add colour and texture.

LENTILS

A small leguminous seed about half the size of a pea, and available in various colours depending on whether they come from Egypt and Turkey (generally orange), or China and India (more likely to be green or brown). They were one of the first cultivated crops in the East, and are richer in protein than any other pulse except soya beans. Lentils provide a good source of vitamins, iron and calcium. One of the quickest-cooking varieties, they are easy to digest, making them especially useful.

Uses: Allow approximately 30-45 minutes to cook brown or green lentils; allow up to 30 minutes for split red lentils to cook to a mush. Lentils are good in curries, stews and soups. Add nuts and shape into croquettes to be fried. Split lentils can be used to thicken liquid. You can also make them into a sauce to serve with spaghetti, or as a base for vegetarian Shepherd's Pie.

MUNG BEANS

A small round bean that is usually green when found in British shops, though other colours are also grown. Mung beans are part of the cuisine of both India (where they are made into a flour called green gram), and China (where they are usually sprouted). They are easy to digest, and when sprouted are a good source of nutrients, especially vitamin C.

Uses: Allow approximately 30-40 minutes to cook. Use in casseroles, stews and soups. Grind beans to a flour and use as a quick way of adding protein to any dish. Mung beans go well with brown rice, also in curries. Try sprouting mung beans and add them to salads or stir-fried vegetables.

SPANISH LENTIL SOUP

½lb/225g/1 cup whole lentils, soaked overnight
2 tablespoonsful vegetable oil
1 onion
1 green pepper
1 clove garlic
1 stick celery
½lb/225g/8 ounces tomatoes, peeled and chopped
1½ pints/850ml/3¾ cups vegetable stock
1-2 teaspoonsful dried oregano
Seasoning to taste
Parsley to garnish

Put the lentils into a pan of fresh water, bring to the boil and continue boiling for 10 minutes. Lower heat and simmer for 20 minutes, or until beginning to soften.

Heat the oil in another pan and add the chopped onion, pepper, garlic and celery. Cook gently for 10 minutes. Add the tomatoes, drained lentils and vegetable stock. Flavour to taste. Cook gently for 10-20 minutes more, or until all the ingredients are tender. Purée or push through a sieve, reserving two or three tablespoonsful of the lentils to add texture to the soup. Reheat. Serve garnished generously with parsley.

SESAME SOYA FUDGE

4oz/115g/¾ cup sesame seeds
2oz/55g/½ cup soya (soy) flour
Honey to mix
1 tablespoonful finely chopped orange peel
1oz/30g/¼ cup sunflower seeds

Put the seeds into a bowl, stir in the flour, then add enough honey to make a firm mixture. Add the orange peel and sunflower seeds, and knead briefly so that all the ingredients are well blended.

Lightly grease a shallow tin, spoon in the sesame soya mixture, and press down, smoothing the top. Leave it in the cool until it begins to firm up. Cut into squares and eat within a few days.

This basic recipe can be adapted in numerous ways. Maple syrup gives a completely different flavour, or try tahini with chopped raisins or dates to sweeten the fudge. Lemon peel can replace the orange. You can omit the sunflower seeds and add vanilla essence for extra flavour, or a spoonful of ground almonds and some almond essence. A pinch of ground cardamoms gives an exotic taste.

PEAS

These are the usual maincrop peas that have been dried and are either left whole, or split. The outer skins are removed from split peas, making them even quicker to cook. They have been used as a vegetable for thousands of years, remains having been found in the ruins of Troy and in pre-dynastic Egyptian tombs. The word *pease* is of Sanskrit origin. Peas are now used in most parts of the world, and are not only an exceptionally good source of protein, minerals, and some vitamins, but are also rich in natural sugars.

Uses: Allow approximately 1-1½ hours for whole peas, 30 minutes for split peas. Yellow split peas are used to make pease pudding, but are also good in dhal, a spiced purée from India. Use mashed split peas to make loaves, thicken soups, shape into patties. Whole peas can be added to stews and casseroles.

PINTO BEANS

These look very much like borlotti beans, but are more of a beige colour. Pinto beans have been cultivated for centuries by the native peoples of North and South America, and are still grown mostly in those continents.

Uses: Allow 45 minutes-1 hour to cook. Especially good in loaves and rissoles, also casseroles and stews. Can be added to salads for a change.

SOYA BEANS

There are two kinds of soya beans grown at present, one used to make oil and flour, the other grown for eating. Although they first appeared in Chinese records over 4,500 years ago, and are still widely grown in China, many North American farmers are now concentrating their efforts on cultivating this bean, which has the highest protein content of all the pulses. Soya beans also contain iron in an easily assimilated form, trace elements, vitamins, and linoleic acid.

Uses: Allow 1½-3 hours to cook. Add to stews, curries and casseroles. Easier to use as soya grits, which have been broken up so they cook more easily. Add soya flour to sauces and soups to add protein, or use in place of eggs to bind when making cakes or pastry. In bread, use 1oz soya flour to 8oz wheat flour. Soya flour is available in three types: full fat, medium, and fat-free.

SEAWEEDS

What they are: Plants and algae that grow in the sea, usually on the seashore between high and low water marks. Some edible varieties can be found on British beaches, but most of those on sale are imported.

Origins: Seaweed must be one of the oldest crops eaten by human beings. It was used by ancient peoples, including the Chinese, the Greeks and the Romans, not just as a food, but also as a medicine and as a fertilizer. Over a hundred varieties can be used for culinary purposes.

Principal nutrients: Nutrients vary according to the species, where it was harvested, and at what time of year, but all seaweeds are an excellent source of essential minerals and trace elements. The most important of these is iodine, a mineral necessary for the proper functioning of the metabolism, and since iodine is found in very few foods, it may be a nutrient many people are short of. Seaweed also contains the essential twenty amino-acids, and is an excellent source of vitamin B12—the one vitamin that vegetarians and vegans are in danger of missing out on as it is present in very few non-animal foods.

Buying and storing: Seaweed is usually sold in dried form and packed in cellophane packets. They usually come with complete instructions on how to rehydrate and use them. A wide range of seaweeds is on sale in most wholefood and health food shops, and you can choose from kelp, nori, arame, wakame, kombu and hiziki, all of which are dried and will keep indefinitely in a cool dry place.

Uses: Seaweeds can be hydrated and added to sautéed vegetables, flavoured with soya sauce. They can also be fried and used as a garnish. Arame is good added to soups. Wakame goes well with beans, also with miso soup. Laver is found on the beaches of Scotland and Wales, and is used much like spinach, though it is probably best known as the main ingredient of laver bread.

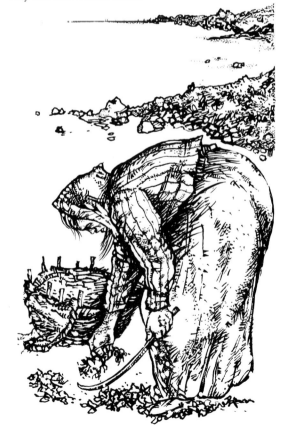

STIR-FRIED VEGETABLES WITH SEAWEED

2oz/55g wakame seaweed
½ small white cabbage
2 onions
1 red pepper
2 tablespoonsful vegetable oil
½ clove garlic, crushed
1 teaspoonful mustard seed
Pinch of ground ginger
3oz/85g/1½ cups bean sprouts
Soya sauce

Soak the seaweed in hot water for 20-30 minutes. Drain well, cool, then chop into pieces.

Finely slice the cabbage, onions and pepper.

Heat the oil and add the garlic, mustard seed and ginger. Cook gently for a few minutes, then add the prepared vegetables and sauté for 15 minutes, stirring occasionally. Add the wakame, raise the heat, and cook for a minute or two. Lower the heat again, add a spoonful or two of cold water, and cook for 5 minutes. Stir in the beansprouts, sprinkle with soya sauce, and cook just long enough to heat through. Serve with rice.

Other seaweeds can be cooked in much the same way.

SEEDS

What they are: Seeds are the mature fertilized ovules of certain flowering plants which are suitable for eating, either to give flavour, or for their nutritional value—or both. Seeds are not as well-known as nuts, yet are a good source of a wide variety of nutrients, and because they are so small, can easily be added to many dishes.

Origins: Seeds have been used as food for many centuries all over the world. In Hindu mythology, the god Yama blessed the sesame seed, and it is regarded by Hindus not only as an excellent food, but also as a symbol of immortality. Alfalfa was first used in the Middle East as food for horses, who did so well that the Arabs started using it as human food, calling it 'the father of all foods', and using it in a wide variety of ways.

Principal nutrients: These vary from one seed to another, but all seeds are good sources of protein, calcium, minerals, some vitamins, and unsaturated fats.

Buying and storing: Seeds are best purchased in small amounts. Store them in a screw-top jar in a cool place. Do not chop or crush them until just before using them.

ALFALFA SEEDS

The seeds of one of the oldest cultivated plants, which has deep roots enabling it to get extra minerals that other plants cannot reach. Alfalfa seeds contain up to 19% protein, compared with 16% in beef, though you would be unlikely to eat your way through a quarter-pound lump of alfalfa! One of the best ways to eat the seeds is to sprout them, which boosts their protein content to 40%.

Uses: In the Third World, alfalfa is used as a food supplement. The seeds can be sprinkled on to savoury or sweet dishes, or can be sprouted and used as a salad ingredient or sandwich filling.

FENUGREEK SEEDS

A tiny dark seed from a leguminous plant, the leaves of which were once used for fodder, hence the name 'Greek hay'. Fenugreek seeds have been used in medicine and healing for thousands of years, and are a good source of protein, iron, and vitamin D.

Uses: Use the seeds to make tea, or lightly toast them and sprinkle them over dishes. Best sprouted, when they have a spicy curry-like flavour. The sprouts can become bitter if cooked for more than 2 or 3 minutes.

PUMPKIN SEEDS

A flat green seed taken from pumpkin gourds which are specially grown for their seeds. In China the pumpkin was called 'Emperor of the Garden', and much revered. Nowadays most pumpkins are grown in the USA, where a new shell-less variety has been bred to make it easier to reach the seeds. Pumpkin seeds are rich in iron.

Uses: Add to salads, granola, and muesli. Sprinkle over savoury or sweet crumbles. Dry roast with soya sauce for a nibble.

THREE SEED NIBBLE

5oz/140g/1 cup pumpkin seeds
5oz/140g/1 cup sunflower seeds
Soya sauce
5oz/140g/1 cup sesame seeds

Mix together the pumpkin and sunflower seeds, then sprinkle with just enough soya sauce to moisten, making sure it is evenly distributed. Spread the mixture across a heatproof plate or shallow tray, and put under a hot grill. Cook for about 5 minutes, stirring frequently, then add the sesame seeds. Continue cooking, still stirring, until the seeds are browned and the sauce has dried to make a coating. (If the pumpkin seeds explode too energetically, lower the heat slightly.) Leave to cool, then store in an airtight jar. Nice as a nibble, but also convenient as a topping for rice and vegetable dishes, or any kind of stir-fries.

SESAME SEEDS

The tiny seeds of an easy-to-grow annual plant that is widespread throughout the Far East, Turkey and the Middle East. They are a particularly good source of calcium (containing ten times as much as milk), and can be eaten regularly, especially by people who do not eat dairy foods.

Uses: Add to any baked goods including bread and biscuits. Use to coat croquettes before frying. Much used in sweets such as sesame crunch bars, halva and Indian sweets.

SESAME ORANGE SWEETS

3oz/85g/⅔ cup sesame seeds
3oz/85g/¾ cup soy flour
2-3 tablespoonsful honey
2 tablespoonsful finely-grated orange peel
Orange juice to moisten
Sesame seeds to coat (optional)

Stir together the seeds and flour, add the honey and peel. The mixture will be stiff at first—it helps to heat the honey. If liked, add just a spoonful or two of juice to moisten. Divide the dough into small pieces and roll into balls. They can be left as they are, or lightly coated with seeds. Set aside to firm up.

SUNFLOWER SEEDS

North American native peoples once cultivated sunflowers, feeding the leaves to animals, using the petals as dye, and obtaining oil and food from the seeds. Although still widely grown in North America, sunflower seeds mean especially big business in Russia. In fact you can take the seeds from the sunflowers in your own back garden, but removing them from the husk is a fiddly job. They are, however, well worth it with their rich concentration of nutrients including B complex vitamins, many minerals, protein, and vitamin E.

Uses: Sunflower seeds have a sweet taste which goes well with many dishes. Sprinkle them over crumbles and soups, mix them into pastry and baked goods, add them to muesli. Ground sunflower seeds can be used to bake very nutritious biscuits. Try dry roasting them together with other seeds.

SOYA MILK

What it is: An alternative to cows' milk which is made from soya beans with oil and sometimes raw sugar added. It is ideal for anyone who wants to avoid cows' milk, and does not cause allergenic problems, though it is best to think of it as a completely different product from cows' milk, since especially when it is drunk raw, it tastes completely different.

Origins: Soya milk is relatively new in Britain, and has been introduced principally to help the many people who want to reduce their consumption of animal products.

Principal nutrients: Like the soya bean from which it is made, this milk contains protein, including all the essential amino-acids. It is a useful replacement for animal milks, especially where allergy is suspected, but soya milk is known sometimes to affect thyroid function, so should be given sparingly to young children.

Uses: Can be used in exactly the same way as milk. Try it in drinks such as milk shakes, sauces, sweet rice puddings and other 'milk'-based dishes. Pour on to muesli or other breakfast dishes; use it in tea and coffee. You can also make yogurt with soya milk.

SPROUTED SEEDS, GRAINS AND BEANS

What they are: When treated with moisture and warmth, seeds become activated and manufacture the vitamins and elements needed to produce a new plant. In this highly active state the amount of such nutrients is dramatically increased within just a few days.

Origins: Though not widely used in the Western world, at least until recently, sprouted seeds have been used in the East for at least five thousand years, and are an important part of their national cuisine.

Principal nutrients: Sprouts are low in calories, high in protein, vitamin A, some of the B complex vitamins, and in particular vitamin C. Some sprouts may contain the important vitamin B12.

Buying and storing: Many health food and wholefood shops now sell bean sprouts, as well as greengrocers and speciality shops. Make sure they are as fresh as possible (or grow your own!). Can be stored in a jar or airtight bag in the fridge for a few days—even under these conditions the vitamin C content can go on increasing.

Uses: Sprouts can be used as fresh vegetables. They are tasty in salads and sandwiches, or added to stir-fried vegetables. Sprinkle into soups and stews at the last minute—never overcook sprouts. Include sprouts in nut roasts, rissoles and omelettes.

CHINESE SPRING ROLLS

For pastry:
    ½lb/225g/2 cups wholemeal (wholewheat) flour
    1 egg
    Cold water to mix
For filling:
    2 tablespoonsful vegetable oil
    2 spring onions (scallions)
    2oz/55g/1 cup mushrooms
    4oz/115g/2 cups bean sprouts
    2 tablespoonsful cooked sweetcorn
    Strip of fresh ginger
    Bunch of watercress
    Seasoning to taste
    Soya sauce
    Vegetable oil for frying

Put the flour into a bowl, add most of the egg, and enough of the water to make a firm dough. Knead briefly, wrap in clingfilm, and set aside in the cool for 30 minutes.

Meanwhile heat the oil and cook the finely-chopped onion for a few minutes. Add the finely-chopped mushrooms and cook a few minutes more. Remove from the heat and stir in the drained sweetcorn, minced or chopped ginger, and shredded watercress. Add seasoning and a little soya sauce.

Roll out the pastry as thin as possible and cut into 12 squares. Divide the filling between them. Roll each one to make a packet, folding the sides so the filling stays in place, and use the rest of the beaten egg to moisten the edges before pressing them firmly to seal.

Heat some vegetable oil and shallow or deep fry the rolls for 5 minutes, turning if necessary. When nicely browned, drain and serve at once.

Spring rolls can also be made using lightly-cooked pancakes (see Caraway Beetroot Pancakes, page 163, for a batter recipe). They are then filled and fried in the same way.

RAW BROWN SUGAR

What it is: Sugar is the sweetener extracted from sugar cane, a perennial plant that grows naturally in the West Indies and around the Indian Ocean. Although both brown and white sugar are made from cane, white has been refined to such an extent that it is almost pure chemical, with no nutritional value whatsoever. Raw brown sugar, on the other hand, is unrefined, still contains some of the goodness of natural molasses and

other nutrients, and is free of added chemicals.

Origins: The use of sugar cane dates back to around 300BC, and sugar has long been used as a food rather than just as a sweetener. Workers in the fields would chew on the cane for nourishment and energy. The over-consumption of white sugar started when sugar began to be refined, so that it was now possible to eat very large amounts of concentrated sucrose, and the lower cost of producing sugar made it possible for everybody to afford it. It is only in recent years that raw brown sugar has become popular as an alternative to white sugar.

Principal nutrients: All sugars, including the more 'natural' honey and maple syrup, dull the appetite and the taste buds when consumed in excess, and all are harmful to teeth, so therefore should be consumed extremely sparingly. However, raw brown sugar does contain some nutrients such as calcium, phosphorus, magnesium, sodium, potassium and iron, and gives foods a better flavour than white sugar. In general, the darker the sugar the more nutrients it will contain, and the stronger will be its flavour.

Buying and storing: Many people confuse brown sugars. There are some on the market which are no more than dyed white sugar, and contain no nutritional benefits at all. Look for the word 'raw' on the pack, which should also give the country of origin. The sugar itself will tend to be sticky in texture as it has not been washed after crystallization. Choose from four varieties: Demerara, light Muscovado, Muscovado and molasses.

Uses: Use wherever a recipe calls for white sugar, in drinks, dessert dishes, jams and marmalades. Add to baked dishes; make sweets; use a little to flavour savoury dishes such as relishes, sauces, red cabbage and apple casserole. Ideal when making cakes and biscuits. Good in ice cream. Always question whether it is necessary to add sugar to a recipe, and add as little as you need to—remember that we are nearly all hooked on sugar, so adding sugar 'to taste' will almost always be more than is necessary either for flavour or for health.

TAHINI

What it is: Tahini is a pale creamy paste made from crushed sesame seeds, sometimes with a little sesame oil added. If made from roasted seeds, the colour is darker and the flavour stronger.
Origins: Tahini has been an important food for centuries in such countries as Turkey, Greece and Cyprus. It is popular in Arab cookery too.
Principal nutrients: Tahini contains all the goodness of sesame seeds in a concentrated form, including vitamins, minerals, calcium, protein and iron. It is easy to digest, and considered by some to be soothing for the stomach. It is very high in fat, and should therefore be used sparingly.
Buying and storing: Can be purchased in screw-top jars from health food, wholefood, and some speciality shops. Make sure it is always covered, and keep in a cool spot.
Uses: A very versatile food with a distinctive and delicate flavour. Try it with spicy falafels, or make into a sauce for vegetables and rice. Make a dip by adding oil, lemon juice, and garlic or herbs. Mix with water and lemon to use instead of milk in tea or coffee. It also goes well with sweet recipes. Make a cream by mixing it with honey, and use over fruit salads or fruit crumbles. Mix with cake crumbs, peel and spices, and roll into balls for a quick nutritious sweet.

TOFU

What it is: Tofu is bean curd made by grinding soya beans into an emulsion, then using salt or a mild acid to curdle it. The result is a firm white curd, usually sold in slabs. It has a very mild flavour, so it can be used in both sweet and savoury dishes.
Origins: Tofu is thought to have originated in China, where it is still used as a staple, more than two thousand years ago, though it is only in recent years that it has become known in the West. It is still one of the first solid foods given to babies in China and Japan.
Principal nutrients: Like the soya bean from which it is made, tofu is an excellent protein food, yet is low in calories. It contains the eight essential amino-acids found in soya beans, and is easy to digest.
Buying and storing: Check that any tofu you buy is fresh. If there is no date on the pack, ask. Once the pack is opened, keep tofu in cold water in the fridge, changing the water daily. It should keep for up to a week in this way.
Uses: Tofu is available in two textures, firm and soft, though either can be used in any dish. The firm variety is best deep-fried, added to flans and quiches, or eaten raw with soya sauce. Use the softer tofu to make sweet cheesecakes or whips, or as a substitute for cottage cheese. Make tofu mayonnaise.

CAULIFLOWER PÂTÉ

1 tablespoonful vegetable oil
½-1 onion
1 medium cauliflower
4 tablespoonsful tahini
2oz/55g/1¼ cups wheatgerm
Soya sauce to taste
Seasoning to taste
Fresh chives to garnish

Heat the oil and sauté the chopped onion until soft. In a separate pan, steam the cauliflower until cooked. Mash the cauliflower or push through a sieve, stir together with the onion, and add tahini to make a smooth paste. Use wheatgerm to thicken, then flavour to taste with soya sauce and seasoning. Spoon into a serving dish and chill. Top with plenty of fresh chopped chives, and surround with raw vegetables, melba toast and corn chips.

see page 136 for a recipe for *DEEP-FRIED TOFU*

MOUSSAKA

½lb/225g/2 cups minced soya TVP
3-4 tablespoonsful vegetable oil
1 leek
2 teaspoonsful dried mixed herbs
Seasoning to taste
Cold water
2 aubergines (eggplants)
4oz/115g/1 cup grated Cheddar cheese
½ pint/285ml/1⅓ cups thin white sauce
Tomatoes to garnish
Parsley to garnish

Hydrate the minced TVP according to the instructions on the packet.

Heat half the oil and sauté the very finely-chopped leek until it begins to soften. Add the drained TVP and cook a few minutes more. Stir in the herbs, seasoning, and a few spoonsful of water to moisten. Cover and cook for 20 minutes.

Meanwhile peel the aubergines, cut into thin slices, and fry on both sides in the remaining oil, using more if necessary. Drain well. Layer a third of the aubergine in an ovenproof dish, top with half of the TVP mixture and some of the cheese. Repeat, and then finish with the aubergine. Pour on the white sauce, making sure it is well-distributed. Top with a final sprinkling of cheese. Bake at 375°F/190°C (Gas Mark 5) for 30 minutes. Garnish with slices of tomato and the parsley.

DEEP-FRIED TOFU

1lb/455g/2 cups tofu
Wholemeal (wholewheat) flour
Seasoning to taste
1-2 eggs
Approx. 2oz/55g/1 cup breadcrumbs
Vegetable oil for frying
Tomato sauce to serve

The tofu must be well-drained. A good way to do this is to wrap it in a clean tea towel, put a weight on top, and leave it for an hour. Cut into four same-size pieces and dust with the flour, seasoning it first. Whisk the eggs and dip the tofu into them, then drop into the breadcrumbs and turn so the tofu is thickly and evenly coated with them. Set aside briefly.

Heat vegetable oil and shallow fry the tofu, turning it once. When crisp and golden, drain well on paper towels. Serve with hot tomato sauce.

TVP (TEXTURED VEGETABLE PROTEIN)

What it is: TVP is processed from soya or field beans to make a meat-like product that can be used in a variety of ways, is quick to prepare, and compares well with meat for its high protein content, while being low in price.

Origins: TVP is a new product designed to replace some or all of the meat in various dishes, and popular with the catering trade, particularly as an extender.

Principal nutrients: These depend on the beans used to make the TVP. In general, though, TVP is a good source of protein, minerals and vitamins. Soya bean TVP gives higher amounts of nutrients. It is also low in calories.

Buying and storing: TVP is dehydrated—add water or vegetable stock when you want to use it unhydrated. It will keep indefinitely if put in a cool, dry place, preferably in a closed container. Hydrated TVP will keep for a few days in the fridge. The unflavoured variety is best, as you can then add your own flavourings. Flavoured TVP may well have monosodium glutamate added, which can cause problems for some people, and may also be coloured.

Uses: Buy minced TVP and use as you would use minced meat—in Shepherd's Pie, a bolognese sauce for spaghetti, to make burgers. Chunks can be used in stews, pies and curries. Be imaginative with the sauces you serve with TVP and you will find it tasty and quick to prepare—a useful 'convenience food'!

VEGETABLES

What they are: Vegetables are edible plants, and come in many varieties—the edible part can consist of roots, stems, leaves, pods, seeds or fruits. Some fifty varieties are available in British greengroceries throughout the year, about half of them home-grown, the rest imported from around the world, though British farmers are now producing many of the more exotic varieties originally introduced from abroad. A variety of vegetables should be eaten by everyone each day, and with so many to choose from, and such a variety of ways to cook and serve them, they need never be boring.

Origins: Though sometimes unpopular in the past with the wealthy, who were too busy filling themselves up with pheasant and boar and had no space left for bulky vegetables, they have always been the mainstay of the poor, who collected various kinds from the countryside around them, and always had a pot of vegetable broth bubbling over the fire. The Romans introduced many new varieties, together with imaginative ways of cooking them, and the British became masters at growing vegetables. By the sixteenth century, however, interest in vegetables had waned, and during the reign of Henry VIII they were hardly used at all. They became popular again during the Elizabethan period, and have now become very much a part of the British pattern of eating, though often still thought of as trimmings to go with the meat. Until quite recently many people grew their own vegetables in their garden or allotment, and considerably more varieties of vegetable were available. The growing of vegetables for one's own consumption has declined enormously since the Second World War, though there has been a recent trend towards more garden and allotment cultivation. Many of the vegetables sold in greengrocer's shops today are restricted to the easiest-to-cultivate and therefore most lucrative varieties, and many of the older—and tastier—varieties are in danger of dying out.

Principal nutrients: Although most vegetables contain vitamins and minerals, not all of them are particularly good sources. Green vegetables are in general good sources of folic acid, a B vitamin found in almost no other foods. Some contain vitamins A and C, and many are useful for mineral salts, especially iron. Dietary fibre is present in vegetables, but in rather small amounts as most are at least 90% water. Cooking vegetables destroys much of the vitamin content, so minimal cooking is important and eating raw vegetables a good idea, though you cannot eat anything like as much raw vegetable as you can when it is cooked.

Buying and storing: If you cannot grow your own, at least try to buy locally-grown vegetables in season, and use them while they are still fresh. For the sake of variety, these can be supplemented with other vegetables which are forced or imported, though these shouldn't be your mainstays. Buy your vegetables from a good greengrocer, and choose carefully, avoiding anything that looks wilted or yellow, blemished or damaged. Organically-grown vegetables are preferable to those produced with the aid of artificial growth promoters, not so much because they are nutritionally superior but because they have not been sprayed. Don't, however, let the absence of organically-grown vegetables in your neighbourhood stop you from eating vegetables—almost any source of vegetables is better than none. Most vegetables will keep for a short time if placed in a cool, well-ventilated spot. Some will keep for a long time, but don't forget that they will rapidly lose their vitamin content. Anything packed in polythene should either be unwrapped, or holes should be made for ventilation.

ARTICHOKES, GLOBE

An unusual vegetable with a globe-shaped head. It is usually imported from Mediterranean countries, though it can be grown in Britain. Buy when the leaves look firm and are closely folded together. Often only the subtly-flavoured heart is served, but the leaves are also tasty, and can be dipped into sauces, dressings or melted butter. Only the fleshy base of the leaves is eaten.

Uses: Can be baked whole and served with a sauce, or stuff the centre with a favourite filling. Alternatively, simply boil until tender and serve hot or cold with a selection of dips.

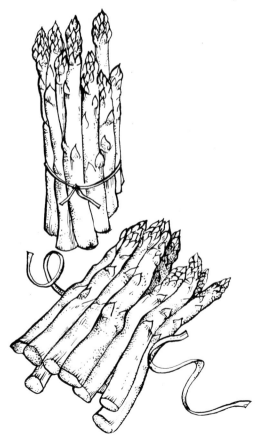

ARTICHOKES, JERUSALEM

A knobbly-looking vegetable which is actually a rhizome. Though grown in this country, they are not widely-known. Jerusalem artichokes have a firm white flesh and a smoky flavour—do not buy if they look wrinkly. They have a high potassium content. Cook with lemon juice to keep the flesh white. Easiest to peel if cooked first.

Uses: Good puréed to make winter soups. Can also be boiled or fried in butter. Add to stir-fried vegetables for a taste and texture something like water chestnuts. Add to a soufflé or serve in a white or cheese sauce.

ASPARAGUS

Asparagus is the very young shoots of a plant which is a member of the lily family. It is mostly imported from Mediterranean countries. It is available only for a short period at the beginning of the summer, and is expensive, so is used as a luxury item rather than as a day-to-day vegetable. Can be thick white stems, or thinner and greener—don't buy if they look woody or tired. Try to cook as soon as possible after purchasing.

Uses: The best way to eat asparagus is to cook it lightly, then serve it with butter or Hollandaise sauce. Can also be used in quiches and flans, or in soufflés—it goes especially well with eggs. Try serving it in a cheese sauce.

AUBERGINE (EGGPLANT)

This shiny, dark purple, oval-shaped vegetable originated in South America. It is now available most of the year. Buy only firm, unshrivelled aubergines. The water content is high, and it can be bitter. To remove this bitterness, slice the aubergine, sprinkle with salt, leave 30 minutes, then rinse with water and pat dry. Aubergines are low in calories, but not particularly high in nutrients. They are avoided by macrobiotics.

Uses: Stuff aubergine halves and bake. Slice or cube and fry aubergine with onions and tomatoes, as in ratatouille. Use to make moussaka, or blend with garlic and make into a dip.

AVOCADO PEAR

A subtropical fruit that is used as a vegetable rather than a fruit. Those on sale in Britain are usually imported from Israel or South Africa. Avocados are becoming more popular, and deserve to be. Apart from their delicious smooth, creamy taste, they are a natural 'super food', rich in protein, vegetable oils, B complex vitamins and minerals. To check if they are ripe, press gently. If still hard, leave to ripen at room temperature.

Uses: The simplest way to serve is to halve, brush with lemon, then fill with nuts or cottage cheese, or dressing with herbs. Can also be chopped up and added to salads. Try avocado blended to make a dip, or make a dressing with it. Avocado soup is chilled for summer days, or bake avocados and eat hot.

GUACAMOLE DIP

2 ripe avocados
2 tablespoonsful lemon juice
¼ small onion
Seasoning to taste
Pinch of paprika
Pinch of chili powder
Parsley to garnish

Mash the avocado flesh with the lemon juice. Finely chop the onion and stir into the avocado mixture with the seasoning and spices to taste. Chill briefly.

Serve in a dish garnished with fresh parsley sprigs. Surround it with corn chips, potato crisps, crackers, raw vegetables such as carrot, cauliflower, pepper and celery, all to be dipped in the guacamole before being eaten!

You can make guacamole in a blender if you prefer.

BEANS

There are a number of varieties available fresh from spring through to autumn, most of them home grown. Runner beans and broad beans are probably the best known. Beans are a reasonably good source of folic acid. The shells should look smooth, free of blemishes, and a good colour. Store in the fridge for a few days if not needed at once.

Uses: Young broad beans are good raw or very lightly cooked, and added to green salads, potato salad, or mixed with other beans and eaten hot. Older broad beans go well in creamy sauces, or add them to vegetable hotpots or casseroles for a quick source of protein. Runner beans go well with tomatoes. Add them to a Salad Niçoise. Serve in a cheese sauce, or add to a quiche.

BEETROOT (BEET)

A plum-coloured round-shaped vegetable which is usually sold ready-cooked, its peel left to be removed just before you serve it. Beetroots are at their best in the late summer, though they are available for most of the year. Buy the smaller ones, which are sweeter, and if you can buy them uncooked, you can also eat them raw. Beetroot tops are nice too—cook them like spinach.

Uses: Cooked beetroot should be sliced or diced and served with dressings, or hot in a white sauce. Complementary flavours include ginger, caraway and soured cream. Borscht is an exotic beetroot soup. Young, raw beetroots are delicious simply grated and added to other vegetables such as celery and apple.

BROCCOLI

Though broccoli is not well known to the British, it is becoming more popular, and some varieties grow well in this country. There are three main types of broccoli. Sprouting broccoli has small tender shoots; Cape broccoli has a single larger head shaped rather like a cauliflower, usually purple; and calabrese has a very good flavour and is imported mostly from Italy—hence it tends to be expensive. Broccoli is a good source of folic acid and vitamin C.

Uses: All broccolis go well in salads, especially with mayonnaise dressing. Make fritters by dipping the heads into a batter and deep frying—good in tempura vegetables. Add cheese sauce and a sprinkling of walnuts.

BRUSSELS SPROUTS

These tiny cabbages were originally grown in the Netherlands, which explains their name. They are a good vegetable for winter, with a nut-like flavour that is actually improved by a touch of frost. Choose small, evenly-sized sprouts with no sign of wilting around the edges. Keep in the fridge for a few days if not needed at once. Brussels sprouts are a good source of folic acid and vitamin C when eaten fresh.

Uses: Good in soups, vegetable hotpots and flans. Go well with mushrooms. Nuts to add are brazils, almonds and peanuts as well as the traditional chestnuts. Young brussels sprouts, finely grated, are tasty if left raw and added to a salad. For a change try them in a curry.

CABBAGES

A variety of cabbages is available throughout the year, and all are excellent sources of vitamin C and minerals, providing they are not overcooked. Most cabbages available in Britain are home grown. Buy in season, choosing those that are firm and a good colour. Favourites to look out for include white cabbage, red cabbage, savoy cabbage and spring greens.

Uses: All can be thinly sliced and used in salads, white and red cabbage together making an interesting combination—in a coleslaw for example. Red cabbage combines well with apple and sweetcorn. It needs to be cooked slowly as it is quite hard. You can also pickle it. Add white cabbage to soups and stews, or serve with carrots. Mix cooked cabbage and potatoes with a little cheese, make into cakes, and fry. Stuff cabbage leaves with a cooked grain, beans and onions.

RED AND WHITE SLAW

½ small red cabbage
½ small white cabbage
1 apple
¼ small onion
2oz/55g/⅓ cup cooked sweetcorn
2oz/55g/3½ tablespoonful peanuts
2oz/55g/⅓ cup raisins
For dressing:
4 tablespoonful vegetable oil
2 tablespoonful cider vinegar
1 teaspoonful honey
Seasoning to taste

In a bowl mix together the finely shredded cabbages, grated apple and onion. Stir in the drained sweetcorn, peanuts and raisins. Combine the salad dressing ingredients in a screw-top jar and shake well, then pour over the cabbage. Toss gently, then chill for 1 hour before serving.

CAULIFLOWER

This vegetable is now available almost all year round, though it is cheaper and better in summer. Look for a firm, close-textured head with no brown flecks. As it has a delicate flavour, do not overcook. For the same reason, do not keep a cauliflower too long before using it.

Uses: Florets can be used raw in salads—try mixing them with Chinese leaves, tomato, banana and nuts. Crème Dubarry is a classic cauliflower soup. Add cheese sauce, and serve topped with breadcrumbs and popped under the grill, or use the mixture to fill vol-au-vents or a flan. Purée, add tahini, and make a pâté. Cook with garlic and onion in tomato sauce for a completely different taste.

CELERIAC

This knobbly root vegetable appears only in winter, and is not well known. It has a creamy white flesh giving a subtle celery-like flavour. Pick only those that are firm and heavy.

Uses: Grate and add to salads. Make into fritters. Purée and use as a vegetable, or as a filling for fritters. Add to bean casseroles. Cook and serve with Hollandaise sauce.

CELERY

There are two varieties now widely available. The self-blanching kind is available during the summer and autumn, the maincrop during the winter. Though dirtier and therefore less attractive looking, the winter celery has a better flavour. Choose crisp, unblemished stalks—if there are leaves, they will indicate how fresh the celery is. Can be kept in the fridge for some days.

Uses: Most widely used in salads, or with dips. Celery can also be cooked in soups, and added to stews and casseroles. Mix it into a tomato sauce to add to spaghetti. Braised celery topped with almonds is delicious.

CHICORY (ENDIVE – U.S.)

A head of chicory should be white to pale green, plump and well formed. This Mediterranean vegetable has a slightly bitter taste, and adds interest to salads. If the edges of the leaves are a stronger green, it will probably be more bitter. Such chicory is better cooked. Chicory contains some iron and folic acid.

Uses: Use whole leaves to line a bowl before filling with a salad mixture, or chop the leaves and add to other vegetables. Add to quiches. Braise the whole heads in butter and lemon juice. Serve in a white or cheese sauce. Goes well with the taste of peppers.

CHINESE LEAVES

These large heads of leaves that look rather like a paler version of cos lettuce are only just becoming popular here, though they have been used in China for centuries. Available most of the year, they make an excellent salad ingredient, are sweet and crisp, and are especially useful in the winter. They keep well in the fridge.

Uses: Add chopped to salads—good with fruits such as apricot and banana added too. Cook gently and sprinkle with seeds. Stuff the leaves, roll them up, and top with tomato sauce. A delicious addition to stir-fried vegetables.

COURGETTES (ZUCCHINI)

Courgettes are baby marrows, either specially grown, or actually cut from marrow plants before they have had time to mature. They grow well in Britain, though they are more often used in Mediterranean-style dishes. They are at their best in the early summer, and shouldn't be too large or the skins will be tough. Keep in the cool for as short a time as possible. Do not peel them.

Uses: Grate and add raw to salads. Include in soups, but add near the end of the cooking time as they quickly overcook. Slice lengthways and stuff—a lentil mixture is tasty—then bake. Fry in oil, coating each slice first in wheatgerm. Serve in a cheese sauce. Use on vegetable kebabs.

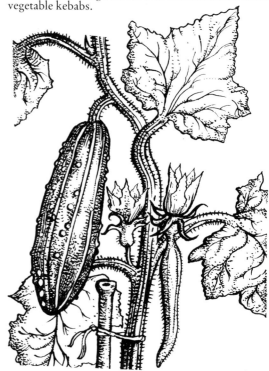

CUCUMBER

There are two kinds from which to choose—the uneven-skinned ridged variety, which looks rather ugly but has a better taste, or the hothouse cucumber, which has a smooth skin. Though you can get them all year round, they are better in summer. Choose those that are firm, round, and not too large.

Uses: Mostly used in salads and sandwiches. Try adding sliced or grated cucumber to plain yogurt to serve with a curry. Cook in a quiche. Make a chilled cucumber soup, or cook and serve in a white sauce.

FENNEL

This strange pale green or white vegetable is not yet well known here. It has a crisp, watery texture, and an aniseed taste. Buy when firm and well-shaped. Darker green bulbs will be tougher.

Uses: Slice and add to salads. Cook with tomatoes and herbs. Goes well with mozzarella cheese. Braise and serve with white or orange sauce, or just with butter and lemon. Eat in chunks like apple—especially good after a meal.

LEEKS

A favourite winter vegetable that grows well in Britain's back gardens. A member of the onion family, it is sold as thick stems, though the smaller these are the sweeter will be their taste. Do not buy if wilted or yellowing. Leeks can be very dirty—to wash them slit them lengthways and wash well under running water. Leeks contain some vitamin C.

Uses: Blanch lightly and add to salads, or serve with a vinaigrette dressing. Can be used raw if young, but chop very fine and do not use too much—the taste is strong. Cook and serve in a white or cheese sauce. Add to stews and soups. Leeks go well with tomatoes. The tougher green tops are best chopped fine and added to bean hotpots and long-cooking casseroles.

LETTUCES

One variety or another is available at any time of year in Britain, most of them home grown, except for crisp iceberg lettuces which are sometimes imported. Kinds to look out for include softer round lettuces, cos, and the curly, rather bitter-tasting endive, which is used more on the Continent than here. All lettuces should be firm and crisp with no sign of discolouration. The softer summer lettuces will only keep a day or so, while some of the crisp varieties will keep up to a week in the fridge. Lettuces contain some vitamin A, especially in the outer leaves.

Uses: Lettuces are used mostly in salads. Try combining two or three different sorts of lettuce to make an interesting salad. When you have a surplus, or they are especially cheap, make cream of lettuce soup. Cook with onion to make an alternative vegetable. Stuff leaves with rice and nuts.

MARROW (SUMMER SQUASH)

A long, heavy autumn vegetable which should be smooth and glossy. When ripe the skin can easily be pierced with a thumbnail. Marrows keep well in the cool, or you can put an underripe marrow in a warm spot. The smaller ones have a better flavour.

Uses: Cube, steam lightly, chill, and serve with yogurt and herbs. Make ratatouille using marrow instead of courgettes. Serve in a white or cheese sauce. Make into soup. Cut marrow rings, stuff them and bake. Older marrows make good jams and chutneys—marrow and ginger jam is a traditional favourite.

OKRA (LADIES' FINGERS, BAMIA, BINDI, GUMBO)

A small dark green finger-like vegetable that originated in the West Indies, and is imported. It is usually available from mid-winter to spring. Do not buy if tired-looking, and preferably not over 4″ (10cm) long, or they will be likely to be tough.

Uses: Add to soups and stews. Serve with onion, celery and peppers in a tomato sauce. Batter and deep fry. Especially good in curry or other spiced dishes.

MUSHROOMS

Three kinds of mushroom are available, the best being the wild field grown mushrooms you have to find and pick yourself—but make sure you know what mushrooms look like! Commercially-grown button mushrooms and flat mushrooms are the same variety, the button mushrooms being younger and not yet opened out. Buy mushrooms with a firm texture and a good colour. As they dehydrate quickly, use them within a day or so.

Uses: Nice raw in salads, or cook them in egg dishes such as quiches, omelettes or soufflés. Dip in batter, deep fry, and serve with Hollandaise sauce. Cook with garlic, wine and tomatoes in Greek style. Add to pizzas, or make into a sauce for pasta, or simply fry or grill.

ONIONS

Onions were one of the very first cultivated foods, and have been a basic in the cookery of many cultures for centuries. In Britain there is a choice of varieties available throughout the year, most of them home grown. When buying onions, avoid any that are bruised or damaged, or sprouting. Keep them in a cool, dark spot, and they should last a long time. Look out for tiny pickling onions, the milder red-skinned shallots, and spring onions to add to salads. Larger varieties include Spanish onions which, because they have plenty of sun, tend to be sweeter, and the British maincrop, which are stronger and best served cooked.

Uses: Use to add flavour to stews and casseroles. Onions go well with eggs, so add to omelettes and soufflés. Make French onion soup. Use in curries. Stuff whole onions with breadcrumbs, cheese, nuts and herbs. Use spring onions or Spanish onions in salads. Shallots are good in creamy sauces.

PEAS

These are best when grown locally and picked when young—which is usually late spring and early summer. Pods should be brightly-coloured, smooth and undamaged. Apart from maincrop peas there are two speciality varieties which are often imported but are well worth trying. These are petits pois, which are tiny and very sweet, and the flat mange tout (snowpea), which is eaten whole. Peas are an excellent source of protein, folic acid and vitamin C.

Uses: Use in pea soup. Add to casseroles and stews. Good in cream sauces. Use to add colour and protein to all sorts of dishes including omelettes, flans, tomato sauces for pasta, macaroni cheese, pizza topping, and stir-fried vegetables.

PEPPERS (CAPSICUMS)

These are members of the chili family, and have only recently started being grown in Britain. Most varieties start out green and then turn yellow or red, the taste being a little sweeter when they are ripe. Buy peppers that are firm and smooth. Once cut, put in a plastic bag and store in the fridge. They are a very good source of vitamin C, but should be eaten when fresh to obtain maximum benefit.

Uses: Add to salads, flans, quiches and vegetable soups. Cook with onions and walnuts and use to stuff crêpes. Stuff whole peppers with breadcrumbs or cooked grain, pine nuts and raisins, and bake. Make a Mediterranean-style ragoût and sprinkle with seeds.

see page 146 for a recipe for *STUFFED PEPPERS*

STUFFED PEPPERS

1 large red pepper
2 large green peppers
1 large yellow pepper   *(or use one colour only)*
4oz/115g/¼ cup cooked grain (bulgur, rice,
    wheatberries)
1 tablespoonful vegetable oil
2 spring onions (scallions)
1 large stick celery
2oz/55g/½ cup chopped almonds
2oz/55g/⅓ cup raisins
Fresh parsley
Seasoning to taste
2oz/55g/½ cup grated Cheddar cheese

Cut the peppers lengthways, remove stems and seeds.
Blanch them in boiling water for 2-3 minutes, then
drain, rinse in cold water, and drain again. Arrange
close together in an ovenproof dish.

   Heat the oil and sauté the chopped onions for a few
minutes, then add the finely-chopped celery and cook
a few minutes more. Stir in the almonds and cook
gently until they begin to colour. Add the grain.
Remove from heat and add raisins, a good amount of
chopped parsley, and seasoning to the mixture. Use to
fill the pepper halves. Sprinkle with cheese. Bake at
350°F/180°C (Gas Mark 4) for 35-40 minutes or
until peppers are cooked.

POTATOES

Originally grown in South America, potatoes didn't
reach Europe until the sixteenth century, and only
really become popular in the nineteenth. By then they
were a staple food in Ireland, and much used
throughout Europe. Today they contribute about a
third of the vitamin C in the diets of people who eat
little fruit or fresh vegetables other than potatoes. They
are in fact quite low in vitamin C, but we do eat a lot of
them. They contain protein, and are an excellent and
versatile ingredient which can be served frequently
without being boring or fattening. At 80 Calories per
100g, potatoes are low in calories—it is the ways they
are cooked and served that give potatoes their unfair
reputation as a fattening food.

   New potatoes should feel slightly damp, and the
skins should rub off easily. Out-of-season new
potatoes from abroad may be stale or, worse still,
treated with preservatives, so be careful when buying.

   Old potatoes should be firm and free from mould or
bruising. The best part of potatoes is their skin, so try
to eat them unpeeled, though do check that the skins
haven't been sprayed to stop the potatoes sprouting.
Store potatoes in a cool, dark, dry place and they will
keep for a long time.

Uses: Cook new potatoes lightly and serve with mint
or garlic; make into a potato salad. Add mashed
potatoes to soups to thicken them or make them into
cakes or croquettes and fry them. Use potatoes in
curries, flans and stews. Chips are a good food if the oil
is really hot so the outside is sealed at once and the
potato absorbs relatively little fat. Make bubble and
squeak, or Shepherd's Pie with a vegetable or lentil
base. Jacket potatoes served with a choice of toppings
is one of the quickest and easiest meals to prepare.

PUMPKIN

These large winter squashes with their bright orange flesh originated in North America, where they grow to huge sizes. Our cooler British climate keeps them from getting much above 15lb (7kg) each. Because of their size, they are often sold in ready-cut sections. When buying pumpkin like this, check that it has only recently been cut, and that the flesh looks firm and non-fibrous. Cut pumpkin should be used as soon as possible, though if you don't need it for a day or two you can cook it, then cover it and keep it in the fridge. Pumpkin has only a fifth of the calories of potatoes and half those of spinach, yet can be made into very filling dishes.

Uses: The most popular way to serve pumpkin is in a sweet, spicy pie. Puréed pumpkin can also be mixed with onion, pepper, nuts and cheese to make a savoury pie. Pumpkin soup is unusual and has a lovely colour. Baked or roasted pumpkin can be served as a vegetable topped with butter. Cubed pumpkin can be added to stews and stir-fries.

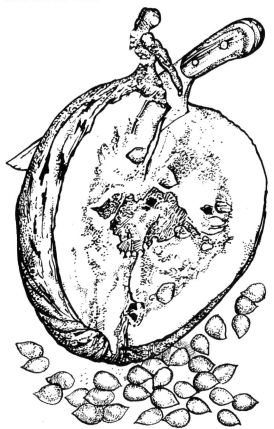

RADISHES

These small red root vegetables have a crunchy texture, and a peppery taste that comes from the mustard oil they contain. They are thought to stimulate the appetite. Available most of the year, British radishes are gradually being supplemented by more exotic varieties from abroad, each of which has a slightly different appearance, though all have the distinctive peppery taste. Buy radishes with their leaves attached if possible, and do not remove them until you are ready to serve them. Store in a cool place.

Uses: Radishes are mostly used in salads and as a garnish. Boil older ones and served them topped with butter or parsley sauce.

ROOTS

A number of the vegetables already described in this section are root vegetables, but there are some that are traditionally linked together as winter roots, and are used in combination in stews, hotpots and soups. These include carrots (especially valuable for their vitamin A content), parsnips, swedes and turnips. A more recent addition to the list is salsify, which looks like a small parsnip and is also called 'oyster plant' because of its unusual taste. All these vegetables, except for carrots, are best and cheapest during the winter. Choose firm, undamaged vegetables, and look out for worm holes. They will keep for some time if stored in a cool, dry, well-ventilated place.

Uses: Use together in vegetable stews. All can be finely grated and added raw to salads. Purée and serve as a vegetable, or mix with egg and use as a flan filling, or to flavour a soufflé. Serve in cheese, white or tomato sauce. Parsnip can be sliced thinly and fried. Carrots, the only root crop that is available fresh all year round, can be steamed when young and sweet, and served with a little butter and lots or parsley. Later they are good in a garlic sauce.

SPINACH

Now available in different varieties so you can buy spinach much of the year, though the leaves are more tender in summer. Spinach is a reasonably good source of iron. Look out for fresh, crisp leaves, and handle with care, for spinach is delicate. Do not wash until just before using it. It can be kept in the fridge for a short time, but is best eaten as soon as possible after picking or buying. Seakale beet or Swiss chard is actually a vegetable of the beetroot family, but it looks and tastes very much like spinach, and should be treated and cooked in the same way.

Uses: Cook with onion and nutmeg, fill pancakes, top with cheese sauce. Cook and mix with ricotta cheese and egg and use to fill pasta rolls or to make lasagne. Try spinach curry. Add to soups and soufflés. Young leaves can be washed, dried, shredded and eaten raw, maybe with a sprinkling of almonds.

SQUASH

These small marrows are very popular in the USA, but are only just becoming available in Britain. They come in a wide variety of colours, shapes and sizes. Buy only if firm, glossy and undamaged.

Uses: Can be used in much the same way as marrow. Add to soups and stews, or stuff with a favourite mixture. Serve as a vegetable by baking and then puréeing, adding butter and herbs to taste.

BASIC VEGETABLE STOCK

¾-1lb/340-455g mixed vegetables*
1oz/30g/2½ tablespoonsful margarine
Chopped parsley
Bouquet garni
3 pints/1¾ litres/7½ cups water
Seasoning to taste

Chop the vegetables and fry them in the melted fat for 5 minutes, taking care not to burn them. Add the parsley, bouquet garni and water, bring to a boil, then cover and simmer for at least 30 minutes, preferably an hour or longer. Cool slightly, then strain off the stock. Use it at once, or keep it in the fridge for up to 3 days. Stock can also be frozen in ice trays—use the cubes as you need them.

*You can use any kind of vegetables for stock, including peelings (wash them well first), celery tops, and the outer leaves of cabbages, Brussels sprouts and lettuces.

SWEETCORN

Another popular North American vegetable, which is now widely-grown in Britain. Fresh corn on the cob usually appears only for a short season in late summer, and these should be eaten on the day of purchase as the natural sugars soon turn to starch once the vegetable is picked, and the taste will be less sweet. Buy plump, well-shaped corns, and do not remove the husks until just before cooking.

Uses: There is nothing to beat lightly-cooked corn on the cob, and it needs only to be topped with a little butter, margarine or tahini. Alternatively, the kernels can be sliced off with a sharp knife to be used in soups, stews, vegetable casseroles and flans, or to be added to egg dishes or stuffings to add colour. Mix with broad beans and a dressing to make Succotash. Nice in salads, especially mixed with bean sprouts.

TOMATOES

Once used only as a decorative plant, tomatoes were considered dangerous to eat, and are still shunned by macrobiotics. Now they are grown in a wide variety of shapes and flavours, and are much used around the world, particularly in Mediterranean countries. When buying them, check that they are firm and undamaged. Under-ripe tomatoes can be left in the fridge if you want to slow down their ripening process, but soft fruit should be kept at room temperature and used as soon as possible.

Uses: Tomatoes are most popular in salads, or cooked to make sauces to serve with pasta or to spread over pizzas before adding the topping. They also go well with aubergines, as in Middle Eastern dishes—add spices and serve with yogurt. Add them to stews, flans and quiches. Make cream of tomato soup, or Gazpacho, a chilled soup. An unusual starter is a savoury tomato sorbet. Soft tomatoes can be used to make a sauce that can be frozen until needed. Green tomatoes make excellent chutney.

WATERCRESS

A crop which is native to Britain and still grows wild in places, though most of the watercress on sale has been specially cultivated. Look for glossy dark green leaves and long stems. Because of spraying and poisonous effluents, wild watercress should be avoided unless it is clearly growing in clean water. Watercress should really be eaten while fresh, but can be kept for a day or so if put in a perforated polythene bag in the salad drawer of the fridge. Watercress is often eaten for its iron content, but in fact this is no higher than many other green vegetables—parsley has five times as much.

Uses: Usually served in salads and sandwiches. Try it in watercress soup, add it to flans, or make a watercress quiche. Unusual if added to stir-fried vegetables. Chop leaves and stir into mayonnaise.

VINEGAR

What it is: A rather sharp acidy liquid, obtained by fermentation from a fruit or vegetable source. Malt vinegar is a highly-processed variety and best avoided. Try to use vinegars made from wine or, best of all, apples.

Origins: Wine and cider ferment naturally to form vinegar, and the preservation of food in vinegar is a technique which has been used for many centuries.

Buying and storing: Buy vinegars with the minimum amount of additives. Store in a sealed bottle in a cool, dark place. Do not buy too much at one time.

CIDER VINEGAR

This is made from whole apples, and in colour can vary from yellow to dark amber. Together with honey, cider vinegar has had more claims made about its beneficial qualities than almost any other wholefood. Nutritional research has failed to substantiate most of these claims, though cider vinegar has been used in healing for many years. It is said to have germ-killing and antiseptic properties, and to help lower the blood pressure. The one claim that cannot be denied is that it tastes nice!

Uses: Add to salads and cooked dishes. Can be flavoured by adding herbs and spices—the chosen herbs should be steeped in the vinegar for 3-4 weeks. Use as a gargle for sore throats, make a hot drink with honey, or inhale the steam. Use in pickles and preserves (see the section in the chapter 'Producing Your Own Food').

WINE VINEGAR

This can be made from either red or white wine, and usually contains a blend of wines. Wine vinegar is very popular in Mediterranean countries.

Uses: Use in salad dressings, and add small amounts to stews, sauces and soups. A hotter vinegar can be made by adding garlic and chili peppers, or it can be flavoured with herbs and spices. Use to preserve fruit and vegetables.

FLAVOURED VINEGAR

1 pint/570ml/2½ cups good quality red wine vinegar

A few sprigs of fresh marjoram, thyme, tarragon, rosemary, raspberry leaves or mint (or a mixture)

Pinch of salt

Heat the vinegar very gently, then pour into a large screw-top jar. Add herbs and salt. Leave for a minimum of 2 weeks—the flavour will be better if you leave it for anything up to 2 months. Strain and bottle. Use as you would ordinary vinegar, especially in salad dressings.

WHEATGERM

What it is: This is the germ of grains of wheat, a tiny embryo weighing only one-fortieth of the whole grain, but containing all the nutrients needed to grow a new plant. It is highly perishable, which is why it is removed from white flour, so that the flour's shelf life can be extended.

Origins: It was only when flour refining began in earnest around 1870 that wheatgerm was 'discovered'. Up until then it had been an integral part of all flours, and though its special nutritional value may not have been appreciated, the bread that was baked from it was far more nutritious. Though nutritionists fought to have it returned to its rightful place, they were scorned for most of the early part of this century, and it is only with the recent interest in wholemeal flour and bread that wheatgerm has again become popular.

Principal nutrients: Wheatgerm oil is the richest known source of vitamin B6, also of vitamin E. In addition, wheatgerm contains vitamin A, iron, calcium, and twelve amino-acids.

Buying and storing: Look for raw, unprocessed wheatgerm. Stabilized wheatgerm has been treated to stop rancidity, and has lost some of its nutrients in the process, though it is still a very valuable food. Buy any wheatgerm in small quantities from a supplier you know to have a fast turnover—health food, wholefood and speciality shops sell it, as do chemists. Store in a screw-top jar in the fridge. Do not use it if you suspect it has gone off.

Uses: Add wheatgerm to everything—it has a mild flavour and is easy to digest. Goes well with breakfast cereals, muesli, sauces, stuffings, baked goods, bread, scrambled egg, yogurt, honey, peanut butter. Use instead of flour when rolling out pastry—this will give it a nutty texture. Coat fritters or croquettes with it when frying. Use to thicken soups.

WHEATGERM BREAD

½oz/15g/1 tablespoonful dried yeast
1 teaspoonful honey or raw cane sugar
¾ pint/425ml/2 cups warm water
1¼lbs/565g/5 cups wholemeal (wholewheat) flour
4oz/115g/1cup wheatgerm
Pinch of salt

Cream together the yeast, honey or sugar, and a little of the warm water, then set aside in a draught-free spot for 10 minutes, or until frothy. Sift together the flour, wheatgerm and salt. Make a well in the centre and pour in the yeast plus the rest of the water. Use your hands to mix well. Turn the dough on to a floured board and continue kneading until it is smooth. Leave covered in a warm spot until doubled in size. Knock the dough back, knead again briefly, then flour hands and shape the dough into a loaf. Put into a well-oiled tin and leave in the warm to rise to the top.

Bake at 375°F/190°C (Gas Mark 5) for 35-40 minutes, or until the loaf sounds hollow when tapped. Put on to a wire rack to cool.

YEAST

What it is: Yeast is a fungal growth which produces fermentation by the use of enzymes. It is used as a raising agent in baking, and in brewing and winemaking. Live yeast is usually available only in dried form, but can be bought fresh from some shops. It is produced in a variety of ways. A new easybake dried yeast is now available, which contains vitamin C to encourage fermentation.

Origins: Yeast was discovered by the early Egyptians, who were so impressed by the way it made bread rise that they devised many sorts of high-baked loaves as an art form as well as to eat.

Principal nutrients: Contains some B vitamins.

Buying and storing: Dried yeast can be stored for ages providing it is kept in a covered container in a cool dry place. Fresh yeast is best bought in small amounts as and when you need it, and should keep for up to a week in the fridge. If it begins to brown round the edges it can still be used, but trim off the discoloured part and then use the rest at once.

Uses: Use yeast in breads, rolls and pizza bases. For brewing and winemaking, use brewers' yeast.

YOGURT

What it is: A thick creamy substance usually made from cows' milk, either full fat or skimmed. It is one of the finest natural foods, but is often sold with artificial colourings, flavourings and preservatives. Nowadays yogurt made with goats' and ewes' milk is also becoming more popular, the advantage being that the milk is produced on a small scale and less likely to be contaminated with antibiotics and hormones. Yogurt can also be made with soya milk.

Origins: Yogurt is thought to have been used first by the nomads of eastern Europe at least a thousand years ago. Other names for yogurt include tako, laben raid, zabady and kefir, and the taste and texture of these traditional yogurts can vary considerably.

Principal nutrients: Yogurt is high in protein, and low-fat varieties are widely available. Some nutritionists believe that the bacteria and enzymes in yogurt help to maintain a healthy intestinal environment. The main thing to remember is that yogurt is as good as the milk it is made from, especially where the fat content is concerned. There is no difference in nutritional terms between live and pasteurized yogurt, though you may prefer your yogurt to be bacteriologically alive rather than sterile.

Buying and storing: Yogurt is sold just about everywhere these days, though live unflavoured varieties are usually only available from health food and wholefood outlets. Those sold in supermarkets may still be live—it depends whether they have been pasteurized after bacterial action or not. Never buy flavoured yogurts. You can always flavour plain yogurt using natural ingredients of your choice.

FROZEN BANANA YOGURT

3 ripe bananas
6 tablespoonsful honey
2oz/55g/⅓ cup raw cane sugar
½ teaspoonful finely-grated lemon rind
¾ pint/425ml/2 cups plain natural yogurt

Mash the bananas and mix with the honey, sugar and lemon rind. Lightly blend in the yogurt. Turn it into a tray and freeze until it begins to firm. Beat the mixture, then return to the tray, cover, and freeze until set firm. Serve in scoops, garnished with roasted hazel nuts.

Seasonings

What garlic is to salad, insanity is to art.
Augustus Saint-Gaudens

Herbs

Herbs can be used either fresh or dried. Use between a third and a half of dried herbs as you would fresh, since they are much more concentrated. Buy herbs in small amounts and use them quickly, as they soon lose their flavour.

To dry herbs: Pick them when young, preferably early in the morning when the sun has just dried the dew. Wash if necessary in cool water, then gently shake or pat dry. Hang them in loose bunches, tips downwards, in a warm, dry, shaded spot to dry. If you prefer, lay the herbs on a flat tray and put in an airing cupboard. When crisp, break off the leaves and store in opaque, airtight jars. Crumble them just before using.

TOMATO BASILICA WITH MOZZARELLA

1lb/455g large tomatoes
½lb/255g mozzarella cheese
Olive oil
Seasoning to taste
Fresh basil

The tomatoes should be ripe but still firm. Wipe them to clean, then cut crossways into evenly sized slices. Slice the mozzarella. Arrange attractively on a serving dish, overlapping the tomatoes and cheese.

Mix together the olive oil, seasoning, and a good amount of finely-chopped basil. Trickle this over the other ingredients. Chill before serving topped with large sprigs of basil.

ANGELICA

What it is: A white-flowered plant that originated in the Baltic, so grows best in cold climates. Can reach up to 8′ in height.

Flavour imparted: Pleasantly aromatic.

Uses: The roots are most commonly used to flavour gin, vermouth and liqueurs such as Benedictine. The candied stalks are best known as decoration for cakes and sweets. Try adding angelica when cooking fruit such as apples, pears or rhubarb. Gives an interesting flavour to marmalades and jams.

BASIL

What it is: Sweet basil is a garden herb that grows well if carefully tended. Though it is said to have originated in India, it is now particularly popular in Mediterranean countries, especially Italy.

Flavour imparted: Delicate and slightly sweet.

Uses: The perfect herb to use with tomatoes, also courgettes. Try it with scrambled eggs, rice and other grain dishes. Good on salads. Mix into cheese spreads or dips for a change. Add to sauces.

VEGETABLE KEBABS WITH HERBS

1 large green pepper
12 button mushrooms
2 large courgettes (zucchinis)
8 cherry or small tomatoes
6 small potatoes, steamed until just cooked
1 large onion
8 stuffed olives
Bay leaves
For marinade:
3 tablespoonsful vegetable oil
1 tablespoonful white wine vinegar
Pinch of garlic salt
1 teaspoonful dried basil
1 teaspoonful dried rosemary, crushed
1 teaspoonful dried oregano
Seasoning to taste

Cut stem from pepper, remove seeds, and cut the flesh into large cubes. Wipe the mushrooms to clean. Cut the courgettes into thick slices. Wash and dry the tomatoes. Halve the potatoes (skins should be left on). Cut the onion into thick segments and then separate the layers. Put all the vegetables into a bowl and pour on the marinade. Leave overnight in the fridge.

Thread all the ingredients on to skewers, arranging them attractively, and including the olives and bay leaves. Lay them on a baking sheet. Cook under the grill for 10-15 minutes or until all the ingredients are just tender, turning the skewers frequently, and basting with any left-over marinade. Serve with rice.

BAY

What it is: A well-known evergreen garden shrub that can grow up to 12′ in height.
Flavour imparted: Very distinctive on its own, though combines well with other flavours.
Uses: An essential ingredient of bouquet garni. Add a whole leaf to stews, casseroles, soups, and remove before serving. Or use to flavour milk before making a sauce. Crush and add to vegetable dishes—goes especially well with cabbage.

CHERVIL

What it is: A cultivated herb that grows well in pots, and has attractive crinkly leaves.
Flavour imparted: Like aniseed. Said to be the most delicately-flavoured of all herbs.
Uses: Nice in salads. Also goes well with egg dishes—try adding it to omelettes and soufflés, maybe with other herbs too. Can also be used as a garnish.

155

CHIVES

What it is: A very common garden herb that grows in a grass-like clump, and has hollow leaves. Particularly popular in Britain. It is a member of the onion family.

Flavour imparted: Mild and oniony, though it actually contains an oil similar to that found in garlic.

Uses: Fresh chives should be snipped with scissors before sprinkling over a wide variety of dishes including salads, omelettes, casseroles and savoury pancakes. Good too with cheese dips, especially cottage and curd cheese. Add to mashed potatoes.

HERB OMELETTE

8 eggs
4 tablespoonsful fresh herbs, mixed
Seasoning to taste
2oz/55g/¼ cup butter or margarine

Break two eggs into a bowl and whisk well. Add ½ tablespoonful of herbs, salt, and freshly-ground pepper. Melt ½oz (15g) fat in a heavy based pan, pour in the eggs, and cook gently for 2 minutes. Tilt the pan and use a spatula to lift the omelette on one side so that the liquid runs underneath. Repeat this until the eggs are just beginning to set. Add the remaining ½ tablespoonful of herbs, fold, and serve at once. Cook three more omelettes in the same way.

Omelette aux Fines Herbes is traditionally made and served like this, relying on fresh free-range eggs and flavourful herbs like tarragon, parsley, chives and chervil to make it a very special omelette. You can, of course, adapt it by adding cheese, strips of pepper, sweetcorn or cream to the eggs as you whisk them.

DANDELION

What it is: The same small yellow-coloured flower that grows wild and is generally considered to be a nuisance. In fact it contains vitamins A and C, iron and potassium. Dandelion tea may help to relieve liver complaints, and is a mild diuretic, known in France as *pis en lit*.

Flavour imparted: The young leaves have a sharp, green taste.

Uses: Apart from making a tea with the leaves and a coffee with the ground roots, you can use dandelions to add flavour and nutrients to any number of dishes. Pick the leaves when they are young and unblemished, wash carefully and pat dry. Then snip and add to salads, cheese or egg dishes, pulses, or use as a garnish with casseroles, bakes, etc.

DILL

What it is: A plant originally grown in the Mediterranean, but now cultivated in Britain too. Is thought to have a carminative effect, and is often used in children's medicines.

Flavour imparted: Subtle, rather like caraway (it contains the same oils but in a different balance).

Uses: Chop the mild-flavoured feathery leaves and add them to salads and sauces. The seeds go well with pickled vegetables. Add them also to coleslaw, sauerkraut and potato salad. An unusual but delicious apple pie can be made by stirring just a few dill seeds in with the fruit.

CHILLED CUCUMBER DILL SOUP

1 onion
1¼ pints/850ml/3 cups vegetable stock
2 cucumbers
1 clove garlic, crushed
1 bunch dill, chopped
Seasoning to taste
Pinch of nutmeg
Paprika to taste
¼ pint/140ml/⅔ cup plain natural yogurt

Slice the onion and cook for 5 minutes in the stock. Cube the cucumber and add to the stock with the garlic; cook 10 minutes more. Add the chopped dill, bring to the boil, then simmer the soup for 15 minutes, or until the cucumber is tender. Set aside to cool.

Purée the ingredients, or rub through a sieve. Stir in seasoning, nutmeg and paprika, then gently add the yogurt, mixing it well. Chill the soup. Top with extra dill if liked.

FENNEL

What it is: A tall bushy plant originally brought to Britain by the Romans. Said to be an excellent aid to digestion: Italians still eat slices of the bulb after a heavy meal.

Flavour imparted: Mild and sweet, with a hint of liquorice.

Uses: The seeds, slightly crushed, make a delicious tea. They can also be sprinkled over cakes, bread and biscuits. Use the chopped leaves as a garnish for salads, soups and nut loaves. Fennel is especially good with rich dishes.

GARLIC

What it is: One of the earliest herbs used in cooking, garlic has been in use for at least 5,000 years. It is a member of the onion family. The clove or bulb can vary in size and shape, and can have a white, pink or mauve skin. Though grown and used throughout much of the world as much for its food and medicinal value as for its taste, the best garlic is said to come from the warmer climates.

Flavour imparted: Can be raw and harsh, or sweet and mild. Pink-skinned garlic tends to be more subtle in flavour.

Uses: Rub a clove of cut garlic around the bowl when only a slight flavour is required, as for salads and fondues. Peel, chop, or put through a garlic press for a stronger taste. Garlic can be added to most dishes. Try it with vegetables, cheese and egg recipes, in soups and stews, on pizzas, with pasta, and in sauces. Garlic bread is another popular way to enjoy this herb.

HORSERADISH

What it is: Horseradish is another herb which has been used since earliest times. It grows up to 3′ tall and has leaves similar to those of the dock; it is often found growing wild. A natural antibiotic, it also has antiseptic qualities and is gently laxative. Horseradish is, weight-for-weight, one of the most nutritious vegetables there is!

Flavour imparted: Strong and bitter.

Uses: The roots are used to make the classic horseradish relish. Can also be added to sauces and dips. Use sparingly.

HYSSOP

What it is: An attractive plant that has clusters of blue flowers. To the ancient Greeks it was 'the holy herb', and much valued for its cleansing properties.

Flavour imparted: Aromatic, with a bitter aftertaste.

Uses: Add chopped leaves to salads, sauces and bakes. Especially good with pulse dishes such as bean stews and lentil purées.

LEMON BALM

What it is: An easy-to-grow plant with strongly fragrant leaves. Contains oils said to help dispel flatulence. Some herbalists also believe that it can ease depression.

Flavour imparted: Subtle and lemony.

Uses: Make tea with the fresh leaves (the lemony quality will not keep in the dried leaf); add one or two crushed leaves to other milkless teas or fruit drinks. Goes well with eggs and savoury rice dishes and salads.

LOVAGE

What it is: A garden herb that can grow to 5′ in height; pale yellow flowers. Much loved in Elizabethan times, it has been out of favour since then, though with a renewed interest in herbs it is being rediscovered and grown in an increasing number of gardens.

Flavour imparted: Like celery but with a sharp tang.

Uses: One of the ingredients that goes well in bouquet garni. Chop lovage and sprinkle it over salad. Especially good with tomatoes and potatoes.

MARJORAM

What it is: There are various kinds of marjoram. Sweet Marjoram, much used in Mediterranean cuisine, grows easily in Britain, and is best known for its flavour, though it was once used for its aroma alone.

Flavour imparted: Delicate yet slightly bitter.

Uses: Use in soups, casseroles and stuffings. Good with egg dishes—try it in a soufflé. Add to scones and bread for a change. Does something special to a fruit salad. Marjoram mixes well with other herbs.

MINT

What it is: There are a number of mints in common use, the most popular being Peppermint, Spearmint and Pennyroyal. All belong to the same family, and apart from adding flavour to food, are widely considered to have a beneficial effect on the digestion. Mint is also used to help alleviate feelings of nausea.

Flavour imparted: Fresh and sharp. Some mints are sweeter than others.

Uses: Whole or chopped leaves are good with new potatoes, in mint sauce, and mixed with other vegetables, especially young peas. Use as a garnish for cold soups and cold drinks. Mint tea is also easy to make, and delicious. Add chopped mint to yogurt with garlic or onion and pour over a cucumber salad. Use to flavour a Waldorf Salad or a fruit salad. Nice with grain dishes, especially when served cold.

OREGANO

What it is: A member of the marjoram family, sometimes called Wild Marjoram.

Flavour imparted: Like marjoram, but stronger and with bitter undertones.

Uses: Traditionally used in Italian cookery with such dishes as pastas and pizzas, though it also goes well with hotter Mexican dishes, and tomatoes cooked Spanish-style with onions. Try adding it to mushrooms, also lentils. Do not use too much.

PIZZA

For base:
    ½oz/15g/good tablespoonful fresh yeast, or
      ¼oz/7g dried yeast.
    Pinch of raw cane sugar
    ¼ pint/140ml/⅔ cup warm water
    ½lb/225g/2 cups wholemeal (wholewheat) flour
    Pinch of salt
    3 tablespoonsful olive oil
For topping:
    ¾lb/340g tomatoes
    ½lb/225g Edam cheese
    1 small green pepper
    4oz/115g/2 cups mushrooms
    12 black olives
    2 teaspoonsful oregano
    Seasoning to taste
    Olive oil

Dissolve the yeast and sugar in half of the water, and set aside in a warm place for 10 minutes, or until it begins to froth. Sift the flour and salt into a warm bowl and add the yeast mixture, the rest of the water, and the oil. Mix well until it comes away from the sides of the bowl, adding a drop more water if necessary to bind. Turn on to a floured board and knead for 5 minutes. Put in a clean, floured bowl, cover with a damp cloth, and leave in a warm spot until doubled in volume. Punch the dough down, divide into four, and roll out to make medium-sized circles no thicker than ¼" (6mm). Arrange on greased floured baking trays.

    Brush the tops with a little oil. Slice the tomatoes and arrange on the pizzas. Cover with slices of the cheese. Cut the pepper into rings and divide between the four. Top with a sprinkling of sliced mushrooms. Add the olives, oregano and seasoning, and trickle a little oil over each pizza.

    Bake at 400°F/200°C (Gas Mark 6) for 20-30 minutes, or until dough is crisp.

PARSLEY

What it is: One of the most popular herbs in Britain, having been used for centuries. Two types of parsley are available, the traditional crinkly variety and a flat-leaved parsley. Parsley features in many legends and folk tales. It is especially rich in vitamins A and C, also iron and calcium.

Flavour imparted: Mild, aromatic, yet quite distinctive.

Uses: It is most popular as a garnish, which means that it is often pushed uneaten to the side of the plate! Add it instead whilst cooking such dishes as sauces, stews, casseroles and bean bakes. Try a parsley soufflé, or adding a generous handful to scrambled eggs. Mix into dips such as hummous, cheese or tahini. Put parsley butter on new potatoes. Add to grain dishes.

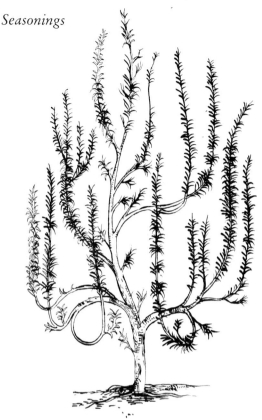

ROSEMARY

What it is: A bushy garden shrub with spiky leaves, which can grow up to 6′ tall. Very fragrant. Rosemary is also used as a powerful medicine that acts on the heart and blood vessels.

Flavour imparted: Delicate and rather sweet, somewhat soapy.

Uses: Use fresh or dried leaves, crumbled or finely-chopped. Add them to vegetable casseroles and soups—especially good with peas and potatoes. Try rosemary with pastry, dumplings, scones and biscuits for a change. It is traditionally used with rich meat dishes. Instead of adding the leaves loose, you can tie them in a muslin bag and remove them before serving the dish—the flavour will be more subtle and you won't have the sharp bitty texture to contend with.

SAGE

What it is: A hardy evergreen with broad, flat leaves. Grown and used throughout Europe since Roman times, it has always been valued as an aid to digestion as well as for its flavour.

Flavour imparted: Warm and strong. A little like eucalyptus.

Uses: Nice with cheese dishes, also with pulses. Add fresh chopped leaves to tomatoes or to make herb butter. Try with cream cheese, adding lemon juice to make a spread, or with cottage cheese. Sage and onion stuffing is delicious with vegetables. Use sage sparingly.

BRAN AND ROSEMARY BISCUITS

6oz/170g/1½ cups wholemeal (wholewheat) flour
2oz/170g/½ cup bran
4oz/115g/1 cup margarine or butter
Cold water to mix
1-2 tablespoonsful dried rosemary, crushed
2oz/55g/⅓ cup sunflower seeds

Sift together the flour and bran, then use fingertips to rub in the fat to make a crumb-like mixture. Stir in just enough cold water to bind to a dough, knead briefly, then wrap in clingfilm and set aside in the cool for 30 minutes. Adjust the liquid if the dough seems too dry, and knead to distribute the rosemary and coarsely-chopped seeds. Roll out on a floured board and cut into circles.

Arrange on a lightly-greased baking sheet and bake at 350°F/180°C (Gas Mark 4) for 20 minutes, or until crisp and golden. Let the biscuits get completely cold before putting them into an airtight container. Serve them lightly buttered with soup, or topped with cream or cottage cheese as a snack.

SAVORY

What it is: There are two kinds of savory in general use. Summer savory is considered to have more medicinal qualities, and is often added to cough mixtures. If planted between rows of bean crops it is said to keep away blackfly. Winter savory is used as an aid to digestion.

Flavour imparted: Mild, with a touch of spiciness. Winter savory is stronger than summer savory.

Uses: Especially good with bean, pea and lentil dishes. Add savory to salads, egg dishes, vegetables and tomato sauces. Use in herb butters. Good when added to rice and used as a stuffing.

SWEET CICELY

What it is: A fern-like herb that grows mainly in the north of England and Scotland, and is easy to grow even in damp, shady spots. Has clusters of pretty white flowers.

Flavour imparted: Sweet and aniseedy.

Uses: Sweet cicely can at least partly replace other sweeteners in many dishes. Use with sharp fruits such as gooseberries, greengages and plums. Also good in fruit juices. Cicely can be used with savoury dishes like bakes, salads and vegetable casseroles—it marries especially well with parsnips. Popular in France.

TARRAGON

What it is: Tarragon is a small bushy herb with long, slender, pointed leaves. It is native to parts of Russia. The variety called French Tarragon is best for cooking.

Flavour imparted: Fresh, very distinctive.

Uses: The most popular use is in Tarragon Vinegar, made by steeping 2oz of leaves in 1 pint of wine vinegar for 4 weeks, then straining. Tarragon also adds its distinctive taste to such sauces as Hollandaise and Bernaise. It goes nicely with mayonnaise too. Try tarragon butter with young asparagus or broccoli to enjoy these vegetables at their best. Chopped leaves can be added to egg dishes and salads.

THYME

What it is: A small garden bush with tiny leaves. Its fragrance is attractive to bees, hence the wide variety of thyme honeys that are available. Thyme is believed to have powerful antibiotic and antiseptic properties.

Flavour imparted: Pungent and warming, with a sweet undertone.

Uses: Cream sauces are particularly good with thyme added. It also goes well with soups such as Borscht, stuffings, nut roasts and salads. Aubergine, peppers and courgettes is a vegetable combination that tastes good with a little thyme added—try it in ratatouille.

Spices

All spices should, if possible, be kept whole, and ground just before they are needed. If you buy the powdered variety, do so in small quantities, as their essential oils begin to evaporate at once, and they soon become stale and dull. Store spices in airtight jars.

GREEN TOMATO CHUTNEY

2lb/910g green tomatoes
1lb/455g apples
1lb/455g onions
1lb/455g sultanas
1 teaspoonful ground ginger*
1 teaspoonful allspice*
1 pint/570ml/2½ cups cider vinegar
¾lb/340g/2 cups raw cane sugar*

Peel and chop the tomatoes, apples and onions. Put into a large saucepan with the sultanas, spices, and ⅓ pint (190ml) cider vinegar. Simmer the mixture gently for about an hour, or until everything is well cooked, adding more vinegar if necessary. Stir in the rest of the vinegar and the sugar, and cook steadily until the chutney thickens.

Transfer to warmed jars, making sure you fill them right to the top, cover with paper, then screw on the tops firmly (metal tops will rust if they come into contact with the chutney). Store in a cool, dry, dark place.

*This is a not-too-hot and rather sweet chutney. Use more spices and less sugar if you prefer.

ALLSPICE

What it is: Not, as many people think, a mixture of spices, but the berry of a tree native to the West Indies, which explains why allspice is also known as Jamaica Pepper. The small brown berries are usually ground into a powder.
Flavour imparted: Like a mixture of cinnamon, cloves and nutmeg. Mild.
Uses: Use in curries. Also good in cakes, stewed fruit and fruit pies. Try in fruit-based punches.

ANISEED

What it is: A decorative annual plant that can be grown in Britain, though the seeds need a warm, dry summer to ripen. Much of the aniseed on sale in Britain is imported from Spain, where it is grown commercially.
Flavour imparted: Sweet, rather like liquorice.
Uses: Can be used to make a delicious tea, widely believed to be good for helping the digestion. Sprinkle the seeds on bread, cakes and biscuits. Crushed seeds go well with vegetables, especially buttered carrots.

CARAWAY BEETROOT PANCAKES

For batter:
    4oz/115g/1 cup wholemeal (wholewheat) flour
    Pinch of salt
    1 egg
    ½ pint/285ml/1⅓ cup half milk, half water
For filling:
    1lb/455g cooked beetroot
    1 small carton natural yogurt or soured cream
    Seasoning to taste
    1-2 teaspoonsful caraway seeds
    Extra yogurt or soured cream to top
    Fresh dill or parsley to garnish

Sift together the flour and salt. Add the beaten egg, then gradually whisk in the liquid. Beat to get air into the mixture. Put in the fridge for 30 minutes.

When ready to make the pancakes, whisk the batter lightly again. Heat a little oil in a heavy-based pan and pour in a few spoonsful of the batter, tipping the pan so that it spreads. Cook gently, and when the underside is set, flip by hand or with a spatula, and cook the otherside for a minute or two. Keep the pancake warm whilst making the other pancakes in the same way.

Meanwhile, dice the beetroot and put into a small pan, stir in the yogurt or soured cream, and heat very gently. Add seasoning and caraway seeds to taste.

Fill each pancake with some of the beetroot mixture, fold carefully, and top with a spoonful or two of yogurt or soured cream and a good sprinkling of herbs. Serve hot.

CARAWAY

What it is: The seeds of a plant which is usually cultivated, though is sometimes found growing wild. The oil from the seeds is used to make Kummel, the famous liqueur.

Flavour imparted: Slightly sharp.

Uses: Caraway seeds can be used in rye bread, seed cake, or on rolls. They also go well with sauces, cheese spreads, and a variety of vegetables, cabbage in particular. The leaves of the caraway plant can be chopped and added to salad.

CARDAMOM

What it is: A plant native to the East Indies and China. They are usually bought in their fibrous pod, and are best ground just before use as they lose their flavour very quickly. Excellent for the digestion.

Flavour imparted: Aromatic, with a touch of lemon. Very distinctive.

Uses: Curries. Indian desserts. Though much used in Indian cookery, it is also popular in Scandinavian dishes. Used to add a distinctive flavour to coffee in the Middle East. Good with baked apples. Add one or two pods to a cup of tea—with or without milk.

CAYENNE PEPPER

What it is: A powder made from a blend of various capsicums, including both seeds and pods. It originated in Cayenne in South America.

Flavour imparted: Very hot, pungent.

Uses: Devilled eggs, some cheese dishes. Curries. A little cayenne adds bite to stews and casseroles. Use sparingly.

CHILI POWDER

What it is: A powder made from the dried small red pod of a particular chili pepper.

Flavour imparted: Burning hot

Uses: Chili beans, Mexican dishes. Use sparingly.

CINNAMON

What it is: Strips from the bark of a small evergreen tree of the laurel family, native to Sri Lanka. Contains a powerful antiseptic oil.

Flavour imparted: Sweet, rather delicate.

Uses: Add ground cinnamon to all kinds of fruit dishes—especially good in rhubarb pie. Gingerbread, milk puddings, stuffing for apples. In Eastern cookery sticks of cinnamon are put in with meat dishes. Can be used in savoury dishes where a warm rich flavour is wanted. Nice added to both tea and coffee.

CLOVES

What it is: The dried berries of the clove tree. Contains oils that really do seem to help relieve toothache.

Flavour imparted: Very strong, spicy.

Uses: Traditionally used in sweet dishes such as mincemeat, apple pies and fruit cakes. Can also be used with vegetable dishes—try sticking whole cloves into an onion and adding it to a stew. Cloves add something extra to mulled wine and hot chocolate drinks. Use with caution.

CORIANDER

What it is: An annual plant brought to Britain by the Romans, which sometimes grows wild although it is often cultivated in herb gardens. The ripe seeds are used to make the powder.

Flavour imparted: Mild, sweet, and a little musty.

Uses: Curries. Casseroles. Nice in the crumble topping of a fruit dish. Coriander also goes well with Middle Eastern dishes—try it in pilaffs, stuffed vegetables, or sprinkled over a mixture of black olives and potatoes. Good with pea soup. The leaves can be shredded and added to salads and curries.

CUMIN

What it is: The seeds of a plant resembling fennel. Often used in powder form.

Flavour imparted: Something like caraway.

Uses: Add the powder to cream cheese dips or spreads. Good with egg dishes, lentils and other pulses, vegetables such as cabbage, and in sauerkraut. The seeds can also be used—crush them lightly first. Use in curries, sprinkle over a pizza.

CHILI KIDNEY BEANS

¾lb/340g/2 cups red kidney beans, soaked overnight
1 small onion
1 small green pepper
1-2 tablespoonsful vegetable oil
½lb/225g tomatoes, skinned and chopped
3 tablespoonsful tomato purée
2 teaspoonsful mixed dried herbs
1-2 teaspoonsful chili powder, or to taste*
Seasoning to taste

Cook the beans in fresh water, boiling them first for 10 minutes, then lowering the heat and simmering for 50 minutes, or until just tender. Finely chop the onion and pepper and sauté in the oil to soften. Add the tomatoes, purée, herbs, chili powder and seasoning. Mash most of the beans and stir into the other ingredients. Cover the saucepan and simmer for about 15 minutes. Add the remaining beans to give texture, and cook just long enough to heat through.

Chili beans cooked this way can be topped with grated cheese. Serve them with corn bread and a side salad.

*Chili powder can vary in strength, but is usually strong, so don't use too much until you are sure you like it!

FENUGREEK

What it is: A plant much used in Indian cookery (see the fenugreek section in 'A Wholefood Glossary').

Flavour imparted: Sharp and spicy, with a bitter aftertaste and a hint of celery.

Uses: As a flavouring, fenugreek is usually ground into a powder—it is included in most commercially-made curry powders. Use it with rice, vegetables and casseroles, but always sparingly. The lightly-roasted seeds can be sprinkled over cooked dishes, cheese dips and omelettes.

CINNAMON HONEY CAKE

½lb/225g/2 cups wholemeal (wholewheat) flour
Pinch of salt
1-2 teaspoonsful mixed spice
6oz/170g/¾ cup margarine or butter
3-4 tablespoonsful honey
3oz/85g/½ cup raw cane sugar
3oz/85g/3 tablespoonsful candied peel
2 eggs
2oz/55g/½ cup flaked almonds

Sift together the flour, salt and spices. In a small saucepan melt the fat and honey together, and stir in the sugar. Remove from the heat and cool slightly, then add the candied peel and whisked eggs. Combine all the ingredients. Turn the mixture into a greased loaf tin and scatter with the flaked nuts.

Bake at 400°F/200°C (Gas Mark 6) for 15 minutes, then lower heat to 350°F/180°C (Gas Mark 4) for 30-40 minutes, or until cooked. Transfer to a wire rack to cool.

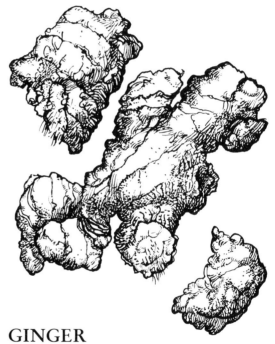

GINGER

What it is: A powder made from the root of a tropical plant. You can sometimes buy fresh ginger which can then be peeled, mashed and used in the same way as the powder—the flavour is richer and sweeter. Buy in small quantities and use when fresh. Ginger is believed to reduce flatulence.

Flavour imparted: Rich, hot and spicy.

Uses: Used in Indian curries, but also in Chinese foods—try it in stir-fried vegetables, or add to the filling for egg rolls. Ginger is also used for beers and cordials, treacle tarts, and cakes such as gingerbread; also ginger biscuits. Try a little sprinkled over melon slices. Crystallized stem ginger is an expensive but delicious addition to fruit salads. Always use ginger sparingly.

BAKED PEARS

4 large pears
Lemon juice
1oz/30g/2 tablespoonsful raw cane sugar
1oz/30g/¼ cup wholemeal (wholewheat) flour
1oz/30g/2½ tablespoonsful margarine
½ teaspoonful ground cinnamon
¼ teaspoonful ground nutmeg
¼ teaspoonful ground ginger
Grated lemon rind

Halve and core the pears. Brush surfaces with lemon juice, then arrange close together in an ovenproof dish, cut side up. Make a crumble by rubbing together the sugar, flour and margarine so that you have a crumb-like mixture. Stir in the spices and lemon rind and sprinkle over the pears. Bake at 375°F/190°C (Gas Mark 5) for 30-40 minutes, or until pears are cooked.
 Serve with yogurt or whipped cream.

MACE

What it is: The outer coating of the nutmeg, which is like a webbing. This is dried and then ground to make a powder. More expensive than nutmeg.
Flavour imparted: Rather like nutmeg, but fuller and sweeter.
Uses: Use whenever you would use nutmeg. Good in fruit cakes or added to whipped cream, also with stewed fruits such as plums and cherries.

MUSTARD SEED

What it is: The seeds of the dazzling yellow mustard plant. These come in various colours and strengths. The seeds are less hot than the more concentrated powder—use which you prefer.
Flavour imparted: Sharp and hot.
Uses: Can be used whenever you want to liven up a dish, as mustard goes well with most ingredients, but use it sparingly. Ideal in pickles, coleslaw, cheese dishes and soufflés. Add a pinch of the powder to salad dressings and mayonnaise. Made-up mustard is usually coloured with saffron or turmeric.

NUTMEG

What it is: The inner part of the fruit of the nutmeg tree. Looks rather like a small walnut.
Flavour imparted: Sweet and spicy.
Uses: Good in sweet dishes such as custards, rice puddings and stewed fruits. Essential to mulled wine. Try a pinch in savoury recipes such as cheese sauces, rice dishes and vegetable casseroles. The Italians add nutmeg to ricotta cheese and spinach, and use it to stuff ravioli or pancakes. Middle Eastern dishes often use nutmeg. Use nutmeg sparingly.

PARPRIKA

What it is: A powder made from dried, ground peppers called Hungarian Red Peppers which are, appropriately, bright red in colour.
Flavour imparted: Very mild and sweet.
Uses: Used in popular Hungarian dishes such as goulash, or a coriander and paprika cheese spread. Try too in paprika sauce, egg dishes, rice and other grain recipes. It is often just sprinkled over the top of pale dishes to add colour.

PEPPER

What it is: There are two kinds of pepper in general use, black and white. In fact both come from the same tropical fruit, the black berries coming from the unripe fruit, whilst white peppers have been allowed to ripen, then have been dried and skinned. Pepper is thought to stimulate digestion and circulation.
Flavour imparted: Strong and spicy. Black peppers are stronger and have a fuller flavour.
Uses: Freshly-ground black pepper brings out the flavour of all foods and can be added as desired. For an unusual sweet, try cottage cheese with honey, peel and spices—and some black pepper. Quiche au Poivre is a classic pepper dish. Whole peppers can be added to pickles.

POPPY SEEDS

What it is: Tiny blue seeds taken from the opium poppy, and often used in the cuisine of such countries as Hungary and Poland. Though much of the plant has narcotic properties, the seeds are drug-free.
Flavour imparted: Mild and nutty.
Uses: Sprinkle over bread, rolls and cakes. Add to cottage cheese or other soft cheeses, or to mashed potatoes. Nice in salad dressings. Try too with pasta when served with a creamy sauce.

PARSNIP CURRY

1lb/455g parsnips
½lb/225g leeks
2 large carrots
3oz/85g/¾ cup cashew nuts
For sauce:
   2 tablespoonsful vegetable oil
   1 onion
   1 clove garlic, crushed
   1 teaspoonful ground turmeric
   1 teaspoonful ground cumin
   2 teaspoonsful ground coriander
   ½ teaspoonful ground ginger
   1 teaspoonful mustard seed
   Seasoning to taste

Peel and cube the parsnip, clean and chop the leeks, slice the carrots. Parboil all the vegetables for 5 minutes until just beginning to soften. Drain and reserve water.

Heat the oil and add the chopped onion and garlic. Cook for 5 minutes or until they begin to colour, then add the spices and cook a few minutes more. Season to taste, and add about ½ pint (285ml) of the reserved water. Bring to a boil, then cover and simmer for 15 minutes. Remove lid and cook gently until sauce thickens. Stir in the vegetables and nuts and cook for 5-10 minutes more.

Curry sauce improves in flavour if made a day or two before needed and then reheated.

VANILLA

What it is: The pod produced by a tropical climbing orchid native to Central America, picked before it ripens. It is cured over a period of time, and ends up as a long black bean-like strip.

Flavour imparted: Delicate and sweet.

Uses: It is better to use vanilla pods than vanilla essence, as the latter may well have additives included—some vanilla flavourings are pure chemical. Although fairly expensive, vanilla pods can be used time and again. Add them to rice puddings, custards and other sweet dishes, then remove the pod before serving, rinse and pat dry. Store a pod in a jar of sugar so the sugar absorbs some of the flavour. Use ground vanilla for a stronger flavour. Vanilla is invaluable when making sweets, ice creams, mousses, banana and coconut pies.

SAFFRON

What it is: The dried orange stigmas of the crocus flower. They can be bought as filaments, or ready ground into a powder. Fairly expensive.

Flavour imparted: Mild, especially as so little is used.

Uses: Mainly used to add colour to a dish, particularly rice.

TURMERIC

What it is: The ground root of a plant native to India. The resulting powder has a distinctive bright yellow colour.

Flavour imparted: Subtle and aromatic

Uses: One of the main ingredients in commercial curry powder. Use when pickling or making relishes. Adds interest in a white sauce. Good with rice and vegetable dishes, unusual in salad dressings. It can be used instead of saffron for colouring dishes.

Other Seasonings

All of the following seasonings have a high salt content, and should therefore be limited in their use. As with sugar, most of us have developed a sense of taste in which a lack of salt seems to be something which needs to be adjusted. This is rarely the case, and we get more than enough salt in our diet without adding any more at all. As a general guideline, while cooking add as little of the seasonings in this section as possible. Leave people to salt their own food and, especially when children are eating, leave the salt pot off the table completely.

WINTER HOTPOT WITH MISO

1oz/30g/2½ tablespoonful miso
1 pint/570ml/2½ cups vegetable stock or water
2 tablespoonsful vegetable oil
3 carrots
1 large onion
1 large turnip
4oz/115g Brussels sprouts
4oz/115g peas, fresh or frozen
Watercress to garnish

Stir the miso into a drop of the vegetable stock and set aside. Heat the vegetable oil in a large pan and gently sauté the peeled and chopped carrots, onion and turnip for 5 minutes, stirring frequently. Add the trimmed and halved Brussels sprouts, the peas (if fresh) and the vegetable stock. Bring to the boil, then cover the pan, lower the heat, and cook gently for 20 minutes. Add the peas (if frozen). Cook 5 minutes more, then check if vegetables are cooked. When tender, stir in the miso and cook for literally a minute more. Serve garnished with watercress. Good with a grain such as rice or wholewheat berries.

GOMASIO

What it is: A highly nutritious condiment used in Japan. Make your own by grinding lightly roasted sesame seeds together with sea salt to make a fine powder. Adjust the proportions to suit yourself: the usual ratio is 8 parts sesame seeds to 1 part salt. If you like you can lightly roast the salt as well. Make only a small quantity at a time and store it in an airtight jar. Gomasio soon loses its taste and goodness.
Flavour imparted: Like a nutty salt.
Uses: Sprinkle over any dish: salads, bakes, casseroles, soups, vegetables, grains, egg and cheese dishes. Best added at the table.

MISO

What it is: A thick soya bean paste produced by lactic fermentation. It has been used in Japan for over 2,000 years, where a variety of different misos are produced, some lighter and milder, others darker and more concentrated. Miso contains all the many nutrients of the soya bean, and is a good vegetable source of vitamin B12.
Flavour imparted: Salty and rich.
Uses: Dissolve a small amount of the paste in liquid and add to soups, gravies, stews and casseroles. Do not use too much, as the flavour is strong and will overpower more subtle tastes. As it is very salty, adjust other seasonings accordingly. Make a spread by mixing miso with tahini and a drop of water.

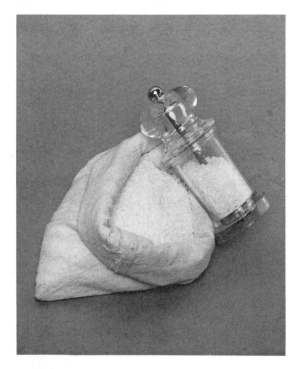

YEAST EXTRACT

What it is: When fresh brewers' yeast is mixed with salt it is broken down by its enzymes. The soluble residue is evaporated under pressure by a process invented in Germany at the turn of the century, but now used throughout the world. There are many varieties of yeast extract on sale, all with salt added, though some manufacturers are now reducing the salt content. Vitamin B12 is sometimes added, and it is an excellent source of several other B vitamins.

Flavour imparted: Savoury, salty.

Uses: Dissolve in liquid and add to soups, stews and casseroles. Also makes a good drink for cold wintery days. Spread thinly on toast. Use sparingly.

SALT

What it is: Natural salt, either sea salt or rock salt, contains a wide variety of trace elements essential to good health, including sodium chloride (common salt) and iodine. Though salt intake should be kept low we do need a little, especially in hot weather. However, we get quite enough from the other foods we eat, and very rarely need added salt. Unlike processed salt, sea salt and rock salt have many nutrients to offer and no chemical additives. They also have a stronger taste, so less is needed.

Flavour imparted: Salty; richer than processed salt.

Uses: Add to foods as needed. If you feel you must add salt to savoury dishes, leave it on the table in a salt mill, and grind it just before eating. Better still, lose the salt mill!

SOYA SAUCE

What it is: Like miso, soya sauce is made by fermenting soya beans. Wheat and salt are added, and the process is a lengthy one—tamari soy sauce, which is the best, takes at least eighteen months to produce. The sauce is rich in protein and other nutrients.

Flavour imparted: Savoury, salty.

Uses: Add to such dishes as casseroles, soups, stews and stir-fried vegetables whilst cooking. A bottle of soya sauce on the table can replace salt. Try sprinkling it over egg rolls, tempura fried vegetables or tofu slices.

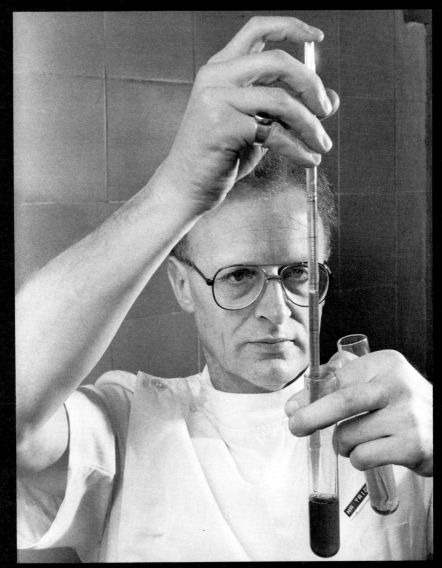

Additives, Pesticides and Other Pollutants

Undertakers have noticed that dead bodies last three
or four days longer than they did fifty or sixty years ago;
this is because they are packed full of the preservatives which
almost all cooked food and commercial frozen foods contain.

Alec Forbes
The Bristol Diet

Additives, Pesticides and Other Pollutants

Concern about the additives and preservatives used in food is not a new thing, yet the original reasons for using them were sound enough. During the industrial revolution of the nineteenth century there was a continuous movement of people from the countryside into the towns, people seeking work in order to earn money with which to feed their hungry families. Unfortunately, the dramatic increase in urban populations created many new problems, not the least being that of how to provide enough food for everyone.

Most foodstuffs were produced in the country. Getting them speedily from there into the cities, and on a large enough scale to satisfy so many hungry stomachs, was impossible. Many foods were simply not available, and what there was was often in a state of decay. In the 1870s science and technology made concerted efforts to solve this problem by finding ways to manufacture food that would stay fresh longer, taste good, and offer nutritional value for money. They were highly successful.

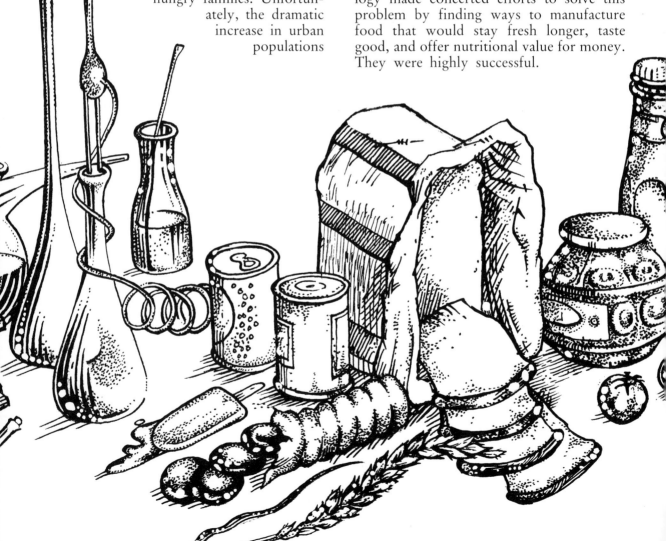

At about the same time, tinned foods, and a little later frozen foods, began to be imported into Britain from America and Australia, adding variety to the diet as well as bringing down prices. Fish and meat, transported under refrigeration, began to appear regularly on the tables of the working class for the first time. The scene was set for one of the biggest changes in attitudes towards food that has ever taken place. Quite suddenly there was choice. People could indulge their preferences, expect to have variety throughout the year. Food began to be seen not just as a basic necessity of life, but as something to be enjoyed.

So far so good. But it wasn't long before the cosmetic aspect of food production began, with manufacturers vying with each other to think up new ideas, create new tastes, and add colour and glamour in order to increase sales and profits from basic products such as bread and sugar. This process has continued virtually unchecked, and since our intake of food has dropped now that most of us are less physically active, the fight for dwindling custom grows ever more fierce.

The sophisticated science of food production is now very big business indeed. At the turn of the century about fifty permitted additives were in use. Today the figure is nearer three and a half thousand, the number having doubled in the last decade, these being used in thousands of products and in millions of combinations. It isn't only the foods we recognize to be highly processed that contain additives. Vegetables such as potatoes, onions and carrots may be sprayed to prevent sprouting or further growth. Lemons and oranges may be dyed and waxed. Strawberries are sometimes sprayed with hormone mixtures to promote growth. Egg yolks are dyed via colouring in the chicken feed.

The food industry insists that such additives are safe, at least in the amounts used. Careful controlling by two major organisations, the World Health Organization and the Food and Agriculture Organization of the United Nations, means that any suspect chemicals may be struck off the list at any time, or at least be closely monitored. New additives are tested on animals before being accepted as safe for humans to eat.

Yet there is increasing concern that these controls are not enough, that testing on animals does not prove what effect they will have on the very different human system, especially in the combinations that will undoubtedly occur as part of the average highly-processed diet. There is concern that though processed foods may cost less per unit, their nutritional value is lower than natural foods, and we therefore end up paying higher prices for our nutrients. Critics are pointing out that cosmetic additives enable manufacturers to use inferior products, dress them up, and sell them at higher prices than they deserve. Ultimately the question must be not only what additives are doing to our health, both physical and mental, but whether most of them are needed for any reason at all.

Some 70% of the food we eat today is processed. It has been estimated that in Britain the average consumption of additives per person is between 7 and 16lbs each year. That's the equivalent of over 22 aspirin-sized tablets of chemicals each day. Can it really be possible that we remain completely unaffected unaffected by them?

Our unhealthy record

Given our improved standards of living and hygiene, safety regulations, and the vast amounts of money spent on hospitals, research and drugs, our health as a nation is not as good as we might expect. We are the world's leaders in deaths from heart disease, a major killer which, interestingly, has increased alongside the expansion of supermarkets. Doctors generally agree that heart disease is at least partially linked with the foods we consume, and it is estimated that some 35% of cancers can be directly caused by what we eat, many more being affected by our diets. Less devastating but nonetheless debilitating to those who suffer from them are such conditions as obesity, hypoglycaemia and diabetes, all linked directly with food.

Hyperactivity in children is causing increasing concern these days, both to their parents and to the puzzled medical profession. Such children sleep little, are over-energetic, unable to sit still and concentrate. As they get older they often experience difficulties with speech and balance, and their learning ability may suffer considerably. This condition is almost certainly linked with a diet too dependent on processed foods. The Hyperactive Children's Support Group has proved beyond doubt that children suffering in this way improve once foods and drinks containing synthetic colours, flavours, and certain preservatives are reduced or stopped completely. In a correctional home in Virginia, USA, youngsters who were switched to a wholefood diet and given no processed food (including white flour and white sugar) showed a marked improvement in behaviour with lessened hyperactivity and an increased ability to concentrate.

Yet because children continue to be drawn to 'fun foods' with their bright colours, sweet flavours and soft textures, items produced with children in mind contain more additives than most foods. Flavoured dessert mixes, fruit yogurts, pies, biscuits, cheese spreads, soft drinks and diet drinks are often packed with additives. A seemingly innocent Swiss roll can contain chemicals known to cause skin rashes, swelling, nausea, breathing problems, blurred vision and vomiting in some people. What makes things worse is that as children's body weight is less than that of adults, the combination of additives they consume from foods has more effect than in an adult.

Another health problem which seems to be on the increase among people of all ages and lifestyles is that of allergies, many if not the majority of which can be linked to chemicals in our food, water and air. Clinical ecologists specialize in such allergies, the first problem being to recognize them. Symptoms are often diagnosed as something else when they are in fact the body's unique way of showing an allergic reaction. Bronchitis, asthma, skin problems such as eczema, digestive upsets, mouth ulcers, constipation, diarrhoea, colitis, abnormal pulse, high blood pressure, fainting fits, fibrositis, some forms of arthritis, headaches and migraines, convulsions, vertigo, impotence, frigidity, behavioural problems such as anxiety, panic and delusions—these and many more symptoms can be forms of allergic reaction.

It is believed that some 5½ million people in Britain are known to suffer in this way, and the figure may be much higher. Allergies can be caused by a variety of substances, and can include aversions to such basic foods as wheat and wheat products, milk, cheese, coffee and eggs, but many can be linked with food additives, and allergic reactions to naturally-occurring substances in food are often exacerbated by the presence of additives. Clinical ecologists frequently find a higher incidence of allergies in people who eat a highly-processed diet, and by testing carefully to find which foods are the most troublesome, have had some amazing results. Unfortunately the medical profession seems reluctant to recognize the value of clinical ecology, despite the evidence, and prefers to treat such symptoms with drugs, which often simply compounds the problem.

To get some idea of the kind of additives your food is likely to contain, take a look at the list below. It has been divided into groups, with a brief explanation of why they are used, and some examples of where they might be found. It has deliberately been kept simple—if you want to go into more detail, there are a number of books now available.

PRESERVATIVES

Purpose: Used to inhibit the growth of bacteria, moulds, yeast or fungi that would affect the taste of the food, and may ultimately result in food poisoning.

Natural preservatives: There are many methods which have been used over the years, and are still sometimes used by the food industry. 'Natural' is in any case a relative term, since the substances used as preservatives (sugar, for example) are often highly refined. Though these techniques have been used for centuries, they are not without their attendant health hazards— salting and smoking have, for instance, been linked with the incidence of stomach cancer and stroke. Natural preservatives include:

Acids (citric, lactic, etc.)
Salt (meat has been salted for centuries)
Sugar (usually sucrose)
Alcohol
Smoke
Vinegar (acetic acid)

Other preservatives:
Sulphur dioxide
Benzoic acid (a derivative of sulphur dioxide)

These two are used in a very wide variety of products, including wine, sausages, fruit juices, pickles, jams, candied peel, sultanas, soft drinks, sauces, and flour for biscuits.

Sodium nitrates and nitrites

Used in meat products such as bacon, ham, tongue and beef, also in some cheeses including Samsoe and Emmenthal and many processed cheeses.

SAINSBURY'S 6 Peanut Delights

EAT WITHIN 3 DAYS OF PURCHASE

INGREDIENTS: CHOCOLATE FLAVOUR COATING (SUGAR, VEGETABLE FAT, WHOLE MILK POWDER, FAT REDUCED COCOA POWDER, WHEY POWDER, SKIMMED MILK POWDER, COCOA MASS, EMULSIFIER: E322; FLAVOURINGS), SUGAR, ANIMAL AND VEGETABLE FATS, PEANUTS, WHEATFLOUR, WHOLE EGG, MARSHMALLOW (GLUCOSE SYRUP, SUGAR, STARCH, EGG ALBUMEN, GELATINE, CITRIC ACID, FLAVOURINGS), INVERT SUGAR SYRUP, EMULSIFIER: E475; SKIMMED MILK POWDER, SOYA FLOUR, FLAVOURINGS, COLOURS: E102, E110, CARAMEL (E150); SALT.

J Sainsbury plc Stamford Street London SE1 9LL

Comments: Sulphur dioxide and benzoic acid destroy vitamin B1, and promote allergic reactions in some people. Sulphur dioxide is also suspected of encouraging genetic mutations. Although the body can dispose of some sulphur dioxide, it is now used in so many foods that there may well be an overload. Foods sold for use in catering establishments are allowed to contain 10% more sulphur dioxide than food sold for home use, so anyone eating out regularly, including children who have school lunches, may be consuming excessive amounts. Sulphur dioxide can be a particular problem for anyone who regularly consumes red wine and potato crisps at the same time. Nitrates are banned in many countries, and have recently been reduced in the USA because of their strong links with cancer, especially of the liver and stomach. Many nitrates reach us through our water supply—the increasing use of nitrates in fertilizers means that they can accumulate in rivers and reservoirs. This water can reach us through processed foods as well as from our taps. Sodium nitrite is known to react with proteins to form nitrosamines in the stomach. As these are known to cause cancer in animals they should be avoided if possible, even though there is as yet no evidence of human cancer being caused in this way.

ANTIOXIDANTS

Purpose: These prevent spoilage due to deterioration in quality, and the development of oxidative rancidity through exposure to oxygen in the air. They are used in processed oils and fats, and foods containing them such as crisps, ice cream, shop-bought cakes and biscuits. Polyunsaturated oils contain their own antioxidant in the form of vitamin E.

EMULSIFIERS AND STABILIZERS

Purpose: To stop oil and water-based liquid separating. There is a wide variety of compounds available to meet varying requirements. Emulsifiers and stabilizers are often used in peanut butter, salad cream, mayonnaise, margarines and low fat spreads.

FLAVOURINGS

Purpose: To replace flavours lost or destroyed during processing, or to make more subtle flavours stronger and tastier.

Natural flavourings:
>   Herbs
>   Spices
>   Essential oils from fruits, berries, seeds, etc.

Synthetic flavourings:
>   Acids
>   Esters
>   Ketones

Comments: It is estimated that there are some 3,000 flavourings in use, which make up the bulk of additives. Many of them have been in use for years and are not suspected of being dangerous, but as natural and synthetic flavourings are increasingly being used in combination, it is becoming more difficult to evaluate their effects.

FLAVOUR ENHANCERS

Purpose: To bring out the natural or diminished flavour of a food. Monosodium glutamate is the most frequently used. Look out for it in tinned soups and other tinned savouries.

Comments: Monosodium glutamate has a long history of use as a flavour enhancer in the Far East, and is much used in Chinese ccoking. Recent research has shown it to cause headaches, dizziness and nausea in some people.

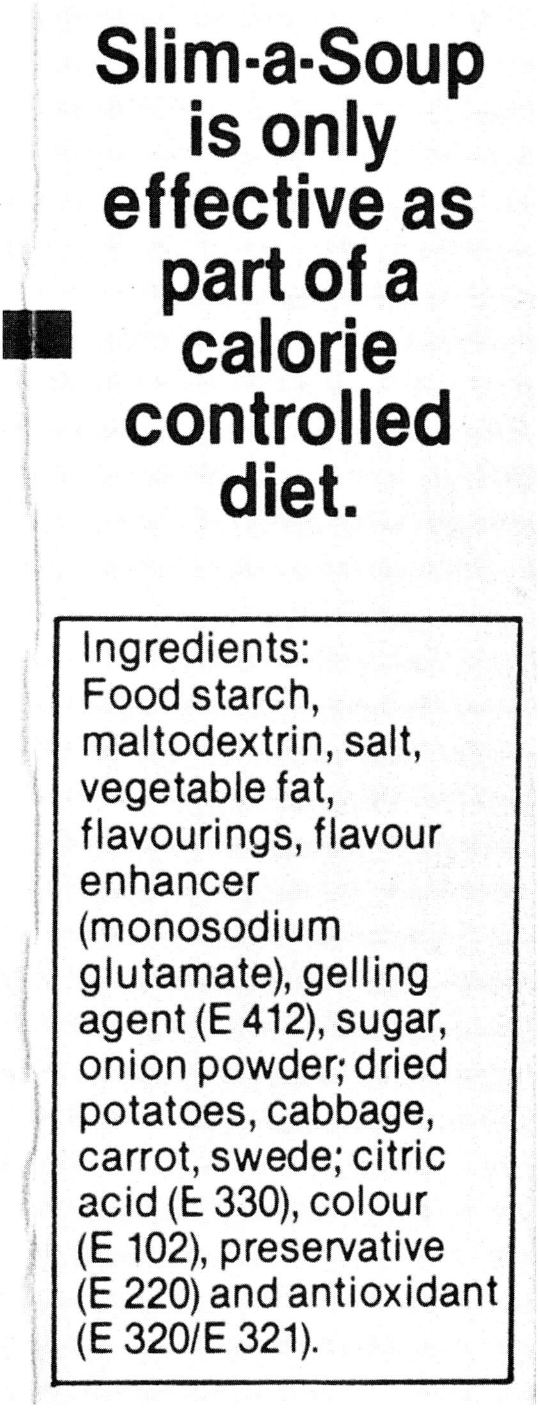

Slim-a-Soup is only effective as part of a calorie controlled diet.

Ingredients: Food starch, maltodextrin, salt, vegetable fat, flavourings, flavour enhancer (monosodium glutamate), gelling agent (E 412), sugar, onion powder; dried potatoes, cabbage, carrot, swede; citric acid (E 330), colour (E 102), preservative (E 220) and antioxidant (E 320/E 321).

General Foods Ltd.,
Banbury, Oxon, England

INGREDIENTS

Raspberry Flavour Jelly Crystals.
Sugar, Gelling Agents (E410, E407, E340, Potassium Chloride), Adipic Acid, Acidity Regulator (E336), Flavourings, Stabiliser (E466), Artificial Sweetener (Sodium Saccharin), Colour (E123).
55 g

Peach Flavour Custard Powder.
Starch, Flavourings, Salt, Colours (E110, E124).
35 g
Sponge, with Preservative (E202), Colours (E102, E110)
Decorations, with Colours (E110, E132, E123).

Trifle Topping Mix.
Hydrogenated Vegetable Oil, Whey Powder, Sugar, Emulsifiers (E477, E322), Modified Starch, Lactose, Caseinate, Stabiliser (E466), Flavourings, Colours (E102, E110, E160a), Antioxidant (E320).
29 g

COLOURINGS

Purpose: To make dull foods attractive, especially when the processing has involved bleaching, or the food has simply lost its natural colour.

Natural colourings:
   Saffron
   Paprika
   Carotene
   Cochineal

Other colourings:
   'Coal tar' dyes

Comments: Many people believe the use of colourings in food to be the least justifiable. Besides being a way to cut the cost of expensive ingredients or cover up inferior ingredients, which means the end-product has lost even more nutrients along the way, colourings are the most dangerous of all additives. Coal tar dyes, which have been in use for more than a hundred years, have been proven to be toxic and carcinogenic in large quantities. The list of permitted colourings is continually being cut as more colours are considered hazardous. Even so, no two countries seem to agree. In 1976 twenty colourings were permitted in the UK, seven of which were banned in other EEC countries.

In Japan only eleven colours were allowed, in India only ten. Since then the EEC has been attempting to bring colourings into line throughout the community using the E numbers, which does at least make it easier to avoid the harmful ones, such as tartrazine (E102).

IMPROVERS

Purpose: To speed up the natural effects of the ageing of flour. This is mainly done using ascorbic acid (vitamin C).

Comments: As an additive ascorbic acid is not harmful, but it shows how nutritionally inferior most of the nation's bread is.

ARTIFICIAL SWEETENING AGENTS

Purpose: For use in slimming and diabetic foods. Also used to sweeten a wide range of more general foods to satisfy our desire for sweet foods without adding calories. Common artificial sweetening agents include:
   Sorbitol (made from glucose, and generally used in diabetic foods)
   Aspartame
   Saccharin (a coal tar derivative)
   Acesulphame

Thaumatin

Cyclamates (banned in the UK in 1969, but may be returned to the list of allowed sweeteners)

Comments: Natural foods have their own sweetness, and by adding excessive sweetening to processed foods the manufacturers are dulling our ability to taste and enjoy natural flavours.

FORTIFIERS

Purpose: To increase the nutritional value of certain foods, especially when this has been impaired by processing. Examples include adding vitamins A and D to margarine, B group vitamins to breakfast cereals, vitamin C to citrus and blackcurrant concentrates, vitamin D to infant milk, bran and calcium to bread, iodine to salt

Comments: Though these additives are rarely harmful, anyone eating a healthy diet should have no need for fortified foods.

MISCELLANEOUS ADDITIVES

This category covers a wide variety of natural and chemical additives used for many different reasons, including:

Anti-caking agents: keep granular foods flowing freely (for example, magnesium carbonate added to salt)

Anti-foaming agents: stop liquids foaming

Glossing agents: Give the desired gloss

Humectants: help retain moisture (in products such as cakes)

Firming agents: to retain texture (acids added to jams, gum added to cream, soft cheeses and fruit yogurts)

UNINTENTIONAL ADDITIVES

All of the above are intentional additives, included by manufacturers for a variety of reasons, but generally used in good faith, and in the belief that the public will ultimately be better satisfied—and will, of course, buy their product again. This, however, is not the complete additive story. Many additives join the foodstuffs we consume through unexpected channels.

Accidental contaminants: These can be anything from nails and flies to toenail clippings and sticking plasters. They are rarer than they used to be, but are still found far more often than they should be. Such wholefood favourites as pulses and grains are, unfortunately, major offenders in that they must always be checked for small stones.

Residues from packing materials: These can be plasticizers, pigments, stabilizers, resins and antistatic agents. Although much is being done to prevent the transfer of such 'additives' to the food which they contain, it is proving difficult to eliminate the problem completely.

CONTAMINANTS FROM THE ENVIRONMENT

Industrial pollution: Plants and animals from areas near factories, smelting plants or major roads may contain heavy metals such as lead and mercury. Fish may be contaminated by water into which factory effluent has been discharged. The effects of nuclear waste discharge on fish is causing particular concern.

Pesticides and weedkillers: This relatively recent problem threatens to be one of the most serious as far as contaminants in food are concerned. In 1984 a Friends of the Earth report was issued on the subject. It said, 'Pesticides are designed to kill. They are currently used to control insects, weeds, plant diseases, and other pests. They are chemical toxins (i.e. poisons) and therefore should be used as sparingly, as safely, and as effectively as possible. Our research . . . shows that the opposite is the case. Instead of being the boon to humans the industry claims them to be, pesticides are becoming a threat in themselves.'

The report goes on to show that the gross overuse of pesticides is reflected in the growing problems of pest resistance, crop damage, wildlife losses and pollution. Pests adapt in order to survive. In 1973 there were only 25 known insects in the world found to be resistant to pesticides. Latest reports put that figure at 432. To combat this, crops are sprayed increasingly often, sometimes just as a matter of routine, even when infestations are not serious. Most pesticides are designed to kill indiscriminately, destroying insects which might be beneficial. Herbicides and insecticides can build up in meat-producing animals that have access to open grazing. They are also responsible for the death of fish, otters, birds of prey, butterflies, geese, swans and bees in particular. Wild flowers too have suffered, many species becoming increasingly rare, many cultivated fields now containing no flowers at all.

There is no legal limit in the UK on the levels of pesticide residues that may contaminate foods. The EEC, the World Health Organization and the Food and Agriculture Organization of the United Nations all give guidelines, but monitoring and enforcement are limited. Clearance may be withheld on products thought to be unsafe, but withdrawal of clearance does not necessarily stop manufacturers using pesticides, and there is no legal penalty if they are found to have done so.

Spraying is another problem. Although only 3% is carried out from the air, its effects are disproportionate. Vapour drift can be hazardous for human beings, livestock, poultry, domestic pets and plant life. The effects can last for days, and for those who come into contact with such sprays the problem is compounded by the difficulty of identifying the substance used in order to be given the right treatment. Water running through the area may also be contaminated, affecting both fish and drinking supplies.

There have been a number of examples of the effects pesticides can have on the human system, many of them in Third World countries and involving American corporations whose standards abroad are different from those maintained at home. The worst ever disaster of this sort took place in Bhopal in central India in December 1984, when a poisonous gas, methyl isocynate, leaked from a tank at a Union Carbide factory. As the heavy gas rolled along the ground it affected everyone in its path, killing over 2,500 people and injuring fifty thousand more, leaving behind a story of blinding, brain and lung damage and sterility that would affect the survivors for the rest of their lives. Mr Ghandi, India's prime minister, announced within days plans to stop the construction of factories using lethal gas and toxins near residential areas. Yet disasters of this kind are frequent in the Third World. According to OXFAM figures, more than 22,500 people die each year in developing countries from the use of pesticides no longer widely used in the West. Compared with such statistics, the lethal nature of pesticides in our environment would appear to be of no cause for concern, but pesticides are designed to kill, however carefully their use is monitored. They are highly dangerous and toxic chemicals, and their value *must* be questionable.

The Friends of the Earth report called for immediate changes in the industry, to include statutory controls on the use of pesticides, a reduction in their overall use, more systematic arrangements for monitoring the effects of pesticides on health along with greater disclosure of information on the many hazards associated with pesticides. Maybe most important of all, the report calls for more research into systems of integrated pest management that would employ natural or introduced predators and parasites, combined with careful timing of planting, crop rotation, and the use of pest-resistant plant varieties. Such a system, if employed with care and determination, would ultimately reduce the need for chemical toxins, and so eliminate many of their problems.

Meanwhile, it is not enough simply to avoid crops grown in Britain in this way. In the USA, for example, a tighter rein is kept on the use of pesticides that are believed to be dangerous. Companies manufacturing them, reluctant to lose profits, often sell banned chemicals to the Third World, where restrictions are less stringent. Third World countries then send these foods back to the West, where those that are tested are frequently found to contain residues of those prohibited chemical pesticides!

DRUGS IN FOOD-PRODUCING ANIMALS

Animal husbandry is now deeply involved in chemical technology too. Drugs are fed to food-producing animals to fatten them up as quickly as possible, to make their flesh or produce (eggs, for example) the right colour for the supermarkets, to prevent the illness and disease that can easily run rife in the unnatural conditions under which many of them are reared. The animal itself acts as a filter, but without doubt some of these antibiotics, hormones and growth promoters end up in the systems of the human beings who eat such meat.

Again the government claims to be monitoring the situation. Restrictions include rulings that certain drugs can only be given to an animal when it is young, or that there should be a withdrawal period prior to slaughter, to allow residues of drugs to be flushed from the animal's system. Even so, there is growing concern about the overuse of such drugs. Steroid feeds used to promote growth in cattle have been proven to be cancer-forming under certain conditions. Hormones have been known to build up in children, resulting in girls starting to menstruate at the age of five, and boys and men to grow breasts. Stilboestrol, a synthetic female hormone used in pig breeding, which has strong links with the incidence of cancer in women, has only very recently been banned in Britain, having been proscribed in Europe and the USA for some time. There is also concern that anyone consuming meat containing antibiotics may, over a period of time, retain a build-up within their own system so that, should they need to be given the drug themself, their body will not respond to it.

Many different drugs are used in animal farming, and the following categories describe some of their uses.

Growth boosters: Apart from hormones and hormone-like drugs, mass medication with antibiotics and with copper and arsenic compounds is widely used. British farmers have resisted EEC attempts to restrict this abuse, which has led to the poisoning of pasture by manure from animals dosed in this way. The arsenic compounds are similar to those used in the early and hazardous treatment of syphilis.

Antibiotics: Disease is rife among a large proportion of modern livestock, which invites the overuse of antibiotics, the development of resistance to them, the spread of disease into the human population, and the impoverishment of the doctor's armoury against infectious diseases. The trade in calves is notorious in this respect.

Anti-mastitic agents: Mastitis, an inflammation of the lining of the udder with a catarrh-like discharge into the milk, is rampant in British cows, which receive 17 million 'shots' a year of concoctions of antibiotics and steroids from a range of 50 or more different preparations.

Hormones and hormone-like drugs: These boost productivity. ICI had to withdraw their 'safe' product *Methallibure* as its use in sows led to the birth of deformed piglets.

Insecticides and parasiticides: These include organo-phosphorus compounds and *Levamisole*, a drug which acts potently on the immune system and is very cautiously prescribed by doctors. These compounds are widely used to treat worms in farm animals. In a new device to curb fly infestations in poultry droppings the insecticide is administered in the birds' feed.

Tenderizers: Enzymes are injected into animals just before slaughter. Although some of the cuts of meat are upgraded in this way, organs such as the liver may be seriously damaged, and the practice is cruel.

Tranquillizers: Terrified pigs are very difficult to handle in markets and slaughterhouses, and they may be injected with tranquillizers to calm them just before killing.

WHAT THE MAJOR SUPPLIERS SAY

When asked which meat, if any, in their shops had been obtained from animals not tested with growth-boosters, and if there was any testing for residues, this is what some of the major suppliers replied:

'It (the infrastructure of the red-meat industry) is an area in which we are still finding our way . . . we recognize that we still have much to learn . . . We are not therefore in a position to say that growth promoters are not used in our meats.'
Marks and Spencer

'The analysis carried out to substantiate the presence of such drugs is very involved and cannot unfortunately be carried out in our laboratories.'
Safeway

'In view of the MAFF's comments we have not in the past considered it necessary for us to carry out routine tests for residues of any injected substances into food animals.'
British Home Stores

'We do not routinely test the meat for residues of drugs, hormones or growth-boosters.'
Sainsbury

'This is a very difficult question to answer . . .'   *Harrods* (and they didn't!)

'As many of our meats used in products sold in the store are purchased through second and sometimes third parties, we are not in a position to provide the information you require.'
Fortnum and Mason

(Source: The Vegetarian Society (UK) Ltd.)

THE TESTING OF FOOD ADDITIVES ON ANIMALS

The reason why manufacturers of additives and preservatives are allowed to use them to pollute our food hangs on a single thread—that they have been tested. Such testing is certainly rigorous. It involves using literally thousands of animals in a series of tests, including the LD50 test, in which animals are dosed with different amounts of the test substance until the dose is established which kills half of them (the Lethal Dose to 50% of them).

In 1983, experiments in Britain to test food additives were carried out on animals as follows:

Mice	6,241
Rats	6,372
Guinea pigs	454
Rabbits	9
Dogs	60
Birds	952
Fish	38
Total	14,126

Acute toxicity tests (short term, lasting up to 14 days)	4,867
Sub-acute and chronic toxicity tests (lasting weeks or years, with repeated dosages)	3,606
Teratology tests (dosing pregnant females to see effect on foetuses)	196
Studies on the distribution, metabolism and excretion of additives	775
More than one of the above	256
Other types (unclassified)	4,426
Total	14,126

Official Home Office statistics also reveal that as part of the testing of food additives, 1,255 animals were subjected to aversive (unpleasant or painful) stimuli, including electric shocks. Presumably these studies were to elucidate what punishment animals would be prepared to undergo and still eat or drink the substance involved.

Thus a lot of scientists spend a lot of time studying a lot of suffering animals. It proves little about human beings. Research carried out in the USA indicates that animal tests are successful in identifying carcinogens only some 37% of the time, which means they are wrong more often than they are right. In addition, there is disagreement about how to extrapolate from the results of tests on small groups of animals to large groups of human beings living under very different conditions. This disagreement can lead to widely differing conclusions being drawn from the same test.

There are always, of course, the classic examples of animal tests which have either not detected the danger inherent in a substance when used on humans (thalidomide being one of the worst), or vice versa (penicillin was tested on human beings before it was tried on guinea pigs—to whom it proved to be toxic. If it had been tried on guinea pigs first we might never have known its value). Animal systems may be similar to ours, but they are not the same. Possibly the most important issue as far as the pointlessness of testing substances on animals is concerned, is that the substances are only tested one at a time, each in isolation. Human beings consume these substances in millions of combinations, over a long period of time. The effect they create *must* be very different.

Avoiding additives

In today's profit-oriented world, and living on a small island where more and more chemicals are being used to force food to grow from soil that has little to give, it's impossible to avoid additives completely.

You can, however, reduce your consumption considerably, and at the same time build up your health and immune system by eating foods full of nutrients so that your body is better able to cope with any chemicals you may consume.

The first step is to reduce your consumption of processed foods. Anything in tins, packages, or frozen is going to contain some additives. If you must buy processed food occasionally, learn to read the labels. Now that ingredients must be listed by law, you can at least choose, for example, frozen peas that contain no sugar (minted frozen peas are invariably also sweetened). Get a book listing the E additives and make a note of those proven to cause adverse reactions of one kind or another—remember that some E additives are natural, some, like lecithin, even beneficial. When buying children's food in particular, be aware of the chemicals and what they can do to growing youngsters' bodies and minds. Teach your children to enjoy natural foods and get them off to a better start in life.

Unintentional pollutants are even more difficult to avoid. Those that get into meat, poultry and fish are best avoided by becoming vegetarian. If you must have your pound of flesh, try buying it from a wholefood butcher whose suppliers will have reared their meat animals under natural conditions, using only the minimum amount of drugs. Or alternate the shops where you buy your meat, and buy different cuts from different animals. You are in more danger of a build-up of antibiotics or hormones if you stick to one kind of meat from one butcher.

Fish may well be dyed (kippers are naturally a pale colour until Brown FK—For Kippers—is added), is frequently sprayed to preserve it, and may well be from polluted waters. To be sure, shop at a reputable fishmongers, and if in doubt, ask.

Pesticides and weedkillers are also impossible to avoid completely. Many of them are absorbed into growing plants. Vegetables may, for example, contain high concentrations of nitrates absorbed through the water in the soil. Other additives may collect on the skins, and these can be removed or at least reduced by giving tougher vegetables a good brush and washing well in water (do not soak vegetables as this leaches away many of the nutrients). Do the same with fruit. Avoid buying fruit and vegetables that look too perfect, as you can bet they will have been grown under artificial conditions with the aid of chemicals, possibly dolled up with dyes and wax, and will taste about as good as the plastic they so closely resemble.

Ultimately, advice on avoiding additives in food can be summed up in three short paragraphs:

Buy organic whenever possible: As the general public is becoming more aware of the dangers inherent in our food, demand for organically-grown products is increasing. Encourage growers by buying their produce whenever you can, even if they are more expensive. They are worth it for their increased nutrients, reduced chemicals, and infinitely better taste. If you can't find a source of organic produce, ask local retailers. If the demand is there, they may well decide to supply what people want instead of what they want people to have.

Vary your foods: Without needing to resort too often to expensive out-of-season imports, you'll find that a wide variety of all kinds of good food is generally available nowadays. By using as many of them as possible in different combinations you'll not only avoid a build-up of one particular chemical within your system, but you will also be taking in a wide variety of nutrients, including valuable minerals and trace elements, and will therefore benefit from better health and increased resistance to disease. Don't let cooking become a habit. Make a point of trying out new ingredients, new cooking techniques, and new combinations. **Check labels:** It's quite likely that you are going to have to shop at supermarkets every now and again, but this isn't necessarily a bad thing. By checking labels you can find out exactly what has gone into a product, and though some of the lists are horrendous, some of them may pleasantly surprise you. More enlightened supermarkets are making a real effort to supply more wholesome products alongside their processed counterparts. Many of these are imported from other EEC countries where restrictions are more severe. A growing number are coming from the USA, where concern about additives in food is leading to changes in manufacturers' policies, and where labelling often takes pride in announcing 'free from preservatives and colourings', 'low in fat', 'natural flavourings' and so on. As with organic suppliers, you can encourage supermarkets to supply more of these wholesome products by buying them. Again, their prices are going to be higher than those of processed foods because they are made with better-quality ingredients, but isn't your health worth paying slightly more for?

Food and The Body

*The egotistical nature of modern man causes him
to place himself and the foods he eats into very different
categories. However, throughout the study of nutrition it becomes
increasingly apparent that at very elementary levels
there is little to distinguish us and our food.*

Miriam Arlin
The Science of Nutrition

Food and the Body

Unless you suffer from some disorder, 90-95% of the food you eat is digested and absorbed. The time this takes can vary, excitement sometimes speeding it up, fear sometimes slowing it down. Food can stay in the stomach for anything from one to eight hours, or even longer. Eventually, though, it becomes part of you, going towards rebuilding cells, affecting the way your brain works, helping your nerves to cope with day-to-day living. It will give you energy, keep you warm, help your system fight off infections.

The food you eat affects not just the life you lead, but your very being.

One of the reasons is that protein, present in most of the foods you eat to a lesser or greater extent, is made up of the same basic amino-acid compounds as the protein present in your body. Most plants and animals are constructed of the same elements which are combined to form the same components—fats, carbohydrates and proteins. We share a large number of biological features, such as the carrying of genetic blueprints of heredity in our cells, and having the ability to release energy through the oxidation of simple nutrients. The enzymes that control the life processes of cells in plants and animals work in much the same way, and in many cases identical enzymes are used for exactly the same purpose.

We are all part of the whole, sharing more than just space on the planet. Ecologically, we benefit each other. It is only when we turn away from natural foods, overload our system with chemicals, with foods too rich, too sweet and too heavy, that our bodies start to falter and weaken, affecting our health, our minds and our moods. The one big difference between human beings and all other forms of life is our ability to choose. Most of us have the resources to be able to live healthily. We are very privileged to be able to choose health when so many poor and undernourished people lack that choice, yet too many people today are still choosing to live unhealthy lives, and it's time for a change.

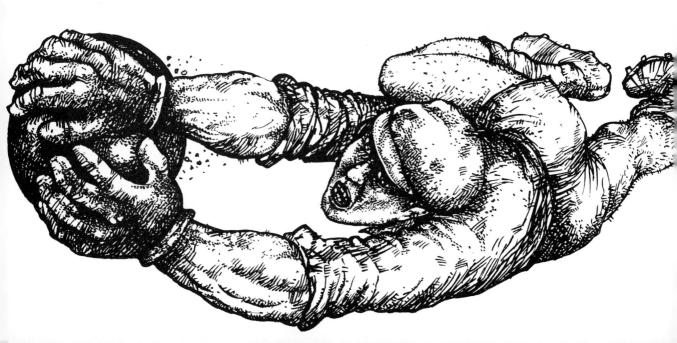

A walking miracle

To understand how the body is affected by food, it helps to have some basic knowledge of human anatomy. With such knowledge you can get to know your own body, which, though it may appear to be much like everyone else's, has its own unique quirks, patterns, and ways of functioning. Take exercise, for example. Everyone knows it's good for you. But not all exercise systems are good for all people. One person will prefer keeping in touch with their body through gentle yoga stretches, another will jog or climb mountains, or work out at a gymnasium. Finding the right system for both your body and your personality isn't always easy, but it's worth doing. In the same way, finding the right foods, and the eating pattern that lets you enjoy and benefit from them, can change the way you feel. The way to start is to learn to listen to your body, to know yourself inside out. Given the chance, your body will tell you what it wants.

You are an ecosystem

Cells and tissues form the basis of the separate systems of the body, each system consisting of a group of structures or organs which carry out an essential function, and each of which is dependent on all the others. For example, the bones, joints, ligaments and muscles are all concerned with movement, which is in turn controlled by the nervous system, this being dependent on an adequate circulation of blood and supply of oxygen, which reaches the blood via the respiratory system. You can almost imagine the body as its own ecosystem contained within a wrapping of skin.

Each of the body's systems is complex, most of them performing more than one function. Here is a simple explanation of some of the more important aspects of the workings of the human body:

The skin does more than just act as a protective covering. It contains the ends of the sensory nerves so that it registers touch, pain, heat and cold. By secreting sweat it helps in the removal of body wastes as well as playing an important role in the regulation of body temperature.

The skeleton is what gives the body support, maintains its shape, and protects vital internal organs such as the brain, spinal cord, heart and lungs, and the digestive and reproductive systems. Made up of 206 bones, it is strong but relatively inflexible.

The joints are what enable movement, 101 of them linking bone to bone, transferring weight, joining one part of the body to all the others, each lubricated and protected to reduce friction and damage. They come in a variety of sizes and shapes to perform a variety of movements from simple hinge joints to those which allow a full circle of movement. The largest is the knee joint, an important joint because of its role in maintaining the erect posture of the whole body. The twenty-six joints of the backbone are also important, each of the vertebrae moving only a little relative to all the others, but working together to allow the spine to bend in all directions. Inflammation of the joints is what we call arthritis.

The muscles are the key to movement—without them neither skeleton nor joints could work. Generating heat, which is why exercise makes you warm, they work mostly in pairs—one actively contracting, the other lengthening passively—to create movement. Such movement can be voluntary, as in walking or reaching to pick something up, or involuntary. The heart itself is a muscle. Muscles are an important medium through which you communicate with the world, the muscles of your face showing your displeasure, fear or happiness. And it takes far more muscles to frown than it does to smile!

The circulatory system is what keeps every tissue and organ of the body supplied with nourishment. These functions are carried out by the blood, the heart pumping 3,200 gallons of it through the blood vessels of the body each day, carrying with it a valuable supply of oxygen. About a third of the red cells in blood consist of haemoglobin, a protein that can combine with oxygen, and thus makes the perfect medium via which to transport it. The blood is moved round the body by the pumping action of the heart. The way you breathe also affects the movement of blood through your system: the stronger and more rhythmic your breathing, the better the flow.

The lymphatic system is a secondary circulation system, a sort of back-up to the first, which drains the tissue fluids. Lymph is a fluid that resembles blood, but contains no red corpuscles. It acts as a liaison between the blood and the tissues of the capillaries, though unlike blood it is not circulated by a central pump, its movement depending mostly on compression of the lymphatic vessels by muscles around the body, and through suction created by the movement of your breathing. The lymphatic tissues form an essential part of the body's defence system against bacteria, viruses and toxins, carrying the harmful agents to the glands which act as filters, and at the same time stimulating the body to create antibodies. In this way they are usually prevented from entering the general circulation, being destroyed or neutralized before they can cause harm.

The respiratory system uses the lungs and air passages to transfer oxygen from the atmosphere to the tissues and, at the same time, removes carbon dioxide, releasing it outside the body. The normal rate of respiration for adults is 14-18 breaths per minute, this rate usually being adjusted without conscious control, affected by impulses such as the build-up of carbon dioxide in the blood. Speech, singing, laughter, crying, yawning, the shallow breathing associated with concentration, rapid breathing from fear or excitement, or after physical exercise—all these affect not just your rate of breathing, but your whole body, by adjusting the amount of oxygen available at any given time. When you breathe in through your mouth, the air reaches your lungs more quickly and is therefore colder; air that has passed through the increased surface area of your nose is warmed and moistened in order to give your lungs less of a shock.

The nervous system is the most highly developed of all the body systems. It correlates the activities of all the systems of the body. The brain is the centre, receiving and storing impulses which form the basis of memory, whilst also transmitting impulses via the nerves in other parts of the body. Only during sleep is there a diminished supply of blood to the brain, when the body's metabolism and heat production are also reduced, the heart rate slowed, blood pressure dropped and voluntary muscles relaxed. Though there is no satisfactory explanation of the basic function of sleep, it is generally agreed that prolonged loss of sleep can be extremely dangerous. Together with the spinal cord, the brain forms what is called the central nervous system, the nerves connecting it to the various organs and muscles of the body. A second system of nerve cells and fibres works relatively independently, its purpose being to control involuntary muscles within the body such as those in the blood vessels, and glands such as those that produce sweat and saliva.

The digestive system exists to turn basic foods into a form in which the body can absorb and utilize them. Digestion starts in the mouth, where food is broken down by chewing and mixing with saliva. It takes food three seconds to pass down the gullet to the stomach, where gastric juices continue breaking down the food, at the same time destroying most of the bacteria that may be present. From there it passes to the small intestine which, at about twenty feet in length, is considerably longer than the large intestine. Almost all the absorption of nutrients occurs through the intestine walls. Any substances that have not been digested so far—fibre in particular—will go on to the large intestine, and will absorb water before being expelled from the body. From beginning to end, the digestive process can take from one to three days, or even a week if little fibre is consumed.

Food and energy
It can be seen from all this that the body, though a system within itself, needs to take in elements from the world outside in order not only to work efficiently, but to survive at all. Without air and water we can survive only a short time. Assuming we are reasonably healthy, and have built up some kind of store, we can go without food much longer—in fact, some people think that fasting is an excellent way to give all the body systems a rest, enabling the digestive system to be thoroughly cleansed so that it works more smoothly once food is taken again. However, food is essential to life. It provides us with the energy the body needs to maintain life: energy for breathing, for our heart to beat, for our brain to function, for our body to move. Food *is* life.

The energy in food is calculated in terms of heat, the units of heat being called 'calories'. The term calories, when used to describe how much food energy we need, is actually the unit called the kilocalorie. It is equal to 1000 calories, and is written either as kcal or Calories with a capital C. How many Calories we need depends very much on our weight and what we are doing. For example, most crash diets recommend dropping your daily Calorie intake to 800 or less, though this is not sufficient for someone living a normal life, and should only be used as a short-term eating pattern. The highest daily mean energy output recorded for any group is 4,880 Calories a day expended by rickshaw pullers in Calcutta! You will use more Calories if you are heavier. Some people use far more than average simply because of their metabolism. Charts telling you how many Calories you should be eating can only be a guide—a better guide is simply to find the foods on which you feel best, and eat enough of them to stay energetic and healthy without getting fat *or* thin.

Energy is, however, only one of the things we get from food. Food also provides us with essential amino-acids, vitamins, minerals and trace elements.

Proteins
Proteins make up the largest proportion of the body, apart from water. Some 17% of the body is protein, including hair, nails, skin and muscle tissue. The red pigment in blood, haemoglobin, is mostly protein. Protein is used principally for growth, but also for maintenance and repair. Any excess intake can be used for energy, but this is an expensive and wasteful way to get it—it also puts a strain on the body as protein is complicated to process, speeding up the body's metabolic rate.

Protein is made up of twenty essential amino-acids. Of these, eight are only found in the food we eat, and the body can make the rest itself.

Essential amino-acids
Leucine
Isoleucine
Lysine

Methionine
Phenylalanine
Threonine
Tryptophan
Valine

Amino-acids the body can make
Alanine
Glycine
Serine
Proline
Hydroxyproline
Cystine
Tyrosine
Glutamic acid
Aspartic acid
Cysteine

Additional amino-acids essential for children
Arginine
Histidine

Complete protein foods provide the proper balance of the eight essential amino-acids that we cannot synthesize in our bodies. However, by combining different so-called 'incomplete' proteins you can more than double the useful protein content of each, and at the same time use less expensive, easier-to-produce foods whilst cutting your consumption of calories and fats.

Best sources: Complete proteins are meat, poultry, seafood, milk, cheese, soya beans, yeast and eggs. Other high-protein foods include nuts, pulses, dairy produce such as yogurt, and cereals. Sprouted grains, beans and seeds are also high in protein.

Comments: Apart from the recognition of the value of combining 'incomplete' proteins, it is now being realized that we need far less protein than used to be thought necessary, and that proteins from plant foods may well be better than those from animal sources. It is recommended by some nutritionists that 10% of our daily calories should come from protein, but others consider even

this to be too high. In fact, protein deficiencies are almost unknown in Britain. When they do occur the symptoms are anaemia, tiredness, lack of muscle tone and poor resistance to disease.

Fats

Fats are required for the absorption of fat-soluble vitamins such as A and D (mostly from animal sources) and E and K (from vegetable sources). Fats also contribute to the texture and palatability of food, giving a feeling of satisfaction. Fats under the skin help to protect our bodies from injury, and internal fat protects important organs. As they are high in calories, fats are a highly concentrated form of energy. Fat in our diet has increased over the past fifty years from 35% to 40%, and in Britain today each of us eats an average of 5oz a day. In the USA 40-45% of total calories consumed are fat, though this figure is dropping as Americans become aware of the problems created by a high-fat diet. By contrast, the proportion of fat consumed in Third World countries can be as low as 10%.

Fats are divided into three kinds:

Saturated fats: These are usually solid at room temperature, and mostly come from animal and dairy foods, but also from plants such as coconut. They are the fats consumed in the largest amounts, and the ones causing most concern. Saturated fats are implicated in the build-up of cholesterol within the arteries, eventually causing arteriosclerosis and heart attacks. High saturated fat intake is also suspected as being a factor in the development of cancer, particularly of the bowels, a cancer that has increased enormously in the West as the consumption of fat has increased, yet is virtually unknown in the Third World.

Monounsaturated fats: These occur in many foods, and do not clog the arteries as do saturated fats, but neither do they help clear them. Olive oil is a good example of a monounsaturated fat.

Polyunsaturated fats: These are liquid oils at room temperature because of their high content of unsaturated fatty acids. Such oils can also be used to make soft margarines, but not all soft margarines are made with polyunsaturated oils—check the label to be sure. Vegetables oils are the sole sources of a member of the fat family called linoleic acid, an important one as the body cannot make it. It is believed that linoleic acid actually helps clear arteries clogged by saturated fats.

Most foods contain all three types of fats, but in widely varying proportions. Although the initial appearance of the fat is one way to judge its type, this can be confusing. Polyunsaturated fats are usually liquid, but when hardened in the manufacture of margarine they can be changed into saturated fats.

Cholesterol has been linked with a number of diseases, and as saturated fats cause cholesterol to be deposited in the arteries they should be kept to a minimum. However, there are different kinds of cholesterol, and we do need a certain amount for a variety of body functions. Cholesterol aids the metabolism of carbohydrates, it is the principal supplier of some essential hormones including sex hormones, and it is cholesterol in the skin that is converted to vitamin D from sunshine. The important thing is that our bodies make their own supply of cholesterol, two-thirds being produced in the liver and intestines.

Best sources: Fats should be kept to a minimum since they are highly concentrated and very rich in calories. We all need a certain amount of fat, but should try to choose oils higher in polyunsaturates such as corn, soya, sunflower or safflower for cooking, and restrict our intake of those foods especially rich in saturated fats (beef, pork, mutton,

butter, lard, hard margarines, milk, cheese, and manufactured foods containing cheap vegetable fats such as biscuits, cakes and ice cream). Most nuts are a good source of polyunsaturated fats.

Comments: Overconsumption of saturated fats often happens because such fats are hidden. It's easy enough to avoid fatty meats and eat less of the fattiest cheeses, but more difficult to eliminate the fats you don't see. Foods to watch out for are ice cream, biscuits, chocolate, salted peanuts and crisps.

Carbohydrates

Carbohydrates are used by the body for energy. They consist principally of sugars or starches which are broken down into glucose (blood sugar) as they are digested. By providing essential energy for the brain and nervous system, carbohydrates free proteins to do vital repair work. Sugars, and particularly starchy foods, provide a major source of energy throughout the world. At the same time, starchy foods also supply vitamins, minerals and some protein, plus valuable fibre, which makes it hard to overeat on them. The Calorie count of starch is about the same as that of protein.

Any reputation that carbohydrates have for being fattening applies only to the refined varieties which can be consumed in large quantities, offer less food value, and, in the case of sucrose (white refined sugar), can cause dependence. Natural carbohydrates are wholesome and valuable foods, and their high fibre content keeps our digestions working efficiently.

A century ago most of our carbohydrate intake came from potatoes and cereals. Only a small proportion came from sugar. Now about a third of the intake of carbohydrates in Britain is in the form of sucrose, which occurs naturally in sugar cane and beet, and also in fruits and some root vegetables such as carrots. Refined sugar contains two sugars, fructose and glucose, and it is in its refined form that most sugar is eaten, added not just to drinks, baked goods and sweets, but also to processed vegetable soups, peanut butter, baked beans, ketchup, and a whole range of so-called savoury foods. Sugar in this form is known to cause tooth decay, obesity and mood swings, and is implicated in many other health problems.

Fructose is a sugar occuring naturally in some fruits and vegetables, and honey contains a relatively high proportion of fructose. Lactose is a sugar that occurs only in milk. Maltose is formed when starch is broken down during the digestion process; it also occurs when grain is germinated for the production of beer.

Best sources: Jacket potatoes, wholegrains, wholemeal bread, unrefined breakfast cereals, vegetables, fruits, dried fruits, pulses, wholemeal pasta, molasses.

Vitamins

The human body needs a large number of different vitamins, though often in very small quantities. This section covers only a selection of the more important vitamins we need for good health.

VITAMIN A

This was one of the first vitamins to be discovered. It is fat-soluble, and can be stored in the body. Vitamin A protects the lining of most of the organs of the body, helps build resistance to infection, and keeps skin, nails and hair healthy. In particular it is linked with eyesight, and shortage of it causes 'night blindness', an inability to see when there is very little light. In Third World countries hundreds or thousands of cases of blindness are caused by vitamin A deficiencies. Research is indicating that it may also help build resistance to cancer.

Best sources: Carrots, parsley, spinach, watercress, any dark green salad vegetables, apricots, milk, eggs, cheese, fish liver oils, heart and kidney, yellow fruits. Vitamin A is added to margarine.

Comments: There is a crucial difference between the form of vitamin A found in animals (called retinol) and the many kinds available from plant sources, of which the most common is beta carotene. Retinol is toxic in large doses, and taking supplements of this kind of vitamin A is dangerous. Excessive beta carotene can also be a problem, but it does give a warning signal in that overdosers turn orange! If this happens, as it can if a great deal of carrot juice and dark green vegetables are consumed, lay off both until the colour goes away.

VITAMIN B COMPLEX

These are water-soluble, so with most of them any excess will be excreted, which means that you need to take in a daily supply. B vitamins are essential for the utilization of carbohydrates. They also help to keep nerves, eyes and hair healthy, and build up resistance to disease. Anyone who smokes, drinks alcohol, eats an excess of sugar or refined foods, is pregnant, nursing, on the pill or under stress, should make certain to get a regular supply of foods containing the B vitamins.

Best sources: Yeast, yeast extract, wholegrains, wholemeal bread, wheatgerm, yogurt, soya beans, peanuts, fish, kidney and liver. Blackstrap molasses—most widely used to fatten cattle—is an excellent source of B vitamins.

Comments: Vegans may need to watch carefully to ensure a good supply of vitamin B12, which occurs mostly in animal foods, and a deficiency of which can lead to anaemia. Some yeast extracts are fortified with this vitamin. There is increasing evidence that vitamin B6 is prevented from being absorbed at certain stages in women's menstrual cycles, especially when a woman is on the pill. Supplements of vitamin B6 are widely known to alleviate some of the symptoms of pre-menstrual syndrome or pre-menstrual tension (PMS or PMT) for many women.

VITAMIN C

Most animals can synthesize this vitamin within their own bodies. Only guinea pigs, bulbul birds, apes and human beings have to obtain it from the foods they eat. It is a water-soluble vitamin, and therefore needs to be topped up daily. Vitamin C is needed for a variety of reasons. It maintains the strength of blood vessels, helps with the absorption of iron, and keeps gums healthy. It is probably best known, however, for its ability to increase resistance to infection, and it also helps to heal wounds. Dr Linus Pauling believes that it might decrease infections such as colds by 25%, and may even help combat cancer, but must be taken in very large doses (from 1,000 to 10,000mg daily). Other researchers have questioned the wisdom of taking very high doses of vitamin C, pointing out that this practice may also suppress the body's immune system. Vitamin C may also help to reduce the effects of allergy-producing substances. As carbon monoxide destroys vitamin C, people living in cities may need extra, as may women on the pill, children and old people. Smokers too need extra vitamin C—it is estimated that every cigarette can destroy up to 30mg. Taken in pill form, however, vitamin C can create excessive acid in the stomach, and should be taken only after meals. It is therefore preferable to keep supplementation to eating additional foods with a high vitamin C content rather than taking pills.

Best sources: Rosehips, Brussels sprouts, cabbage, citrus fruits, blackberries, salads, green vegetables, strawberries, grain and bean sprouts, green peppers, potatoes.

Comments: Though most people think of citrus fruits as our main source of vitamin C, the highest single contribution in Britain is in fact made by the lowly potato, which, though not enormously rich in vitamin C, is eaten regularly and in generous amounts, particularly as dehydrated mashed potatoes, which are usually highly fortified with this vitamin.

VITAMIN D

This fat-soluble vitamin can be stored, and is needed only in small amounts. It helps form strong bones and teeth by regulating the amount of calcium and phosphorus entering them via the blood. It is found in very few foods indeed, but vitamin D is also called 'the sunshine vitamin', as the body can actually make it when exposed to sunlight. Ultraviolet rays act on the oil of the skin to make the vitamin, which is then absorbed into the body.

Best sources: Eggs, butter, fortified margarine, milk, cream, fish liver oils.

Comments: It's hard to be short of vitamin D if you eat the foods listed above and get out into the sunshine often enough. Many Asians in this country, however, suffer from a shortage of vitamin D, as these foods are not traditionally eaten by them, nor do they expose their bodies as much as Europeans when out of doors. Rickets is still a disease which is present in poor communities in Britain, and many baby foods are enriched with this vitamin to help counteract the shortage. Too high an intake of vitamin D causes more calcium to be absorbed by the body than can be excreted, the excess being stored in the kidneys where it can cause serious damage.

VITAMIN E

Not a lot is yet known about this vitamin, though it is recognized as being important to the body in many ways. It is fat-soluble, and can be stored. Though it seems to help different people in different ways, it seems likely that vitamin E plays a part in fat metabolism (which may help artery troubles by preventing blood clots), and stimulates healing in general.

Best sources: Wheatgerm, vegetable and nut oils, wholegrains, wholemeal bread, eggs, soya beans and some green vegetables. Most foods contain some vitamin E.

Comments: The main function of vitamin E is to prevent fats (both in foods and in the body) from going rancid. If they do go bad, then substances called 'free radicals' are released into the body which can be highly dangerous and are known to cause cancer. Our bodies are protected from such damage by the vitamin E which is naturally present in oils and margarines containing polyunsaturated fats. If, however, oils are used and re-used, the vitamin E is destroyed and free radicals are released. This is an important reason why oils should not be overheated or re-used.

VITAMIN K

This is not a well known vitamin, though research is being carried out to discover more about it. It appears to be essential for normal clotting of blood, and can help in cases of excessive menstrual flow, internal bleeding and haemorrhage. It is fat-soluble, and as it is needed only in very small amounts, a deficiency is unlikely. Vitamin K can also be synthesized by the bacteria in our gut.

Best sources: Yogurt, alfalfa, green vegetables such as spinach, egg yolk, safflower and soya oil, cereals.

Minerals

As with vitamins, the body needs traces of a wide variety of minerals; this section covers only the more important of these.

CALCIUM

There is more calcium in the body than any other mineral, 2-3lbs of it, mostly found in teeth and bones. Calcium in the diet is used to develop and maintain teeth and bones, as well as promoting normal clotting of the blood and functioning of nerves and muscles. Only about 20-30% of calcium in the diet is actually absorbed, and an adequate supply of vitamin D is necessary for this absorption. Although deficiencies are unlikely in Britain, children need a good supply, as do older people, and women who may lose large quantities of the mineral through repeated pregnancies.

Best sources: Milk and cheese are the best sources. Vegetarians and vegans can also get calcium in adequate amounts from soya beans, green vegetables such as spinach, peanuts, walnuts and sunflower seeds. Fortified white bread and hard water can also be important sources.

PHOSPHORUS

Together with calcium, phosphorus forms the hard structure of bones and teeth. It is present in every cell of the body, and plays an important part in reproduction and the transfer of hereditary traits. Phosphorus is also important for the functioning of heart and kidneys, and it is believed that it may help lessen the pain of arthritis.

Best sources: Wholegrains, eggs, seeds, milk, cheese, green vegetables, oranges and dried apricots. In fact, most natural foods contain some phosphorus, so only those living on a diet of highly-processed foods may have an insufficient amount—though many foods are now processed with phosphates.

Comments: The only way in which people might become deficient in phosphorus is if they use antacid tablets for a long period of time.

MAGNESIUM

Magnesium is known as the anti-stress mineral. It is essential for correct nerve functioning as well as for the formation of bones and teeth, and the functioning of the glands and the metabolism. It is also believed that it may help prevent heart attacks. Chronic alcoholics may need extra, also women on the pill. It also has laxative properties—Epsom Salts contain a large amount of magnesium!

Best sources: Nuts, peas, beans, apples, seeds, figs. Magnesium forms part of a substance called chlorophyll which is the green colouring matter in plants—so green leafy vegetables are another good source of this mineral.

SODIUM

All body fluids contain sodium, which works with potassium to maintain the salt concentration of the blood. We need only about 1g a day, whereas we consume an average of 12g. Excess sodium is therefore likely to be the problem, and can be linked with high blood pressure and depleted potassium levels.

Best sources: All foods contain some sodium, including cereals, butter, eggs, milk and cheese. Sodium obtained from such foods should supply sufficient without adding salt (sodium chloride) to food.

Comments: Small babies cannot cope with extra salt, though it is sometimes added to baby foods, mostly to make it taste 'better' to the adult making up the baby's food. Avoid such foods, and never add any salt to any food intended for babies and young children.

POTASSIUM

Potassium is necessary for muscle and nerve function, also for carbohydrate and protein metabolism. It also works with sodium to balance the body's water reserves. Although deficiencies are rare, a number of things can reduce potassium in the body—physical and mental stress, hypoglycaemia (low blood sugar), too much coffee, alcohol and sugar, and taking diuretics.

Best sources: Almost all foods contain some potassium. The richest sources are green vegetables, bananas, milk, citrus fruits, sunflower seeds and potatoes.

Comments: It is unwise to take supplements of potassium except under supervision.

IRON

Iron helps build healthy blood cells. Each cell has a lifespan of approximately 120 days and is then replaced, so the body needs a continuous supply of iron if the blood is to do its job properly. Although we consume many foods that are good sources of iron, a deficiency may arise if it is not absorbed properly, as can happen if vitamin C intake is low. Women in particular may suffer an iron deficiency as they lose a large amount of iron each time they menstruate. Anyone drinking tea or coffee in excess may also be inhibiting their iron absorption. The eventual result of an iron deficiency is anaemia.

Best sources: Meats such as liver and kidneys are usually given as the best sources. Anyone who prefers to avoid meat will find ample iron in green vegetables, molasses, dried fruits such as apricots and figs, wholegrains, pulses and sesame seeds.

Comments: Drinking orange juice at the same meal as a vegetable iron source is eaten helps it to be absorbed, since the type of iron found in vegetables (ferric) is poorly absorbed, and the acid in the orange juice reduces it to the ferrous form.

TRACE ELEMENTS

COBALT

Present in vitamin B12 where it is found mostly in animal foods. Vegans may therefore be deficient in it, though deficiencies are extremely rare. It is essential for healthy red blood cells.

Best sources: Buckwheat, figs, many green vegetables, milk, meat and shellfish.

CHROMIUM

How chromium is used is still uncertain, though recent research indicates that it works with insulin in the metabolism of sugar, and shortage may therefore result in a diabetes-like condition.

Best sources: Egg yolk, yeast, wholegrain cereals, raw sugar, molasses, fruit juices and corn oil.

COPPER

Copper is required to convert the body's iron into haemoglobin, and for the functioning of the nervous system. A large excess can be poisonous.

Best sources: Shellfish, nuts, wholegrains, green leafy vegetables, dried peas and beans. It is also present in tobacco, birth control pills, exhaust fumes, and copper piping, a particular cause of toxicity if hot water from copper pipes is drunk by children.

FLUORINE

Fluorine is found in bones and body tissues, but most of its recent publicity has been to do with the fact that it can build up in the enamel of the teeth to make them stronger. It is now added in generous amounts to toothpastes and mouthwashes, also to some water supplies. There is a fine line between the beneficial effects of fluorine and the dangers of toxicity—many people are now linking it with cancer. In fact it cannot help bad teeth, only those which have not yet finished growing. Excess amounts can cause a mottled effect on the teeth.

Best sources: Naturally-fluoridated drinking water. Other good sources of fluorine are tea, and fish—providing you eat the bones!

IODINE

Only a small amount of iodine is stored and used, but it is very important for the functioning of the thyroid glands which, in turn, affect growth and mental and physical health. Two-thirds of the body's iodine is concentrated in the thyroid glands which are situated on either side of the neck. When the throat enlarges to compensate for a lack of iodine the disease is called goitre.

Best sources: Vegetables grown in iodine-rich soil, kelp and other seaweed, meat, seafood. Some sea salts have iodine added.

MANGANESE

Manganese is involved in the functioning of a number of enzyme systems in the body. It is also important for the formation of thyroxin, the main hormone of the thyroid gland.

Best sources: Cereals, legumes, nuts, green vegetables, spices, egg yolks. Tea is a rich source.

MOLYBDENUM

Molybdenum helps to metabolize carbohydrates and fats, and is also an important part of the enzyme responsible for the utilization of iron, so helps prevent anaemia. A deficiency of molybdenum is now being recognized as one of a group of factors contributing to cancer. The intake of molybdenum is dependent upon how much is present in the soil in which vegetables are grown.

Best sources: Wholegrains, dark leafy vegetables.

SELENIUM

Selenium is a fairly new discovery, and is not yet fully understood. It appears to be concerned with the activity of vitamin E, so may slow down hardening of the tissues. Research is being conducted into the possibility that it may provide protection from some cancers.

Best sources: Seafood, meat, wheatgerm, bran, broccoli, tomatoes and onions.

SULPHUR

Sulphur is important for healthy hair, skin and nails. It may also help keep your brain working properly by maintaining the correct oxygen balance. It is also used to remove toxic substances, including certain drugs, from the body.

Best sources: Meat, eggs, cabbage, beans and fish.

ZINC

Though only necessary in small amounts, zinc is very important, and is involved in numerous functions. It is essential for the efficient working of many body processes, plus the maintenance of enzyme systems and cells that in turn affect such processes as the functioning of the brain, the development of the reproductive organs, keeping the skin healthy, helping growth, and healing wounds. Zinc is also thought to help detoxify alcohol in the liver. Experiments are taking place using zinc in the treatment of schizophrenia. Processed foods contain little zinc.

Best sources: Wheatgerm, wholegrain cereals, mustard, nuts, bran, kelp, brewers yeast, pumpkin seeds, peas, beans, lentils, milk, shellfish and meat.

Some nutritional statistics

The following tables show, first of all, where the fats in our diet come from, second, the calorific value of some everyday foods, and finally, the proportions of basic nutrients in some common foods.

The first table comes from the Ministry of Agriculture, Fisheries and Foods publication *Sources of Fat in UK Foods* (1985), and shows that over half of our fat intake is in the form of saturated fats of animal origin. The other two tables are taken from Vegetarian Society (UK) publications.

WHERE THE FATS IN OUR FOOD COME FROM

Butter, margarine and other fats	37%
Meat	27%
Milk and cream	14%
Cheese	5%
Biscuits	4%
Other sources	13%

CALORIFIC VALUES OF SOME EVERYDAY FOODS

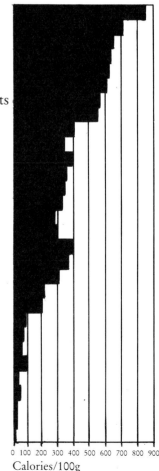

Veg. fats and oils
Butter and marg.
Des. coconut
Brazils & walnuts
Hazels
Almonds
Cashews & peanuts
Sesame
Soya
Pulses
Oats
Rice
Barley
Wheat & rye
Dates & figs
Raisins
Cheddar cheese
Sugar
Honey
Molasses
Chestnuts
Bananas
Grapes
Apples
Potatoes
Carrots
Peas
Cabbage
Tomato
Cucumber

0 100 200 300 400 500 600 700 800 900
Calories/100g

BASIC NUTRIENTS IN SOME COMMON FOODS

Protein ▇ Fat ▨ Carbohydrate ▨

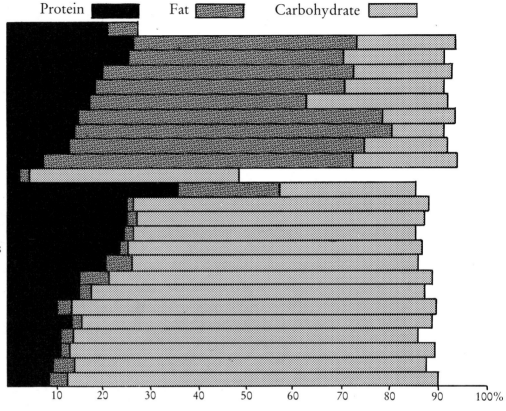

	10	20	30	40	50	60	70	80	90	100%
Beef (lean)										
Peanuts										
Sunf. seeds										
Almond										
Sesame										
Cashew										
Walnut										
Brazil										
Hazel										
Coconut										
Chestnut										
Soya										
Lentils										
Mung beans										
Dried peas										
Haricot beans										
Chick peas										
Oats										
Hard wheat										
Soft wheat										
Rye										
Millet										
Barley										
Maize										
Rice (whole)										

The Holistic Cook

The Holistic Cook

What sort of a person, then, is a holistic cook?

A holistic cook understands that eating is not only about staying alive, and not only about pleasure. A holistic cook knows that we eat in order to feel healthy and energetic, and is ready to put a lot into life in order to get the most out of it. With that in mind, a holistic cook makes the effort to acquire at least a basic knowledge of food and nutrition, of where food comes from, how it is produced, and how it works within the human body.

A holistic cook knows that balance is the key, varying ingredients and types of dishes, all of it served in imaginative ways. The experienced holistic cook senses this balance rather than working hard at it, knowing that the occasional non-food will do little harm to a body that is kept in peak condition by a daily diet of wholefoods.

A holistic cook enjoys cooking. It isn't a chore or a worry. A holistic cook sees mealtimes as an opportunity to be creative, yet relies on a few simple cooking techniques in the knowledge that wholesome ingredients are bound to taste good however they are used. The holistic cook works with the minimum of fuss, having other things to do besides spending the day in the kitchen!

A holistic cook is only too happy to share the kitchen—and the work. The kitchen is seen as a place for happy companionship, a place for women and men to work together—a holistic cook has long since abandoned any notions that the kitchen is where overburdened women prepare meals while the men relax. A holistic cook knows that the kitchen is the heart of a house and is delighted to share it with everyone—the more cooks the merrier; many hands make light work; a pleasure shared is a pleasure doubled—all ways of saying the same thing.

A holistic cook's concern extends far beyond the kitchen. A holistic cook uses simple ingredients produced in ways that are kind to all other forms of life, that do not exploit land or people, that do not pollute the planet. Much of it is home-grown or home-made. What needs to be bought is chosen with thought and understanding, not only about the goodness it contains, but also about how it was produced, where and by whom, with an awareness of its real cost and value.

A holistic cook avoids foods that come in packets, tins and plastic wrappers, firstly because the foods inside will no longer be alive and at their best and tastiest, but also because such wrappings use up valuable resources unnecessarily. They also add to pollution when they are discarded after use.

A holistic cook is very much concerned about all people, not only family, friends and acquaintances. A holistic cook believes in need, not greed, and takes only what is really necessary in the knowledge that there could be enough food for everybody on the planet, and in the hope that what is left will eventually reach those who are starving.

A holistic cook is unaffected by the media-motivated obsession with thinness, dieting, and counting calories. A holistic cook recognizes that everyone is different, and likes it that way, having no desire to conform to unattainable ideals, knowing that the best way to judge whether your body is the way it should be is to be aware of how you feel, how much energy you have, how well you sleep, how often you laugh.

A holistic cook rarely suffers from the minor ailments that plague modern society—constipation, headaches, migraines, indigestion and so on, many of which are associated with bad eating habits.

A holistic cook doesn't preach about the right way to eat, but by example does help to convince other people about the sense of eating holistically.

Above all, a holistic cook sees the preparation of food as a way of showing love, of giving physical and spiritual nourishment, of doing something positive every day to make the earth a better place. To a holistic cook, food is more than just something to eat: it is fundamental to the flow of life. It can be used or abused, it can nourish or destroy. It is the stuff of revolutions. Aware of this, a holistic cook eats with care and with love, and always with gratitude.

About the Author

Janet Hunt, who lives near Bath in the south west of England, is a vegetarian and well-known cookery writer, interested not only in our food and our relationship to it, but also passionately concerned about our current ecological crisis, which makes her the ideal author for *The Holistic Cook*. She started her career in writing by editing and preparing publications for the Vegetarian Society, and has written a dozen cookery books, including six titles in the Thorsons *Best of Vegetarian Cooking* series.

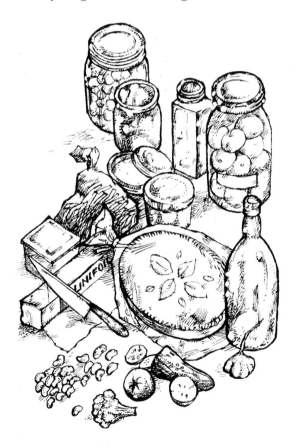

Bibliography

Adams, Ruth (1976) *Eating in Eden* Rodale Press

Barkas, Janet (1975) *The Vegetable Passion* Routledge and Kegan Paul

Berry, C.J.J. (1968) *First Steps in Wine Making* Amateur Winemaker

Betteridge, Karen and Peter Deadman (1973) *Nature's Foods* Unicorn Books

British Nutrition Foundation (1977) *Why Additives? The Safety of Food* Forbes Publications Ltd.

Brothwell, Don and Patricia (1969) *Food in Antiquity* Thames and Hudson

Dumont, René and Nicholas Cohen (1980) *The Growth of Hunger* Marion Boyars

Forbes, Alec (1984) *The Bristol Diet* Century

Friends of the Earth (1984) *Report of the Pesticides Action Network UK* FOE

Hanssen, Maurice (1984) *E for Additives* Thorsons

Hill, Laurence D. (1983) *Month-by-Month Guide to Organic Gardening* Thorsons

Hoffmann, David (1983) *The Holistic Herbal* Findhorn Press

HMSO (1976) *Manual of Nutrition* HMSO

Kushi, Michio (1983) *The Cancer Prevention Diet* Thorsons

Larsen, Egon (1977) *Food—Past, Present and Future* Frederick Muller

Lewis, Christine (1979) *The Food Choice Jungle* Faber and Faber

Lovelock, J.E. (1979) *Gaia: A New Look at Life on Earth* Oxford University Press

Mackarness, Richard (1976) *Not All in the Mind* Pan

Mackarness, Richard (1980) *Chemical Victims* Pan

Mervyn, Leonard (1984) *The Dictionary of Vitamins* Thorsons

Mindell, Earl (1982) *The Vitamin Bible* Arlington Books

Mowett, Farley (1959) *The Desperate People* Little, Brown

O'Brien, Jane (1983) *The Magic of Tofu* Thorsons

Peterson, Vicki (1978) *The Natural Food Catalog* Arco

Polunin, Miriam (1978) *The Right Way to Eat* Dent

Rippere, Vicki (1983) *The Allergy Problem* Thorsons

Schumacher, E.F. (1973) *Small is Beautiful* Blond and Briggs

Sherman, Kay Lynne (1981) *The Findhorn Family Cook Book* Findhorn Press

Shurtleff, William and Akiko Aoyagi (1975) *The Book of Tofu* Autumn Press

Soil Association (1978) *Some Good Companions* Soil Association

Soil Association (1982) *Friend and Foe in the Garden* Soil Association

Taylor, R.J. (1980) *Food Additives* Wiley

Tudge, Colin (1977) *The Famine Business* Faber and Faber

Tudge, Colin (1980) *Future Cook* Mitchell Beazley

Twose, Nigel (1984) *Cultivating Famine* Oxfam

Vegetarian Society (annual) *International Vegetarian Handbook* Vegetarian Society

Wood, Betty (1984) *The Healing Power of Colour* Thorsons

Wynne-Tyson, Jon (1979) *Food for a Future* Centaur

Some Useful Addresses

A stamped addressed envelope would be appreciated when you write to these organizations for help and advice.

Action Against Allergy
43 The Downs,
London SW20 8HG

Chicken's Lib
P.O. Box 2,
Holmfirth,
Huddersfield HD7 1QT

Compassion in World Farming
20 Lavant Street,
Petersfield,
Hants GU32 3EW

Dr Hadwen Trust for Humane Research
46 Kings Road,
Hitchin,
Herts SG5 1RD

Farm and Food Society
4 Willifield Way,
London NW11 7XT
Educational and pressure group for humane farming and wholesome food.

Friends of the Earth
377 City Road,
London EC1V 1NA

Full Moon
Charlton Court Farm,
Mouse Lane,
Steyning,
West Sussex BN4 3DF
Supply the Ecover range of biodegradable household products, including washing-up liquid. These are sold through wholesalers and wholefood shops. If you have trouble in finding a local outlet, write for help.

Good Gardeners' Association
Arkley Manor Farm,
Rowley Lane,
Arkley,
Barnet, Herts EN5 3HS

Health Education Council
78 New Oxford Street,
London WC1 1AH

Henry Doubleday Research Association
National Centre for
Organic Gardening,
Ryton on Dunsmore,
Coventry CV8 3LG

Hyperactive Children's Support Group
59 Meadowside,
Angmering,
Sussex
Aims to help and support hyperactive children and their parents.

National Society for Research into Allergy
PO Box 45,
Hinckley,
Leicestershire LE10 1JY
Aims to help the allergy sufferer through dietary control.

Organic Farmers and Growers Ltd.
9 Station Approach,
Needham Market,
Ipswich,
Suffolk IP6 8AT
A co-operative for farmers wanting to use biological methods.

OXFAM
Banbury Road,
Oxford OX2 7DZ

Sea Shepherd Conservation
12 Royal Terrace,
Glasgow G3 7NY
Sells the Caurnie Soaperie range of products,
including biodegradable washing-up liquid.

The Soil Association
Walnut Tree Manor,
Haughley,
Stowmarket,
Suffolk IP14 3RS
Promotes the knowledge and practice of
organic husbandry.

Vegan Society Ltd.
P.O. Box 3,
Charlbury,
Oxford,
OX7 6DU

Vegetarian Society (UK) Ltd.
Parkdale,
Dunham Road,
Altrincham,
Cheshire WA14 4QG

Working Weekends on Organic Farms
(WWOOF)
19 Bradford Road,
Lewes,
Sussex BN7 1RB

World Wildlife Fund
Panda House,
29 Greville Street,
London EC1 N8AX

Index

Certain page numbers are set off in **bold type** to indicate a longer entry in the glossary sections of the book (e.g. apples 43, **103**, 197, 199).

A

Two forthcoming titles in this series of illustrated books which brings to different areas of everyday life a new awareness of the wholeness and connectedness of every aspect of ourselves and our environment:

THE HOLISTIC GARDENER

Margaret Elphinstone and Julia Langley

Examines gardens and gardening in the context of nature as a whole, and considers gardens as an integral part of a living planet, showing how the holistic garden is a part of the ecology of its environment, and how the activities of the holistic gardener seek to enhance that ecology and extend it, rather than to impose techniques which work against the flow of the living environment.

However, gardening is still a human intervention in the course of nature, and the holistic approach goes on to review the role of the gardener as a human being who is part of the environment, making their own impression upon it.

The book identifies two objectives in creating gardens — to produce food and to create beauty — and these two categories are carried through to the structure of the book, in which the practical chapters are divided into sections covering the edible and ornamental aspects of gardening.

The introductory chapter considers the responsibility of the gardener, and the reasons why we undertake intervention in nature as gardeners. The second chapter gives basic practical information, seeing the garden as an ecological system interdependent with its local environment, and including information on soil, climate and local conditions, artificial additions such as composts, mulches and greenhouses and weeds and weeding. The following chapter looks at plants and how to choose them for particular gardens, always taking account of the place of the plant within its ecological setting.

The next four sections follow identical formats and cover the four basic areas of gardening: vegetables, fruit, flowers and trees and shrubs. The heart of each of the four sections is a glossary of plants with a clear and uniform presentation for each species covered.

The book concludes with a detailed bibliography, a list of sources for supplies and a comprehensive index.

HOLISTIC HEALING

Jill Rakusen and Jan Resnick

Holistic healing is an integrated approach to wellbeing which takes the idea of health in its broadest context, and at the same time takes full account both of the individual person wanting to be healthy and of their physical and cultural circumstances.

The authors put health and healing into the context of our whole approach to life and lifestyle, thus distinguishing it from the many available books on first-aid and medicine which tend to assume that everybody is much the same, and that healing is something which happens outside a social and economic framework.

From the holistic point of view, orthodox drug-and-surgery-based medicine is seen as only one strand amongst an intricate array of possibilities. Holistic healing concentrates on the description of individual experience and does not rely on dogmatic medical theory; it sees interaction, process and change as more important than specialization, structure and stasis; it sees quality of life as the measure of health; it sees healing as both a personal and a social transformation.

As well as setting out the theory and practice of holistic healing clearly and accessibly, *Holistic Healing* makes it clear that faith, trust and intuition are often at least as important in the healing process as technical precision and expertise, and it questions current beliefs about medical 'truth', medical 'facts' and the dissemination of medical 'information'.

There are sections on health and environment, diet, the practice of holistic healing, the politics of holistic health, community and self-help health and women and healing. It includes an illustrated glossary of nearly 150 techniques and approaches, together with a detailed bibliography and index.